Social investment and territorial inequalities: mapping policies and services in the Baltic states

BALTISCHE STUDIEN ZUR ERZIEHUNGS- UND SOZIALWISSENSCHAFT / BALTIC STUDIES IN EDUCATIONAL AND SOCIAL SCIENCES

Herausgegeben von / Edited by Gerd-Bodo von Carlsburg,
Natalija Mažeikienė und / and Airi Liimets

BAND 38

Zu Qualitätssicherung und Peer Review der vorliegenden Publikation

Die Qualität der in dieser Reihe erscheinenden Arbeiten wird vor der Publikation durch die Herausgeber der Reihe geprüft.

Notes on the quality assurance and peer review of this publication

Prior to publication, the quality of the work published in this series is reviewed by editors of the series.

Jurga Bučaitė-Vilkė (ed.)

Social investment and territorial inequalities: mapping policies and services in the Baltic states

PETER LANG

Bibliographic Information published by the Deutsche Nationalbibliothek
The Deutsche Nationalbibliothek lists this publication in the Deutsche Nationalbibliografie; detailed bibliographic data is available online at http://dnb.d-nb.de.

Library of Congress Cataloging-in-Publication Data
A CIP catalog record for this book has been applied for at the Library of Congress.

This monograph is written in the framework of the research project 'Inequality, Urbanization and Territorial Cohesion: Developing the European Social Model of Economic Growth and Democratic Capacity (COHSMO)' funded by Horizon 2020 Grant [no. 727058].

The monograph is approved for publishing by the Council of the Faculty of Social Sciences, Vytautas Magnus University, Lithuania (Ref. No. 16-1).

Reviewers:
Assoc. Prof. Dr. Cristina Stănuş, Lucian Blaga University of Sibiu, Romania
Prof. Dr. Iveta Reinholde, University of Latvia, Latvia.

ISSN 2748-0658
ISBN 978-3-631-84284-3 (Print)
E-ISBN 978-3-631-87742-5 (E-PDF)
E-ISBN 978-3-631-87743-2 (EPUB)
DOI 10.3726/b19662

Peter Lang – Berlin · Bern · Bruxelles ·
New York · Oxford · Warszawa · Wien

This publication has been peer reviewed.

www.peterlang.com

Preface

This book emanates from the COHSMO research project "Inequality, Urbanization and Territorial Cohesion: Developing the European Social Model of Economic Growth and Democratic Capacity" funded by Horizon 2020 Grant [no. 727058] implemented in the period 2018–2021.[1] The project addresses social inequalities and socio-economic differences between neighborhoods, cities and regions across European countries (Poland, Greece, Austria, UK, Denmark, Italy, Lithuania). It focuses on a public investment approach and the role of social policies in delivering economic growth and better quality of life implemented by employing multi-layered and multi-scaled governance forms, tools, and mechanisms. COHSMO pointed to the relevance of a territorial perspective in forming place-driven policies. The project asks whether "place" matters in implementing a social investment policy framework at territorial level? One of the main achievements of our project includes the development and conceptualization of a European Social Model. The model proposes solutions for a more cohesive European countries considering the impact of territorial inequalities and importance of life chances, community participation and complementarity within a social investment policy paradigm. Our research, among other sub-questions, was designed to detect the importance of localities in designing a variety of welfare and economic growth policy tools for sustainable territorial development in different context and regions. Will a shift towards social investment policy be an efficient perspective to counteract rising spatial differences in various administrative systems, welfare traditions, and contexts? Is it necessary to recognize the emerging policy concepts that should underline the importance of governance, institutional complementarity, and provision of services? And finally, how is social-economic equity and well-being at different local, regional, and state levels promoted? Each chapter of this book benefitted from the outcomes of the academic cooperation in this long-term project that employs both qualitative and quantitative research methodological approaches[2].

1 More information on the research project is available here: https://www.cohsmo.aau.dk/.

2 The chapters of this book are based on the material from COHSMO project reports (D.2.2., D..4.4., D.4.6.; D.5.1., D.5.2, D.5.3 deliverables), available online: https://cordis.europa.eu/project/id/727058/results.

We would like to thank all consortium members from Austria (Vienna university), Italy (Milano Politechnico), Poland (Warsaw University), the United Kingdom (Bristol University), Greece (Harokopio University) and Denmark (Aalborg university) for their effective teamwork and inspirational insights that encouraged us to develop the idea of publishing this book. The book would not have been published without continuous administrative support from the Aalborg university team that was responsible for the overall project administration and supervision. We would also like to take the opportunity to acknowledge the contributions of all national teams, early-stage researchers, doctoral students, and post-docs who tackled the extensive field work. The rich and fascinating empirical data invaluably feeds the theoretical and empirical assumptions. International collaboration is always a challenge for researchers from a variety of scientific fields that are trying to combine different views, expectations, and insights. We have been privileged to work with the team leaders Rob Atkinson, Yuri Kazepov, Costanzo Ranci, Anja Jørgensen, Hans Thor Andersen, Pawel Swianiewicz, Carolina Pacchi and many others not mentioned in this personalized list, without whose extensive expertise and commitment the vision of this book would not have been possible for our Lithuanian team. Our young colleagues, both doctoral students and post-doc researchers, contributed substantially, conducting field research, utilizing empirical skills, and exerting considerable efforts in interviewing people from local authorities, business, and local communities. Similarly, we are grateful for the reviewers for their constructive feedback and academic guidance through the jungles of territorial policies and multi-scale governance.

Table of contents

List of abbreviations

ALMP	Active labor market policy.
ECEC	Early childhood education and care.
VET	Vocational education and training.

Jurga Bučaitė-Vilkė

Introduction. Challenging territorial inequalities and social investment policies. Book scope and content

Fuzzy concepts: Territorial differences, territorial cohesion, and social investment policy turn

In 2013 the EU launched the Social Investment Package for Growth and Social Cohesion (European Commission, 2013) to underline the importance of welfare reform policies and respond to growing social, economic, and technological risks in the turn towards expanding social investment policies. Together with the historical Lisbon Agenda (2000), this was a political call to convert Europe into the "most competitive and dynamic knowledge-based economy in the world, capable of sustainable economic growth and more and better jobs and greater social cohesion" (European Council, 2005) and became an indivisible part of reforming national European welfare policies. In academic debate, and in the light of an urgent need for welfare reforms, the emergence of a European Social Model became a background for a re-conceptualization of the role of state and market allocation mechanisms. Social investment as a paradigm was well developed in the academic discussions elaborated by Vandenbroucke, Vleminckx, 2011, Morel et al. (2012), and Hemerijck (2014, 2017) and many more. The determination to overcome the byproducts of demographic change; growing social disparities, the need for sustainable economic growth and increasing labor productivity, has redirected most European countries towards welfare modernization. There is strong empirical evidence that social investment has significantly modified national welfare systems, especially in fostering labor force participation, in revising social spendings, fostering the dual family earner model, and expansion of public services (Nolan, 2013; Hemerijck, 2014, 2017). Further academic arguments emphasize social investment as a political platform to reconsider social spending and its economic effectiveness. The main question here is whether social spending is constructed as a welfare investment that eventually results in higher economic performance, labor productivity and increased human capacities, or treated as simply economic expenses (Morel et al., 2012).

In this book we adhere to the idea that social investment reflects the turnaround in conceptual and analytical policy frameworks that effectively relate social risks and policy responses. Therefore, mobilization and governance structure are important to enable welfare policy implementation (Hall, 1993). Scholars underline the multidimensionality of the social investment perspective that effectively contributes to growth and social inclusion. In addition, the social investment paradigm includes a complex policy mix across different fields, for example, labor market, education, social benefits transfer systems, parenting and family services, elderly care, and gender policies (Heckman, 2006; Solga, 2014; Schindler et al., 2015; Garritzmann et al., 2018 and many others). Hemerijck (2017) based on his long-term commitment to welfare state analysis, summarizes social investment as effecting considerable interventions in three "productive" policy functions: (1) "raising the quality of the 'stock' of human capital and capabilities over the life-course; (2) easing the 'flow' of contemporary labor-market and life-course transitions; and (3) maintaining strong minimum-income universal safety nets as income protection and economic stabilization 'buffers' in ageing societies" (Hemerijck, 2017, p. 19). The importance of strengthening skills and competencies, enhancing productivity over the course of a lifetime, efficiently allocating labor resources and securing income protection and economic stability, define the core of the social investment paradigm (Hemerijck & Vandenbroucke, 2012; Hemerijck, 2014, 2015). What is important for this book is the need for institutional complementaries that are associated with different policy provisions that complement each other. Referring to Hemerijck (2017), isolated social investment policy innovations do not achieve a positive effect if not provided as policy synergy. On the contrary, social investment tools without a systematic approach risk becoming counterproductive and costly, especially in terms of cost-benefit analysis. For example, the implementation of an effective childcare provision system should be accompanied by a comprehensive employment policy for both parents, especially for low skilled and low-income females as well as an overall social protection system (Van Lancker, 2013).

Secondly, an important analytical dimension of the book is a multi-layered concept of territory and territorial inequalities that derive from the conceptual and empirical findings by social and economic geographers, urban planners, political scientists, and urban sociologists. A social investment policy paradigm has been the inspiration to look differently at territorial inequalities that have experienced a resurgence in national states on a different scale from regional or local levels. Therefore, policy awareness of emerging territorial cohesion complements the discussion on a so-called "European social model" that appeals to the values of social welfare, equity, sustainability and good governance. As documented in the growing body of academic literature, the concept of territorial cohesion is employed as an alternative in order to raise awareness of the relationship between spatial inequalities and social-economic growth. In general, territorial cohesion policy that entails the reference to spatial dimensions proposes rather fuzzy policy-making tools that require new decisions on territorial interdependence (Faludi, 2007a). With reference to Faludi, we should be more concerned about "equity, competitiveness, sustainability, and good governance". Following his assertion, territorial cohesion can balance these ideas on spatial scales where a balancing act is needed to reconcile the divergent interests of stakeholders (Faludi, 2007b, p. 25). Despite the diversity of opinion among political advocates as to how territorial cohesion should be reinforced, there is common agreement about the need for a certain level of decommodification as a part of social rights (Faludi, 2007a; Esping-Andersen, 1990). Beyond the classical understanding of decommodification (Esping-Andersen, 1990), it also includes the aspects of quality of life in territories, as for example, public interventions in service provision or urban planning, values, and lifestyles.

In responding to intensive advocacy of sustainable territorial social-economic growth and the need for better territorial equalization, a few challenges arise. The first issue is related to the reduced capacity of a national welfare state to respond sufficiently to territorial disbalances and spatial differentiation problems. The emergence of new social risks, including income inequality, social exclusion, new employment patterns and technological change calls for better "contextualization" of welfare provisions. There is currently much evidence that European regions have become more polarized regarding social and economic development aspects (Puga, 2002; Charron, 2016; Rodrıguez-Pose, 2018). Referring to Andre Rodrıguez-Pose (2018), there are places that matter and places that do not. The largest cities are characterized by a growing population and industries that reflect economic productivity, growing technological hubs, greater skills and growth accumulations. In contrast, rural areas and declining industrialized regions present a picture of declining labor productivity, de-population, social exclusion and social stigma, and lower household incomes. Therefore, by territorial inequalities are treated as irrelevant regarding low-income and low-density places. Remote territories are treated as places of inefficient return of economic development policies and globalization (Glaeser & Gottlieb, 2009; Kline & Moretti, 2014; Rodrıguez-Pose, 2018). In this respect income-support transfers and benefits to sustain employability are used as principal welfare instruments to achieve economic effectiveness. However, the statistical data from different countries demonstrates that misguided investments result in inadequate regional development where unemployment, reliance on in-kind support and weak competitiveness remain a main issue (Fratesi & Rodríguez-Pose, 2016). The misleading reference is that lagging-behind areas have no potential that leads to miscalculation of territorial assets (Barca et al., 2012).

The second issue concerns institutional inability to provide policy solutions for territorial equalization. These concerns address the issue of policy interventions asking at what level should policies intervene in territorial development. There are many reasons and trade-offs explaining the inadequate policy response to the needs of vulnerable territories, for example, imbalance between multilevel coordination and governance levels, low impact interventions, and focus on income-support transfers, politicization of territorial inequalities, and the overlooking of economic and social potential of lagging-behind territories. Institutional quality may also reflect the tensions in implementing effective territorial interventions in terms of competitiveness, capacity to innovate, limits in accountability amongst other issues (Charron et al., 2014; Rodríguez-Pose & Di Cataldo, 2015; Rodríguez-Pose & Garcilazo, 2015). It is obvious that growing regional disparities require a recalibration of public policies addressing territorial social and economic inequalities more effectively than traditional so-called spatially blind policies (Iammarino et al., 2019). One of the possible solutions is place-sensitive policies that better address the territorial capacities especially when left-behind territories are provided with right endowments and infrastructures (Iammarino et al., 2017). On the one hand, regional inequalities and social exclusion work as complementary mechanisms. Low quality institutions and poor connectivity act as stimulating mechanisms for higher levels of territorial disparities as well. As Lammarino et al. (2019, p. 288) summarize, the ambivalence of a place-sensitive approach stating that "too much focus on efficiency through agglomeration may therefore enhance territorial inequity (which, in turn, undermines efficiency), while too much focus on equity through place-based support (without development) undermines overall economic efficiency". Finally, maximization of territorial potential and development of capabilities could provide a framework for the different spatial development patterns of territories whether urban or rural. Advocacy of a place-based policy framework could indicate the agenda for implementing social investment policies that mobilize territorial capacities with institutional endowments. Coordination of top-down instruments and bottom-up initiatives lead to the development of a place-sensitive theoretical framework underpinning the conventional policy tools (Iammarino et al., 2019).

The scope of the book: Territorial impact and social investment policies

This book presents an insight into the discussions on how social investment policies could be responsive to territorial inequalities in terms of better policy coordination, capacities and the adaptability of institutional infrastructures to territorial needs. So far, the SI perspective has paid insufficient attention to the role played by combining different conceptions such as territorial differentiation, territorial cohesion, and local development. The principal objective underpinning the chapters is the question as to whether social investment policies could be tailored differently to address territorial capacities and territorial needs. The conceptual and empirical insights into the design of territorially sensitive social investment policy could be useful for both researchers and political practitioners.

One of the key hypotheses the book tries to address is the assumption that *social investment should shift to higher levels of territorialization* by looking more carefully at contextual conditions and the impact of coordination among multi-governance levels (national, regional and municipal). By so doing, the book inspires us to look differently at the territorial sensitivity of such welfare policy strategies implemented in advantaged developing areas as well as those which are disadvantaged peripheral territories. In other words, the book discusses territorial differences that are critical to developing social investment strategy in urban, rural, and suburban areas. By looking at social investment policy design, we also consider the impact of other factors, such as urban infrastructure, governance design and effectiveness, and territorial capital that play a considerable role in the social and economic development of regions and municipalities.

By combining theoretical notions about territorial cohesion, territorial development, and social investment in one paradigm, it is possible to make the central argument for "territorialization of social investment policy" by postulating welfare policies for territories and assessing their impact (Figure 1). Conceptualization of the connections between territorial relationships and social investment policies as depicted in Figure 1, presents an ideal type of such policy. Figure 1 rests upon two main questions. Firstly, how to evaluate the overall effects of SI policies on minimizing territorial inequalities. Secondly, how to define the development patterns typical for both developing metropolitan hubs and vulnerable regions (1st constituent). Thirdly, how to identify the governance tools and approaches that facilitate or hinder locally sensitive SI strategies (2nd constituent), for example, vertical and horizontal policy coordination tools, centralization and/or decentralization procedures, the impact of local partnerships and higher levels of public engagement. Accordingly, we argue that the territorial dimension of SI policy is analyzed looking at the interplay of factors such as persistence of territorial inequalities, state interventions and modes of subnational and municipal coordination (institutional rescaling) and provision of services to different beneficiaries. On the vertical dimension, we consider general trends of centralization vs. decentralization in implementing social investment policies. On the horizontal level, we observe the design, funding mechanism, implementation, and

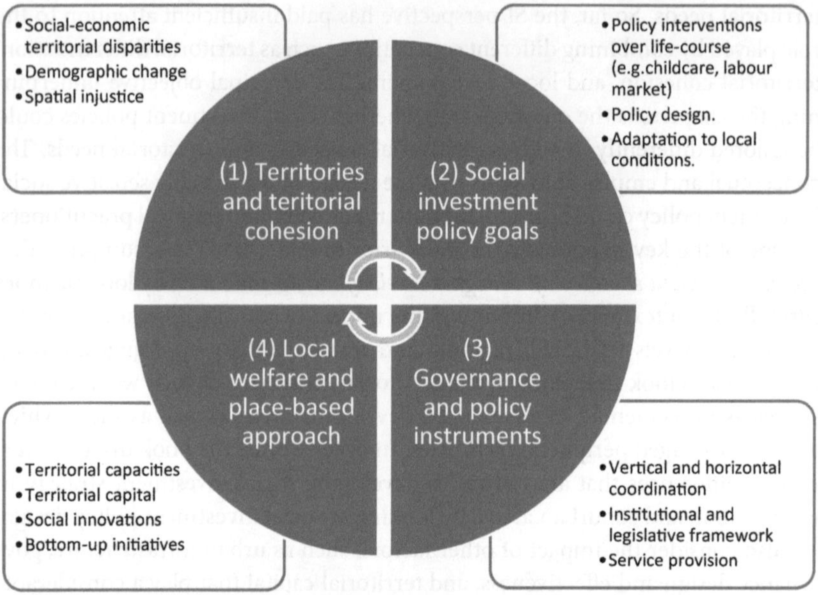

Figure 1. Conceptualization of the linkages on territorial relationships with social investment policies. Source: Own elaborations.

service provision of SI policies (3rd constituent). The last constituent (4) asks about the impact of territorialized social investment policies on better life-chances in areas of different size.

The conceptual approach of this book has some limitations, for example, we need to carefully consider the country-level specifics, such as self-governance systems, regional development policy tradition and legacy, bureaucratic culture, decision-making processes, and public engagement. The second issue is related to democratic capacity. The conceptual framework hinders the possibility of looking carefully at the role of social partners and civil society actors in territorial decision-making and evaluating the variety of bottom-up initiatives of the selected SI policy arenas.

Selection of SI policies: This book presents insights into the regional challenge to develop territorially sensitive policies that focus on local welfare and well-being span, such as early childhood education and care (ECEC), vocational training (VET), and an active labor market (ALMPs). Early childhood education and care, vocational training and active labor market policies implemented at different governance scales – central, and municipal – are a specific focus of the book. In this way, we are in accordance with the conceptual and methodological insights on the social investment paradigm as discussed above. The selected policies play a crucial role in triggering labor market participation, family and work reconciliation and social inclusion. By referencing numerous works on welfare state and social investment perspectives (Hemerijck & Vandenbroucke, 2012; Hemerijck, 2013, 2014, 2015), and a taxonomy of social investment policy functions ("flow" – "buffer" – ("stock") we demonstrate institutional complementarities (conception introduced by Hall and Soskice, 2001). Three elements are distinguished: "(1) the quality of the 'stock' of human capital and capabilities over the life course; (2) easing the 'flow' of contemporary labor-market and life-course transitions; and (3) maintaining strong minimum-income universal safety nets as income protection and economic stabilization 'buffers' in ageing societies" (Hemerijck, 2017, p. 19). At this point childcare services, vocational training and active labor markets complement each other in two ways. Firstly, childcare policy aligned with effective parental leave arrangements and supported by in-kind and in-service incentives contributes to active economic participation of parents, enables to deal with social risks in low-income households. Secondly, active labor market policy instruments enable parents to participate in labor market and create more job opportunities, especially for mothers (flow element). Policy instruments that enable better school-to-work transition and careers contribute to implementation of social investment policies. Additionally, human capital is fostered by vocational training and education to facilitate the flow into productive economic activities.

Promoting SI policies in small-scale countries. Why Lithuania?

The relevance of social investment policy and its implementation in the Baltic states has been intensified by the political discourse on reducing and optimizing public spending for education, public services and social welfare that dates from the 2008 economic crisis. At this point the book fills a gap in the literature on the understanding of the relationship between social inequalities, territorial cohesion, and the switch over to social investment in Lithuania, one of the three Baltic countries. The chapters analyze local and contextual conditions that contribute positively to social investment strategies and their impact on increasing territorial disparities in different regions of Lithuania.

In answer to the question, why is it important to analyze the Lithuanian experience of social investment policy "territorialization", we provide two main arguments. The first argument considers that it is necessary to study in-depth the interaction of social investment strategies and different territorial conditions as well as the impact of social investments on reducing and mitigating social inequalities. Substantial theoretical and empirical research demonstrates that social investment policies are likely to have positive impact only if specific contextual conditions are met. The long-term experience of European countries suggests that social investment policies are expected to have a positive impact on economic growth, social inclusiveness and the reduction of poverty (Vandenbroucke & Vleminckx, 2011; Nolan, 2013; Hemerijck, 2014, 2017). In contrast to the Western experience, these hypotheses have never been tested in Lithuania. Lithuania as a case study presents the opportunity for a consideration of the options for a social investment perspective and the effects of contextual pre-conditions for implementing sustainable social investment policies. In this publication, the authors argue that the success of these policies depends on the contexts in which they are embedded, i.e., the life chances and limitations as well as new opportunities that come with living in rural or urban areas. Lithuania, therefore, might present an interesting case study for the exploration of successes and failures of social investment policies in terms of local autonomy, multi-level governance and inclusiveness of community stakeholders.

The second argument is around the growing social and economic polarization of regions in Lithuania and centralization tendencies in regional development. Over the last decade, the economic marginalization of regions became a crucial indicator, for example, in 2019 the capital of Vilnius generated 42.4 % of national GDP compared to the other regions, of which 72.1 % of total FDI (foreign direct investments) is allocated to capital area (Statistics Lithuania, 2021). The second city of Kaunas generated 19 % of total national GDP in 2020. The Lithuanian experience supports economic growth strategy as the main pillar for territorial policies, mostly stipulated by the EU accession process since 2004 (Burneika, 2013; Puidokas & Daukaitė, 2013). On the contrary, the difficulties experienced by peripheral regions have been mainly addressed either through regional development policies supporting financial subsidies or agglomeration of public infrastructure; for example, merging schools or public hospitals (Daugirdas et al., 2013; Kriaučiūnas et al., 2016; Ubarevičienė et al., 2016). The growing challenges to the implementation of social investment policies, both at central and local (municipal) level indicate institutional inertia and a lack of leadership in finding sustainable solutions for "left behind" territories. The main problems are multi-dimensional. Some are related to insufficiency of multilevel institutional coordination, a failure to balance territorial disparities and national policies' goals, lack of place-based innovations and horizontally integrated development strategies. Others reflect broader public engagements, for example, public mistrust of politicians and bureaucracies or inadequate community leadership in local-welfare decisions.

Book content

The book is based on empirical data from examples selected from different Lithuanian municipalities (urban, suburban, and rural). The case studies represent the local approaches towards implementing early childcare, vocational training and education, and active labor market policies that are studied in a wider socioeconomic and territorial disparities context. Institutional framework, horizontal and vertical governance, and public service provision are the main elements that support the primary question of the book on territorial policy recalibration and sensitivity to territorial development challenges. The involvement and active participation of different social, political, and economic actors also contributes to making social investment strategies more effective. In other words, the authors aim to provide a roadmap for inquiry into the territorial impact of SI policies and identify challenges resulting from the differences in multi-scale governance, service provision and institutional complementarities. Finally, considering the importance of an emerging social investment policy paradigm in Lithuania and challenges facing the construction of territorially sensitive public intervention tools, we raise questions with regard to the book design:

The book comprises a variety of topics that are organized around the central question on re-connecting territorial differences and territorial cohesion, SI policy tools and local social-economic and demographic contexts in the case of Lithuania case. The authors contribute to answering the following theoretical and empirical questions on connecting territorial concepts with social investment policy practices and institutional design:

- What are the means of connecting territorial cohesion, territorial differences, and a social investment approach?
- What are the advantages and risks in implementing social investment policies and can they be adjusted to territorial specificities?
- Are there any relevant territorial differences that impact social investment policy development and the territorial sensitivity of such strategies?
- What are the overall effects of these policies on territorial inequalities and on the problems characterizing the most vulnerable areas?
- What institutional factors, governance mechanisms and instruments could drive welfare policies to become more territorially responsive?
- What are the policy tools and (inter-)institutional mechanisms that facilitate or hinder SI strategies; for example, vertical and horizontal coordination, service provision mechanisms, response to beneficiary needs, involvement of stakeholders, perception of territorial capital and disadvantages?

- Can we rely on the impact of territorially sensitive early childcare education, vocational training, and active labor market policies to sustain better life-opportunities? What is the role of different local stakeholders in implementing SI policies?

In detail, the book is organized into two related thematic parts. The first part contributes to the **theoretical elaborations** on territorial cohesion and SI policies to recalibrate territorial sensitivity policies (Figure 1 for summary; chapters 2–3). The chapter, "Territorial cohesion, spatial justice, and the social investment approach", by George Mavrommatis and Panagiotis Artelaris addresses the multi-dimensional theoretical conceptions of territorial cohesion, spatial justice and territories. The chapter also clarifies how European territorial cohesion policy substantially impacts the re-consideration of territorial inequalities and tackles socio-economic disparities. The place-based policies are promoted as an alternative for peripheral areas to sustain economic and social development patterns. Chapter 3, "A social investment approach for place-sensitive services: What is the potential impact on territorial inequalities?" (Ruggero Cefalo, Marta Cordini and Tatjana Boczy) furthers the conceptual considerations of a territorially driven social investment approach. The authors reflect on how territorial inequalities and multilevel governance structures could be taken into consideration when framing a social investment policy perspective. The provision of capacitating services, the process of rescaling, the persistence of spatial disparities in Europe as well as the characteristics of the emerging knowledge economy, become an essential framework for investigating social investment policy instruments and their impact on territorial development.

The second part of the book is dedicated to context in terms of exogenous factors (socio-economic and demographic profiles of territorial differences) and institutional analysis (chapters 4–7). The chapters consider country level experience, looking at policy achievements and failures in implementing the SI policies at municipal level. The authors assume that territorial differences are important factors in formulating central government rhetoric about rescaling service provision in different welfare policy fields. SI policy design, governance, involvement of organizational actors, institutional mechanisms, and capacities are analyzed to demonstrate efforts made by the government to tackle territorial inequalities. Vertical and horizontal coordination as well as local partnerships are important elements for ensuring better integration of selected SI policies of ECEC (early childhood education and care), VET (vocational education and training) and ALMP (active labor market policy) into territorial development policies.

The chapter "Territorial profiles: spatial inequalities and the importance of socio-economic differences" by Jurga Bučaitė-Vilkė, Viktorija Baranauskienė, and Artūras Tereškinas explores the socio-economic and demographic situation in Lithuanian regions over the last decade (during the period 2008–2019). They provide a statistically based reflection on regional policy changes in the country looking at the heterogenous picture of economic and social growth in urban zones. In contrast, the peripheral areas face the challenges of population decline, labor migration, economic polarization, and higher level of inequalities. The authors conclude that national focus on economic growth parameters might limit the alternatives to re-arrange the territorial development notion along the lines of social investment policies. Aušra Maslauskaitė in her chapter "Promoting social investment policy through the development of early childhood education and care policy: The Lithuanian case" analyses the implementation of a national childcare policy as an instance of collective engagement and territorially driven design. The divergent experiences of urban, suburban, and rural municipalities reveal that the ECEC policy is flexibly adapted to territorial diversity, for example, it reflects demographic change in early-age children group by establishing more childcare facilities. She provides empirical evidence on the growing tendencies towards decentralization in childcare policy regarding potential leadership and social innovations at municipal level. Artūras Tereškinas in his chapter "Active labor market policies as a part of social investment approach" contributes to analysis of the active labor market policy field that represents the case for balancing national standardization and territorial needs. As a part of social investment policy, an active labor market encompasses the strategy for enabling human capital in economic activities. However, centrally planned measures are not aligned with territorial challenges, for example, a higher proportion of older employees that face difficulties related to changing their workplaces due to insufficient professional skills or education hubs. The empirical findings from urban, suburban and rural municipalities indicate a need for early labor market interventions that foster municipal initiatives and social dialogue as a part of the social investment approach. Finally, the chapter on "Social investment and vocational education and training policy: The architecture of combining national standardization and territorial needs" by Jurga Bučaitė-Vilkė deals with challenges faced when re-designing vocational training to be more responsive to socio-economic and demographic issues in municipalities. The impact of a strong regulatory framework in designing vocational education based on municipal decisions is significant as the municipalities have no autonomy with regard to educational network or training content. Chapter 7 concludes that we should consider the variables of vertical and horizontal governance, stakeholder participation, and policy realization (through infrastructure and services) that provide territorially sensitive instruments. As demonstrated in these chapters, there is much room for a recalibration of specific policy tools and mechanisms in order to meet territorial needs and challenges when considering territorial differences in urban, suburban and rural municipalities. Finally, the authors assume that policy cases contribute to the discussion on policy variations and tensions that capture the wider impact of state policy on territorial autonomy and consolidation.

References

Barca, F., McCann, P., & Rodríguez-Pose, A. (2012). The case for regional development intervention: Place-based versus place-neutral approaches. *Journal of Regional Science*, *52*(1), 134–152.

Burneika, D. (2013). *Regioninė politika Europoje*. Vilnius: Vilniaus universitetas.

Charron, N., Dijkstra, L., & Lapuente, V. (2014). Regional governance matters: Quality of government within European Union member states. *Regional Studies*, *48*(1), 68–90.

Charron, N. (2016). Diverging cohesion? Globalisation, state capacity and regional inequalities within and across European countries. *European Urban and Regional Studies*, *23*(3), 355–373.

Daugirdas, V., Burneika, D., Kriaučiūnas, E., Ribokas, G., Stanaitis, S., & Ubarevičienė, R. (2013). *Lietuvos retai apgyventos teritorijos*. /Monografija/. Vilnius: Lietuvos socialinių tyrimų centras.

Esping-Andersen, G. (1990). *The three worlds of welfare capitalism*. Princeton University Press, Princeton, New Jersey.

European Commission (2005) Delivering on Growth and Jobs: A new integrated economic and employment co-ordination cycle in the EU, SEC (2005) 193, http://ec.europa.eu/growthandjobs/pdf/SEC2005_193_en.pdf.

Faludi, A. (2007a). The European model of society. In A. Faludi (Ed.), *Territorial cohesion and the European model of society* (pp. 1–22). Cambridge: Lincoln Institute of Land Policy.

Faludi, A. (2007b). Territorial cohesion policy and the European model of society. *European Planning Studies*, *15*(4), 567–583.

Fratesi, U., & Rodríguez-Pose, A. (2016). The crisis and regional employment in Europe: What role for sheltered economies?. *Cambridge Journal of Regions, Economy and Society*, *9*(1), 33–57.

Garritzmann, J. L., Busemeyer, M. R., & Neimanns, E. (2018). Public demand for social investment: New supporting coalitions for welfare state reform in Western Europe?. *Journal of European Public Policy, 25*(6), 844–861.

Glaeser, E. L., & Gottlieb, J. D. (2009). The wealth of cities: Agglomeration economies and spatial equilibrium in the United States. *Journal of Economic Literature, 47*(4), 983–1028.

Hall, P. A. (1993). Policy paradigms, social learning, and the state: The case of economic policy making in Britain. *Comparative Politics, 25*(3), 275–96.

Hall, P. A., & Soskice, D. (2001). An introduction to varieties of capitalism. In A. Hall & D. Soskice (eds.), *Varieties of capitalism: The institutional foundations of comparative advantage* (pp. 1–70). Oxford: Oxford University Press.

Heckman, J. J. (2006). Skill formation and the economics of investing in disadvantaged children. *Science, 312*(5782), 1900–2.

Hemerijck, A. (2013). *Changing welfare states*. Oxford: Oxford University Press.

Hemerijck, A. (2014). Social investment: "stocks", "flows" and "buffers". *Politiche Sociali, 1*(1), 9–26.

Hemerijck, A. (2015). The quiet paradigm revolution of social investment. *Social Politics: International Studies in Gender, State & Society, 22*(2), 242–56.

Hemerijck, A. (2017). Social investment and its critics. In A. Hemerijck (Eds.), *The uses of social investment* (pp. 3–42). Oxford, United Kingdom:Oxford University Press.

Hemerijck, A., & Vandenbroucke, F. (2012). Social investment and the euro crisis: The necessity of a unifying social policy concept. *Intereconomics, 47*(4), 200–6.

Iammarino, S., Rodríguez-Pose, A., & Storper, M. (2017). Why regional development matters for Europe's economic future. *European Commission Directorate General for Regional and Urban Policy Working Paper, 7.*

Iammarino, S., Rodríguez-Pose, A., & Storper, M. (2019b). Regional inequality in Europe: Evidence, theory and policy implications. *Journal of Economic Geography, 19*(2), 273–298.

Kline, P., & Moretti, E. (2014). People, places, and public policy: Some simple welfare economics of local economic development programs. *Annual Review of Economics, 6*(1), 629–662.

Kriaučiūnas, E., Pociūtė-Sereikienė, G., & Ribokas, G. (2016). Gyventojų aptarnavimo įstaigų tinklo kaitos tendencijos Lietuvos kaimo gyvenvietėse. *Lietuvos socialinė raida Nr. 5, Lietuvos socialinė raida: teritorinis aspektas* (pp. 80–94).

Morel, N., Palier, B., & Palme, J. (eds.) (2012). *Towards a social investment state? Ideas, policies and challenges*. Bristol: Policy Press.

Nolan, B. (2013). What use is 'social investment'?. *Journal of European Social Policy*, *23*(5), 459–468.

Puga, D. (2002). European regional policy in light of recent location theories. *Journal of Economic Geography*, *2*, 373–406.

Puidokas, M., & Daukaitė, I. (2013). Lietuvos regioninės politikos tobulinimo kryptys Europos Sąjungos regioninės politikos kontekste. *Viešoji Politika ir Administravimas*, *12*(1), 65–79.

Rodríguez-Pose, A. (2018). The revenge of the places that don't matter (and what to do about it). *Cambridge Journal of Regions, Economy and Society*, *11*, 189–209.

Rodríguez-Pose, A., & Di Cataldo, M. (2015). Quality of government and innovative performance in the regions of Europe. *Journal of Economic Geography*, *15*(4), 673–706.

Rodríguez-Pose, A., & Garcilazo, E. (2015). Quality of government and the returns of investment: Examining the impact of cohesion expenditure in European regions. *Regional Studies*, *49*(8), 1274–1290.

Schindler, H. S., Kholoptseva, J., Oh, S. S., Yoshikawa, H., Duncan, G. J., Magnuson, K. A., & Shonkoff, J. P. (2015). Maximizing the potential of early childhood education to prevent externalizing behavior problems: A meta-analysis. *Journal of School Psychology*, *53*(3), 243–63.

Solga, H. (2014). Education, economic inequality and the promises of the social investment state. *Socio-Economic Review*, *12*, 269–97.

Statistics Lithuania (2021). Official database https://osp.stat.gov.lt/.

Ubarevičienė, R., van Ham, M., & Burneika, D. (2016). Shrinking regions in a shrinking country: The geography of population decline in Lithuania 2001–2011. *Urban Studies Research*, http://dx.doi.org/10.1155/2016/5395379

Van Lancker, W. (2013). Putting the child-centred investment strategy to the test: Evidence for EU27. *European Journal of Social Security*, *15*(1), 4–27.

Vandenbroucke, F., & Vleminckx, K. (2011). Disappointing poverty trends: Is the social investment state to blame?. *Journal of European Social Policy*, *21*(5), 450–71.

Part I Revising territories and social investment policy in Europe: Concepts, ideas and challenges

Panagiotis Artelaris and George Mavrommatis

Chapter 1 Territorial cohesion, spatial justice and the social investment approach

Abstract: With a focus on economic, social and territorial policy, European Cohesion Policy is increasing in importance as a result of the recent rise in territorial inequalities in the European Union (EU). This paper attempts to reveal connections between the policy concept of territorial cohesion, the normative idea of spatial justice and the social investment approach. It is argued that territorial cohesion and spatial justice are intrinsically linked to the social investment approach. The common ground between territorial cohesion and spatial justice is the goal of delivering an improvement in people's lives regardless of where they live. For its part, the social investment approach is also about expanding people's life opportunities by investing in them and thus increasing their capabilities to participate fully in economic and social life. It is true that social investment policies so far have mostly neglected the spatial dimension as they have not been place-sensitive. However, a place-based social investment approach, working in a coherent way with territorial cohesion policy, has the potential to lead to effective solutions ameliorating some of the EU's current spatial ills and the political reactions they generate.

Keywords: European Cohesion Policy, territorial inequality, spatial justice, capabilities approach, place-based, social investment approach.

Introduction

With a focus on economic, social and territorial policy, European Cohesion Policy is increasing in importance as a result of the recent rise in territorial inequality across the European Union (EU) (Capello et al., 2015; Iammarino et al., 2019). This rise has been extensively documented in many official reports, such as the Territorial Agenda 2030 (Ministers Responsible for Spatial Planning and Territorial Development and/or Territorial Cohesion, 2020). The emphasis on territorial inequalities stems from the possibility that growing spatial disparities could endanger EU economic, social and territorial cohesion and even threaten what is perceived as the European Model of Society (Faludi, 2007b, c; Zaucha & Böhme, 2020).

This chapter attempts to reveal connections between the policy concept of territorial cohesion, the normative idea of spatial justice and the social investment approach. More specifically, it is argued in this study that territorial cohesion and spatial justice are intrinsically linked to the social investment approach. If the common ground between territorial cohesion and spatial justice is to deliver an improvement in people's lives regardless of where they live, then both entail an attempt to expand people's capabilities in a territorialized way. The social investment approach is similarly focused on expanding people's life opportunities by investing in them and increasing their human capital. To put it differently, the social investment approach expands people's capabilities by investing in their ability to participate fully in economic and social life. Nevertheless, territorial cohesion and social investment policies are quite different. The first is highly place-based while the second is mostly not sensitive to place. As a result, there is a risk of policy incoherence in the implementation of these two policies. The question that then arises is how to make them work in a policy-coherent way. This idea is food for thought.

The chapter proceeds, firstly, with a theoretical and empirical discussion of the EU policy concept of territorial cohesion. As becomes evident, territorial cohesion is a very abstract concept with many different metrics and layers of meaning. Secondly, to render this concept more tangible and concrete, we transfer the concept of an 'ideal type' from the realm of sociological and historical research to that of European Cohesion Policy. We describe an ideal type of territorial cohesion emerging from the examination of territorial cohesion policies in seven distinct EU national contexts, namely the Austrian, Danish, Greek, Italian, Lithuanian, Polish and UK contexts. This ideal type of territorial cohesion contains a number of specific characteristics. It provides a more grounded theory of territorial cohesion than the abstract uses of the term in the European Union's documents and policy discourse. Thirdly, we continue with our theoretical endeavors by exposing the links between territorial cohesion and spatial justice; we bring to the fore their commonalities without paying significant attention to their differences. Fourthly, we link the ideas of territorial cohesion and spatial justice with the social investment approach through the capabilities perspective. It is argued that a territorialized social investment approach comes close to the aims of both territorial cohesion and spatial justice. Finally, the chapter closes with a synopsis and some policy suggestions.

Territorial cohesion: Defining a contested EU policy concept

Territorial cohesion is the opposite of spatial inequality; thus, when the aims and goals of territorial cohesion are promoted, spatial disparities between and within places gradually diminish. Territorial cohesion is a competence shared between the European Commission and the various EU countries/governments. It is an ambiguous and contested concept, with many different interpretations and meanings (Artelaris & Mavrommatis, 2020). As a policy concept, territorial cohesion originates from the French tradition of regional thinking. The roots of the concept are linked to regional policy in France (Faludi, 2007a, 2010, 2015), where a decentralized state attempts to diminish regional disparities. More to the point, Jacques Delors (European Commissioner 1985–1995) and Michel Barnier (EU Regional Commissioner) are considered to have played influential roles in expanding European Cohesion policy priorities from the economic and social spheres to the territorial one as well (Holder & Layard, 2011). Faludi has argued that a territorially based European Cohesion policy is basically 'old (French) wine in new bottles' (Faludi, 2004). In short, French regional policy is considered the starting point for the development of the EU Territorial Cohesion policy.

The publication of the European Spatial Development Perspective (ESDP, 1999) is considered the first and most important step towards the creation of a European planning philosophy. In essence, it created the foundations of territorial cohesion policy. According to the ESDP, the main spatial problem in the EU is the heavy concentration of people, activities and economic growth in a few specific metropolitan areas (the 'infamous' European pentagon: the metropolitan areas of London, Paris, Milan, Munich and Hamburg). Accordingly, the main objectives of the European planning philosophy are balanced and sustainable development throughout all EU territory, the promotion of polycentric development, parity of access to infrastructure and knowledge across EU space, and the wise management of natural and cultural heritage. In other words, these are the proposed solutions to the spatial concentration of population and economic activities in the EU.

Territorial cohesion has been described, among other ways, as 'ambiguous' and 'complex', while several studies have been conducted to define its meaning and operational dimensions (see for instance Mirwaldt et al., 2008; Begg, 2010; ESPON INTERCO, 2013; González et al., 2015; Atkinson & Zimmerman, 2016; Avdikos & Chardas, 2016; Faludi, 2016; Medeiros, 2016; Dao et al., 2017; Nosek, 2017; Asprogerakas & Zachari, 2020). The literature characterizes territorial cohesion as a 'vague' policy concept (Atkinson & Zimmerman, 2016) or simply a 'fashionable term' with 'many layers of meaning' (Mirwaldt et al., 2008). Some scholars have suggested that territorial cohesion is an 'elusive' and 'ambiguous' term that cannot be easily translated into a clear and measurable concept (Medeiros, 2016). Others have stated that territorial cohesion is a 'contested', 'multi-dimensional' and 'dynamic' concept that 'lacks clarity' (Dao et al., 2017). It has been also suggested that territorial cohesion is of an 'amorphous' character (Van Well, 2012). To cut a long story short, a strict definition of territorial cohesion is an almost 'impossible' task (Bohme & Gloersen, 2011).

Territorial cohesion as a policy concept contains several dimensions, including, among others, socio-economic convergence,[1] spatial planning, economic competitiveness[2] and policy coordination[3] (Evers, 2012). However, only the last two (i.e. economic competitiveness and policy coordination) appear to contribute added value at the EU policy level, as socio-economic convergence[4] and spatial planning have been implicit in the cohesion policy for a long time (Othengrafen & Cornett, 2013). The fact that some of these dimensions (such as socio-economic convergence and economic competitiveness) conflict with each other (Waterhout, 2007) might hinder the ability of territorial cohesion to achieve its policy goals (Nosek, 2017).

Before we proceed any further, we should note that territorial cohesion is an EU policy construct – an EU policy instrument that was constructed and successively communicated by European policy officers and technocrats working on territorial issues. Along these lines, Dabinett (2011) suggests that 'territorial cohesion is a construct that is not found outside the documents and discourses that constitute the words of EU spatial planners and spatial policy' (Dabinett, 2011:2). Other scholars have stated that territorial cohesion is an EU policy discourse whose meaning is related to the discursive chains it becomes attached to (Servillo, 2010). To put it differently, territorial cohesion can be seen as a 'half-empty' EU policy signifier, depending on who is using the term and for what kinds of reasons (Faludi, 2015).

According to Abrahams (2014), we should not approach territorial cohesion by trying to define it; instead, it might be more appropriate to let the concept remain 'fuzzy'. Instead of asking what territorial cohesion is, it might be more useful to ask what territorial cohesion actually does. How is it translated in different national (EU) contexts? What kinds of uses can various actors make of it? For Abrahams, this is the 'pragmatic' approach to the concept. Along these lines, Van Well (2012) has suggested that territorial cohesion can be viewed as a

1 Convergence concerns reduced disparities among regions over time and is linked to the popular concepts of sigma- and beta-convergence (for a review at the EU level, see Artelaris 2015).

2 According to Colomb and Santina (2014), territorial cohesion pursues economic growth and competitiveness while incorporating concerns about solidarity and equity.

3 Policy coordination can be perceived as horizontal coordination, vertical coordination and territorial coordination (for a review, see Nosek 2017).

4 Avdikos and Chardas (2016), however, suggest a decline in the role and importance of socio-economic convergence in recent years, with a loss of prominence and influence in the policymaking process.

'moving target' whose meaning each member-state (or region) constructs to promote its own priorities and guarantee EU funding. Other writers have wondered whether territorial cohesion has the same meaning in all EU national contexts or whether it is subject to different national interpretations in different EU countries (Mirwaldt et al., 2008).

How do you measure territorial cohesion?

Measuring territorial cohesion is certainly not a simple task, given the insufficient clarity of the concept, its different interpretations among EU Member States (Medeiros, 2016) and the lack of a widely accepted and established methodology (Dao et al., 2017). Measuring territorial cohesion, however, is crucial for at least two reasons (Medeiros, 2016:6): first, to reduce the vagueness of the concept and 'engage the academic community in producing useful studies, which could be of vital importance to better understand and correct territorial imbalances'; second, to use and discuss the concept 'in a more concrete and focused way' at the political level. According to Medeiros, 'Leaving the fate of knowledge regarding territorial cohesion to non-measurable and uninformed academic discussions would only contribute to maintain[ing] the present, elusive status quo of this notion ad eternum' (Medeiros, 2016:6). For Dao et al. (2017), measuring territorial cohesion can make the concept more operational.

Although territorial cohesion is, by its nature, a multidimensional concept characterized by a multiplicity of aspects (economic, social, political and cultural), it has been mainly associated with Gross Domestic Product (GDP) per capita, especially during the first two programming periods (i.e., 2000–2006 and 2007–2013). GDP has been used as the main eligibility criterion for EU funding and as the basic indicator of the effectiveness of EU regional policies. This is in line with the promotion of the objectives of economic and social progress as well as the achievement of a high level of employment and balanced, sustainable development (Weckroth & Moisio, 2020).

However, in recent years, the need for a more holistic framework for measuring territorial cohesion has been acknowledged. It has been argued that conventional single indicators such as GDP per capita or (un)employment rates can be regarded as incomplete measures of territorial cohesion, mainly because they are insufficient to cover several aspects of quality of life and human development.[5] As Commissioner Hahn suggested in 2010, 'there is an inherent need to

5 GDP, for instance, focuses only on monetary issues, excluding non-market activities that contribute to human development and well-being, while labour market indicators

develop more indicators for different thematic approaches… That would facilitate to integrate monitoring and evaluation system in the decision-making process which is of crucial importance as a pace-maker.' (Hahn, 2010). In a similar vein, a few years later, Commissioner Crețu noted that 'GDP alone does not accurately enough reflect the needs of a region, as it leaves out crucial parameters such as quality of life, social inclusion, level of employment or sustainable development. This is why, to complement GDP, the Commission is investigating other indicators…'[6]

The recognition of the multidimensionality of territorial cohesion has given rise to an increasing consensus among academics and practitioners on the need for establishing alternative measurement approaches. Several important efforts in this direction have been made at the EU level, including, inter alia, the studies of ESPON (2007), Medeiros (2011), ESPON (2012), ESPON INTERCO (2013) and Hanell (2015) (for an extensive review, see Zaucha & Böhme, 2020). Although significant breakthroughs have been made regarding this issue, the adoption of a sound and uniform approach remains a daunting task (Zaucha & Böhme, 2020); all these studies are based on different aspects of conceptual and intellectual frameworks of territorial cohesion, analyze different geographic scales and follow different methodological approaches. However, they all highlight the need for a multidimensional approach to measuring territorial cohesion.

More specifically, two main approaches have emerged for the measurement of territorial cohesion (Hanell, 2015). According to the first, the concept can be measured by using a number of relative thematic variables and identifying their patterns and trends. Those variables cover not only the economic and social dimensions of territorial cohesion but also other dimensions explained above (territorial governance and cooperation, sustainability, polycentricity, etc). According to the second approach, territorial cohesion can be measured via Composite Indicators (also known as synthetic indices). A Composite Indicator aims to combine many aspects of the phenomenon or concept analyzed, facilitating the reduction of a multifaceted reality to a single value. These indicators, although they are not without critics (Dialga & Giang, 2017), are considered standard and effective tools for the measurement of multidimensional

also present serious disadvantages, since they cannot capture, for example, the extent of problems in some specific areas (e.g. structurally weaker regions, regions with large numbers of foreign workers on temporary contracts or regions with high levels of brain drain) (Ghai 2003; Artelaris 2017).

6 https://www.europarl.europa.eu/doceo/document/CRE-8-2017-11-13-ITM-019_EL.html

phenomena. Today, the construction of Composite Indicators at the regional level is probably one of the most interesting areas of research, mainly because of the need for better territorial policies (Artelaris, 2021). As a result, several Composite Indicators have been constructed to measure territorial cohesion – using, however, different numbers of dimensions and variables and producing different results.

Examples of the first approach include the ESPON project, namely INTERCO. In this project, a list of 32 top indicators structured along six territorial objectives was selected, covering both thematic issues and policy dimensions of territorial cohesion (ESPON, 2013). The territorial objectives included global competitiveness; innovative territories; fair access to services, markets and jobs; inclusion and quality of life; attractive regions of high ecological value and strong territorial capital; and integrated polycentric territorial development. The choice of indicators was determined by the priorities of the Territorial Agenda 2020 and the Europe 2020 Strategy.

An example of the second (Composite Indicators) approach is the study by Medeiros (2011) based on the methodology used for the Human Development Index (HDI), introduced by the UN in 1990 (UNDP, 1990). The HDI is probably the oldest and most significant attempt to overcome the narrow focus of GDP. In this study, Medeiros proposes a Territorial Cohesion (composite) indicator that takes into consideration dimensions related to socioeconomic territorial imbalances, environmental sustainability, territorial cooperation/governance processes and the polycentricity of the urban system. The results of the study revealed a heterogeneous pattern of territorial cohesion for the EU (NUTS 2 level).

Although the main message of empirical studies is that further research is needed to develop a common framework for measuring territorial cohesion, their findings can be used by policymakers not only as a way to better understand territorial cohesion but also as guiding lights in the process of policymaking and as tools for evaluating the performance and effectiveness of the policies adopted. Measuring territorial cohesion is still a challenging task, calling for additional work.

Creating an 'ideal type' of territorial cohesion?

The purpose of this section is to introduce the notion of an 'ideal type' of European Territorial Cohesion policy. It must be noted that specific national policy environments existed in (many) EU countries before the appearance of the EU territorial cohesion policy. Accordingly, the arrival of territorial cohesion policy in national (EU) contexts did not take place in a policy vacuum, but instead in already-formed environments corresponding to broadly-defined national cohesion/convergence goals. As a result, on the one hand, territorial cohesion had to be adapted in many cases to fit in with existing policies. On the other hand, the arrival of territorial cohesion policy changed many aspects of these pre-existing national policy environments and brought an emphasis on new priorities. In short, territorial cohesion might mean different things in different EU countries and national policy contexts.

Because of this, instead of trying to define the concept of territorial cohesion abstractly at the EU level, it might be useful alternatively to derive it from distinct EU national contexts. Within the COHSMO project, the national policy contexts of Austria, Denmark, Greece, Italy, Lithuania, Poland and the UK were investigated to understand what territorial cohesion policy meant in those different policy contexts and what its respective usages were in each. To put it differently, the notion of an 'ideal type' of territorial cohesion and its main characteristics emerged from the examination of seven different EU member states' national contexts and distinct regional policy traditions.

The concept of an ideal type originates from the work of Max Weber (2014) and his way of approaching dynamic and complex social phenomena that cannot be fully explained but can be interpreted to an extent and thereby rendered at least partly understandable. In Weber's work, the ideal type, or pure type, is a form of analytical construction that enables the researcher to approach reality by simplifying it. However, an ideal type never really corresponds to all facets of reality but only to some, as it does not include all the elements of the phenomenon under investigation but is constructed instead out of certain selected characteristics. It thus lies between the abstraction, or generalizing tendencies, of theoretical thinking and the particularities, or specificity, of historical research and individual case studies. In short, the ideal type can be seen as a way of constructing a logical and coherent analytical instrument for further research, perhaps even a grounded hypothesis.

In this section, we attempt to transfer the concept of the ideal type from the realm of sociological and historical research to that of European Cohesion policy. According to the above, the ideal type of territorial cohesion lies somewhere between the general abstractions of EU policy thinking and the concreteness of each national policy framework under examination. As a result, the ideal type of territorial cohesion includes characteristics emerging from different national contexts (the Austrian, Danish, Greek, Italian, Lithuanian, Polish and UK contexts) without containing all the characteristics of any given case. It is a way of approaching territorial cohesion policy not from the totally abstract and generalizing type of perspective that is usually found within the minds of EU policymakers, but through a more grounded approach, which nevertheless is still a form of abstraction – a grounded abstraction.

It must be noted that some of the characteristics of the ideal type of territorial cohesion are not necessarily regarded as aspects of territorial cohesion within their own national policy landscapes. In many cases, they are not even referred to as such. However, these characteristics are important to include in the effort to construct an ideal type of territorial cohesion. At the same time, the logic of some of these characteristics may not necessarily add up; instead, conflicts and contradictions may emerge between them. Among other reasons, this can be attributed to the fact that territorial cohesion policy in any given national context can unfold on different geographical scales; territorial cohesion policies can involve a number of different actors (at different scales) not necessarily sharing the same objectives. The ideal type of territorial cohesion constructed from the examination of the above-mentioned national contexts includes the following characteristics:

- **An emphasis on balanced development and access to services (and even connectivity)**. From the very beginning, the ESDP spoke of balancing competitiveness with harmonious and equally distributed development. Most importantly, balanced development and access to services have remained strictly spatial concepts as forms of territorialized social inclusion or spatial justice. The implication is that people should not face obstacles because of their location. In this sense, the life-opportunities perspective on individuals, or the emphasis on the freedom of individuals to live decently according to their potential in their places of residence, becomes part and parcel of the balanced-development and access-to-services perspective on territorial cohesion. In short, location should not be a disadvantage. Furthermore, these imperatives have come to be articulated through a policy language that speaks of parity of access or equity of services, facilities, infrastructure and even knowledge. More concretely, this balanced-development and access-to-services perspective comes to be communicated through the concept of 'services of general interest' (SGI), which cover all the fundamentals people need to lead a decent life (jobs, health, education, security, etc.). Through the equal provision of 'services of general interest' in all places, people are spared deprivation of public goods based on where they happen to live. This is a fundamental dimension of territorial cohesion and can be found in many different national frameworks.
- **Polycentric development and the advancement of urban economic growth**. The idea of polycentricity goes hand in hand with the notions, among others,

of economic competitiveness, smart growth and digital connectivity. From the perspective of territorial cohesion's goal of polycentricity, the spatial concentration in specific urban areas of people, activity and prosperity creates obstacles relating not only to the increased costs of concentration (land values, quality of life, time to work, etc.) but also, indirectly, to issues of spatial justice (concentration of economic activity, political representation, facilities, etc.). There is a strong emphasis on measures seen as capable of facilitating urban/metropolitan economic growth through the creation of a polycentric system, thus enhancing the economic competitiveness of the various regions. Furthermore, such policies are part and parcel of a wider form of policy thinking that views economic globalization as unstoppable and stresses the role of cities. Accordingly, the creation of a polycentric urban system (and its functional areas) has come to be perceived as the motto of economic development in a knowledge-economy era; cities are seen as growth poles of economic and social development and are charged with the task of attracting human talent and economic capital. This notion of polycentricity, which originates from the ESDP, can be considered an important element of territorial cohesion policy.

- **A place-based approach**. According to such an approach, activating local development dynamics – in all areas, but especially in underdeveloped ones – on the basis of endogenous resources and local comparative advantages is deemed paramount for any local development efforts to be successful. At the same time, place-based and community-based initiatives must be harnessed to take advantage of territorial diversity. Accordingly, local potential for endogenous development is supplemented with external help, in part from multi-level governance systems. As a result, localities seeking to escape their undeveloped economic structures and bleak economic futures must exploit territorial assets and even create new ones. Furthermore, such a place-based or local development approach takes for granted a 'bottom-up' perspective as local knowledge must be harnessed while abstract and a-spatial theories and policies must be replaced by concrete, place-informed understandings. More importantly, the building of democratic capacities and the broadening of civic participation in policy planning and implementation are deemed important within a place-based approach.
- **Empowering local and regional governments within (but not only within) a European multi-level governance system**. In broad terms, territorial cohesion can be considered part and parcel of the much broader phenomenon of the development of European multi-level governance, which includes several actors performing at different geographical scales. The multi-level

governance theory arose from research on the EU aimed at understanding the relations between Brussels, national governments and regional/local/urban authorities. This theory represented an early recognition of the fact that EU cohesion policies, which were the redistributive EU spatial policies *par excellence*, increased the political power of regional, local and urban authorities. The EU came to be conceived as a political system where authority is shared between various actors at different levels. Within such a framework, the European Commission, along with the sub-national authorities (regions, cities, etc.) and non-state actors (businesses, NGOs, etc.), can bypass national governments and thus develop autonomous policymaking processes. By all accounts, national governments still remain important in policymaking, but they no longer hold monopolistic powers; they are one among a variety of actors. The empowering of regional and local governments within a multi-level EU framework of governance is a characteristic element of territorial cohesion policies.

- **Integration and co-ordination of policies**. The notion of integrated policies refers to policies that take into consideration all dimensions of development (economic, societal, environmental and cultural), all scales of space and time and all levels of governance (European, national, federal, regional and local). According to this approach, the integration of policies can maximize intended results and facilitate stated policy goals. More particularly, territorial cohesion policies depend closely both on the horizontal coordination of all policies with a spatial impact (policy coherence) and on territorial cooperation between different spatial units and various actors at all levels of the multi-level EU governance system. Such coordination between different policies and various governance units is considered conducive to the production of integrated policies, which can provide the best solutions to problems of territorial cohesion across EU space.

Territorial cohesion and the normative idea of spatial justice

The discourse on territorial cohesion has partly led to a re-conceptualization of European regional policy incorporating dimensions of spatial justice (Davoudi, 2005). The main reason for the interest in spatial justice is the significant increase in EU territorial inequality that intensifies spatial injustices and put EU territorial cohesion policy under pressure (Jones et al., 2020). As a result, great strides have been made in academia during the last years toward applying the normative concept of spatial justice to cohesion policy concerns in the EU regional context (Kearns et al., 2014; Jones et al., 2020). Furthermore, European policymakers have even explored the potential effectiveness of the concept of spatial justice as an alternative to the concept of territorial cohesion and territorial cohesion policy (Jones et al., 2019:99).[7]

The idea of spatial justice is based, to a great extent, on the academic debates of the '70s and '80s that supplemented John Rawls' idea of justice (Rawls, 1971) with a territorialized notion of social justice (Davies, 1968; Harvey, 1973; Pirie, 1983; see also Jones et al., 2019:107–110). According to Rawls' (1971) *A Theory of Justice*, the principle of 'fair equality of opportunity' in democratic societies translates into the dictum that social and economic differences can be tolerated only if they are associated with the availability of 'offices and positions' that are open to everyone. Nevertheless, the Rawlsian principle of justice is a-spatial, as his theory does not examine the distribution of injustices in space (Maly, 2016). The spatialization of this principle would entail that people should not be disadvantaged because of their location; location should not hinder or constrain individuals' life opportunities or capabilities.

Thus we see that when social justice is viewed from a territorial perspective, it transforms into spatial justice. The concept of spatial justice originates in the work of Edward Soja (2010) and his ideas about the unequal distribution of injustices in space, especially at the urban level – an approach conceptually close to the economic, social and political disparities perspective. According to Soja, spatial justice (or injustice) is not simply the outcome of economic, social and political processes; it is also a 'dynamic force affecting these processes in significant ways' (Soja, 2010:2). Seeking spatial justice means the geographical extension of economic, social and/or environmental (etc.) justice to places (and population groups) that experience injustice (Soja, 2010:5). Like the concept of territorial cohesion, spatial justice cannot be considered in strictly economic terms. However, in contrast to the concept of territorial cohesion, spatial justice allows for a more plural understanding of development, well-being and quality of life, bringing those notions to the forefront of the discussion (Jones et al., 2019). Nevertheless, the concept of spatial justice remains complex and

7 In the policy context, a few recent studies have explored the contribution of place-based policies to spatial justice. Although place-based policies can contribute significantly to spatial justice in some cases, the positive link is hindered in several countries by factors related to the domestic institutional environment (Keller at al. 2021; Weck et al. 2021), such as a high degree of central government involvement (Petrakos et al. 2021).

contested (Madanipour et al., 2021), while its metrics remain in their infancy, still limited and unclear (Israel & Frenkel, 2018).[8]

Linking territorial cohesion, spatial justice and the social investment approach

As has been argued above, one significant aspect of territorial cohesion has to do with enhancing people's capabilities to live according to their potential, irrespective of where they happen to reside. The capabilities approach emerged as a reaction against mainstream positions in welfare economics, political philosophy and ethics (Claassen, 2016). It is based on two core concepts: functionings and capabilities (Sen, 1985, 1993; Nussbaum, 2000). The former is related to personal features such as what a person is doing or achieving in life. The latter is associated with what human beings can do or achieve, that is, the range of options available to a person. On a policy level, spatial justice considerations originate from the European model of society that was built upon the social-democratic and Christian-democratic canon of European politics and maintained an 'appropriate balance' between the individual, the market and the state (Faludi, 2007b, c). Increasingly, the French principle of 'égalité' became territorialized through the core political belief that citizens should not experience spatial disadvantage. Decades later, Barca (2009) and others argued that an EU '*territorialized social agenda*' should create equality between places as people live their lives and build their capabilities in specific places.

In close relevance to the above, territorial cohesion as spatial justice has been mainly articulated in terms of parity of access to services, facilities, infrastructure and knowledge. It has been communicated through the concept of 'services of general interest' (SGI) that cover all the fundamentals people need to lead a decent life (jobs, health, education, security, etc.). The equal provision in all places of 'services of general interest' ensures that people are not deprived of public goods because of where they happen to live.

The social investment approach transcends the idea of social welfare as merely the provision of general services, facilities, infrastructure, etc. It contends that social welfare should not only provide different kinds of services and cash transfers but also, and more importantly, promote programs and policies that enhance the capability people have to participate fully in economic and social life.

8 See Israel and Frenkel (2018) for a conceptual framework in which a metric of justice can be employed in different spatial contexts.

To put it differently, social investment policy invests in the realization of people's potential. It attempts to strengthen people's capabilities and skills through the promotion of education, vocational training, childcare, active labor market policies, healthcare, etc. The idea of the social investment approach goes back to the late 1990s. As a policy priority, it was built into the Lisbon Agenda (2000). The social investment approach is a distinctive welfare policy paradigm (Hemerijck, 2015, 2018); some writers even argue that it is now dominant in European social policymaking (Cantillon & Van Lancker, 2013). According to the literature, the social investment approach is based on the pillars of social inclusion through work, individual responsibility and human capital investment (ibid). However, this approach has been criticized for putting too much emphasis on investing in people and not necessarily enough on the protection of vulnerable groups or people outside the employment umbrella (Hemerijck, 2018; Boczy et al., 2019). Discussion of the effectiveness and limitations of the social investment approach is still ongoing.

In a sense, the provision of 'services of general interest' and the social investment approach are quite close. Both aspire to help people live decent and dignified lives in the places where they reside. Both aim to assist individuals in living decently and not experiencing disadvantages because of where they happen to live. However, the social investment approach is not so much about parity of access to services as it is about strengthening the capability to participate fully in economic and social life. It is about investing in people to realize their capabilities and augment their life opportunities. As Boczy et al. (2021) argue, territorial cohesion and social investment focus on different levels: the former on the collective, the latter on the individual. Accordingly, territorial cohesion aims to promote the cohesion of spatial units collectively, while social investment aims to help people individually.

From the above, it becomes apparent that the aims and objectives of a territorialized or place-based social investment policy are close to those of territorial cohesion. To put it differently, there are many commonalities between a place-based social investment approach and the aims and goals of territorial cohesion as spatial justice. However, the territorial dimension of the social investment approach remains under-explored as it has been mostly ignored in policy implementation and debate (Boczy et al., 2021). To date, the emphasis on social investment has been formulated at the national and supranational levels. More to the point, programs that invest in people's capabilities have been designed at the national level with the financial assistance of the EU (ibid). As a result, sub-national and local levels have not been seriously taken into account in the design and implementation of social investment policies. This serious flaw can jeopardize territorial cohesion across national territories (ibid). This means that a non-territorialized social investment policy can not only create obstacles to territorial cohesion but also increase spatial disparities. Accordingly, what we need is a place-sensitive (Boczy et al., 2021) social investment approach that is not generic or a-spatial but instead tailored to the needs of different regions, areas and localities, etc. – a place-based social investment policy.

Conclusions: Coherence between social investment and territorial cohesion policies

The EU territories are experiencing a period of rapid and significant change as a result, among others, of the 2008 and 2020 (Covid-19) economic crises resulting in persistent spatial inequalities (Iammarino et al., 2019; Bailey et al., 2020). In this context, European Cohesion Policy, with its focus on economic, social and territorial policy aspects, is increasingly gaining attention and significance. This chapter aimed to reveal existing connections between the policy concept of territorial cohesion, the normative idea of spatial justice and the social investment approach. As we argued, territorial cohesion as the equal provision of 'services of general interest' (spatial justice), is close to the aims of the social investment approach. Both aspire to help people live dignified lives in the places where they happen to reside. Nevertheless, the social investment approach is not so much about parity of access to services as it is about strengthening people's capabilities to participate fully in economic and social life. However, a place-based social investment policy is closer to the aims and objectives of territorial cohesion; there are many commonalities between a place-based social investment approach and the goals of territorial cohesion as spatial justice.

The question that arises in the current, complex and volatile EU environment is how to implement European and national policies to decrease spatial disparities, promote territorial cohesion and foster economic development. In this paper, we suggested that social investment and territorial cohesion policies should work together in a coherent and mutually reinforcing manner. This means that policy efforts should work synergistically and not as adversaries. To that end, we probably need a place-sensitive social investment approach – a set of policies that are place-based and complement the aims and objectives of territorial cohesion.

References

Abrahams, G. (2014). What "is" territorial cohesion? What does it "do"? Essentialist versus pragmatic approaches to using concepts. *European Planning Studies*, *22*(10), 2134–2155.

Artelaris, P. (2015). Local versus regime convergence regression models: A comparison of two approaches. *GeoJournal*, *80*, 263–77.

Artelaris, P. (2017). Geographies of economic crisis in Greece: A social well-being approach. *Geoforum*, *84*, 59–69.

Artelaris, P. (2021). A development index for the Greek regions. *Quality & Quantity*, https://doi.org/10.1007/s11135-021-01175-x.

Artelaris, P., & Mavrommatis, G. (2020). Territorial cohesion as a policy narrative: From economic competitiveness to 'smart' growth and beyond. *Social Inclusion*, *8*(4), 208–217.

Asprogerakas, E., & Zachari, V. (2020). The EU territorial cohesion discourse and the spatial planning system in Greece. *European Planning Studies*, *28*(3), 583–603.

Atkinson, R., & Zimmerman, K. (2016). Cohesion policy and cities: An ambivalent relation. In S. Piattoni (Ed.), *Handbook on cohesion policy in the EU*. Elgar Publishing, Elgar online.

Avdikos, V., & Chardas, A. (2016). European Union cohesion policy Post 2014: More (place-based and conditional) growth – less redistribution and cohesion. *Territory, Politics, Governance*, *4*(1), 97–117.

Bailey, D., Clark, J., Colombelli, A., Corradini, C., De Propris, L., Derudder, B., Fratesi, U., Fritsch, M., Harrison, J., Hatfield, M., Kemeny, T., Kogler, D., Lagendijk, A., Lawton, P., Ortega-Argilés, R., Iglesias Otero, C., & Usai, S. (2020). Regions in a time of pandemic. *Regional Studies*, *54*(9), 1163–1174.

Barca, F. (2009). *An Agenda for a reformed Cohesion Policy: A place-based approach to meeting EU challenges and expectations*. DG Regio, EC.

Begg, I. (2010). Cohesion or confusion: A policy searching for objectives. *Journal of European Integration*, *32*(1), 77–96.

Boczy, T, Cefalo, R., & Cordini, M. (2019). The social investment perspective and its territorial dimension. In DAStU working paper series, n. 03/2019 (LPS.05).

Boczy, T, Cefalo, R., & Cordini, M. (2021). Place-sensitive social investment and territorial cohesion: Implications for sustainability. *Sustainability*, *13*, 7085. https://doi.org/10.3390/su13137085.

Bohme, K., & Gloersen, E. (2011). Territorial cohesion storylines: Understanding a policy concept. *Spatial Foresight Brief*, *1*, www.spatialforesight.eu.

Cantillon, B., & Van Lancker, W. (2013). The shortcomings of the social investment perspective. *Social Policy & Society, 12*(4), 553–564.

Capello, R., Caragliu, A., & Fratesi, U. (2015). Spatial heterogeneity in the costs of the economic crisis in Europe: Are cities sources of regional resilience?, *Journal of Economic Geography, 15*, 951–972.

Christopherson, S., Martin, R., & Pollard, J. Claassen, R. (2016). An agency-based capability theory of justice. *European Journal of Philosophy, 24*(3), 1279–1304.

Colomb, C., & Santinha, G. (2014). European Union competition policy and the European territorial cohesion agenda: An impossible reconciliation? State Aid rules and public service liberalization through the European spatial planning lens. *European Planning Studies, 22*(3), 459–480.

Dabinett, G. (2011). What future for cohesion policy? An academic and policy debate, *Paper presented at DG Regio*, Regional Studies and Slovenia Government Office for Local Self-Government and Regional Policy Conference, 16–18 March 2011.

Dao, H., Cantoreggi Plagnat, P., & Rousseaux, V. (2017). Operationalizing a contested concept: Indicators for territorial cohesion. *European Planning Studies*, https://doi.org/10.1080/09654313.2017.1281230.

Davies, B. (1968). *Social needs and resources in local services: A study of variations in provision of social services between local authority areas*. London: Joseph Rowntree.

Davoudi, S. (2005). Understanding territorial cohesion. *Planning, Practice & Research, 20*, 433–441.

Dialga, I., & Giang, H. (2017). Highlighting methodological limitations in the steps of composite indicators construction. *Social Indicators Research, 131*, 441–465.

ESDP. (1999). European spatial development perspective: Towards balanced and sustainable development of the EU territory, *European Commission, Brussels.*

ESPON INTERCO. (2013). Indicators of territorial cohesion, scientific platform and tools, project: 2013/3/2, Final Report, Luxemburg: ESPON.

ESPON. (2007). Feasibility study on monitoring territorial development based on ESPON key indicators, Part A: Tentative spatial monitoring report, final report. ESPON project 4.1.3. Bonn: Bundesamt für Bauwesen und Raumordnung.

ESPON. (2012). INTERCO indicators of territorial cohesion. Part B. Final report. Scientific.

Evers, D. (2012). A solution in search of a problem: A 'Garbage Can' approach to the politics of territorial cohesion. *European Journal of Spatial Development, 10*(1), 24–24.

Faludi, A. (2004). Territorial cohesion: Old (French) wine in new bottles?, *Urban Studies, 41*(7), 1349–1365.

Faludi, A. (2007a). From European spatial planning to territorial cohesion policy. *Regional Studies, 40*(6), 667–678.

Faludi, A. (2007b). Territorial cohesion policy and the European model of society. *European Planning Studies, 15*(4), 567–583.

Faludi, A. (2007c). The European model of society. In A. Faludi (Ed.), *Territorial cohesion and the European model of society* (pp. 1–22). Cambridge, MA: Lincoln Institute of Land Policy.

Faludi, A. (2010). The process architecture of territorial cohesion policy. *European JournalofSpatialPlanning*,no.30,uuid:a6ebf58b-d926-4dd1-96b7-2171f8432909.

Faludi, A. (2015). Territorial cohesion under the looking glass, EU publications, https://op.europa.eu/en/publication-detail/-/publication/15dd2ed8-9d76-49f2-994e-775b77f0d40a/language-en

Faludi, A. (2016). EU territorial cohesion policy, a contradiction in terms. *Planning Theory and Practice, 17*(2), 302–313.

Ghai, D. (2003). Decent work: Concept and indicators. *International Labour Review, 142*, 113–145.

González, A., Daly, G., Pinch, P., Adams, N., Valtenbergs, V., Burns, M., & Johannesson, H. (2015). Indicators for spatial planning and territorial cohesion: Stakeholder-driven selection approach for improving usability at regional and local levels. *Regional Studies, 49*(9), 1588–1602.

Hahn, J. (2010). *Evaluation of ERDF objectives, 2000–2006* [Press Release]. Retrieved from https://ec.europa.eu/commission/presscorner/detail/en/SPEECH_10_167.

Hamerijck, A. (2015). The quiet paradigm revolution of social investment. *Social Politics, 22*(2), 242–256.

Hamerijck, A. (2018). Social investment as a policy paradigm. *Journal of European Public Policy, 25*(6), 810–827.

Hanell, T. (2015). Measuring territorial cohesion: A macro regional approach. In T. Lang, S. Henn, W. Sgibnev, & K. Ehrlich (Eds.), *Understanding geographies of polarization and peripheralization. Perspectives from Central and Eastern Europe and beyond* (pp. 235–251). London: Palgrave Macmillan.

Harvey, D. (1973). *Social justice and the city* (Edward Arnold, Maidenhead, Berks).

Holder J. and Layard A. (2011), Drawing out the elements of Territorial Cohesion: Re-scaling EU Spatial Governance, *Yearbook of European Law*, 30(1):358–380.

Iammarino, S., Rodriguez-Pose, A., & Storper, M. (2019). Regional inequality in Europe: Evidence, theory and policy implications. *Journal of Economic Geography*, *19*, 273–298.

Israel, E., & Frenkel, A. (2018). Social justice and spatial inequality: Toward a conceptual framework. *Progress in Human Geography*, *42*(5), 647–665.

Jones, R., Goodwin-Hawkins, B., & Woods, M. (2020). From territorial cohesion to regional spatial justice: The well-being of future generations act in wales. *International Journal of Urban and Regional Research*, https://doi.org/10.1111/1468-2427.12909

Jones, R., Moisio, S., Weckroth, M., Woods, M., Luukkonen, J., Meyer, F., & Miggelbrink, J. (2019). Reconceptualising territorial cohesion through the prism of spatial justice: Critical perspectives on academic and policy discourses. In T. Lang & F. Görmar (Eds.), *Regional and local development in times of polarisation: Re-thinking spatial policies in Europe* (pp. 97–119). London: Palgrave Macmillan.

Kearns, G., Meredith, D., & Morrissey, J. (Eds.). (2014). *Spatial justice and the Irish crisis*. Dublin: Royal Irish Academy.

Keller, J., & Virág, T. (2021). A drop in the sea or catalyst for change: Diverse effects of the place based approach in Europe. *European Planning Studies*, https://doi.org/10.1080/09654313.2021.1928047.

Madanipour, A., Shucksmith, M., & Brooks, E. (2021). The concept of spatial justice and the European Union's territorial cohesion. *European Planning Studies*, https://doi.org/10.1080/09654313.2021.1928040.

Maly, J. (2016). Questioning territorial cohesion: (Un)equal access to services of general interest. *Papers in Regional Science*, https://doi.org/10.1111/pirs.12250.

Medeiros, E. (2011). Territorial cohesion: A conceptual analysis, Lisbon: Institute of Geography and Spatial Planning (IGOT) Alameda da Universidade. Retrieved from: https://www.regionalstudies.org/wp-content/uploads/2018/07/medeiros.pdf

Medeiros, E. (2016b). Territorial cohesion: An EU concept. *European Journal of Spatial Development*, *60*. Available from: http://www.nordregio.se/Global/EJSD/Refereedarticles/refereed60.pdf.

Ministers Responsible for Spatial Planning and Territorial Development and/or Territorial Cohesion. (2020). Territorial agenda 2030. A future for all places, Accessed 14 June 2021, https://ec.europa.eu/regional_policy/sources/docgener/brochure/territorial_agenda_2030_en.pdf.

Mirwaldt, K., McMaster, I., & Bachter, J. (2008b). Reconsidering cohesion policy: The contested debate on territorial cohesion. *European Policy Research Paper*, No. 66, University of Strathclyde, Glasgow.

Nosek, Š. (2017). Territorial cohesion storylines in 2014–2020 cohesion policy. *European Planning Studies, 25*(12), 2157–2174.

Nussbaum, M. C. (2000). *Women and human development: The capabilities approach.* Cambridge: Cambridge University Press.

Othengrafen, F., & Cornett, A. (2013). A critical assessment of the added value of territorial cohesion. *European Journal of Spatial Development, 53*, 1–30.

Petrakos, G., Topaloglou, L., Anagnostou, A., & Cupcea, V. (2021). Geographies of (in)justice and the (in)effectiveness of place-based policies in Greece. *European Planning Studies.* https://doi.org/10.1080/09654313.2021.1928050.

Pirie, G. (1983). On spatial justice. *Environment and Planning A, 15*(4), 465–473.

Rawls, J. (1971). *Theory of justice.* Harvard: Harvard University Press.

Sen, A. K. (1985). *Commodities and capabilities.* Cambridge: Cambridge University Press.

Sen, A. K. (1993). Capability and well-being. In M. Nussbaum & A. Sen (Eds.), *The quality of life.* Oxford: Clarendon Press for UNU-WIDER.

Servillo, L. (2010). Territorial cohesion discourses: Hegemonic strategic concepts in European spatial planning. *Planning Theory and Practice, 11*(3), 397–416.

Soja, E. (2010). *Seeking spatial justice.* Minneapolis: University of Minnesota Press.

United Nations Development Programme (UNDP). (1990). *Human development report 1990.* New York: Oxford University Press for UNDP.

Van Well, L. (2012). Conceptualizing the logics of territorial cohesion. *European Planning Studies, 20*(9), 1549–1567.

Waterhout, B. (2007). Territorial cohesion: Discourses underlying. In A. Faludi (Ed.), *Territorial cohesion and european model of society* (pp. 37–59). Cambridge, MA: Lincoln Institute of Land Policy.

Weber, M. (2014). *The protestant ethic and the spirit of capitalism.* Kettering: Angelico Press.

Weck, S., Madanipour, A., & Schmitt, P. (2021). Place-based development and spatial justice. *European Planning Studies.* https://doi.org/10.1080/09654313.2021.1928038.

Weckroth, M., & Moisio, S. (2020). The challenge of spatial justice for EU's cohesion policy. *Social Inclusion, 8*(4), 183–193.

Zaucha, J., & Böhme, K. (2020). Measuring territorial cohesion is not a mission impossible. *European Planning Studies, 28*(3), 627–649. https://doi.org/10.1080/09654313.2019.1607827.

Ruggero Cefalo, Tatjana Boczy, Marta Cordini

Chapter 2 A social investment approach for place-sensitive services: What is the potential impact on territorial inequalities?

Abstract: This chapter presents the Social Investment (SI) approach to social policy and service provision, which considers social policies productive factors that combine social inclusion and economic competitiveness. The territorial dimension has not been extensively explored within the SI debate. Because of the potential impacts on regional and territorial inequalities, local specificities and multilevel governance structures should be considered in research framed by SI. In the following chapter, we begin by describing the Social Investment (SI) approach through a review of the origin, policy strategies and criticisms leveled at SI. Subsequently, we reflect on the territorial dimension of these policies. This dimension results from the interaction between several factors including reliance on the provision of capacitating services, the process of rescaling, the persistence of spatial disparities in Europe, and the characteristics of the emerging knowledge economy. Finally, we explore the relationship between place-sensitive Social Investment and Territorial Cohesion.

Keywords: Social Investment, New Social Risks, Welfare, Territorial Cohesion, Social policy, Service delivery.

Introduction

Given the changing nature of social risks that follow far-reaching structural changes in the economy, technological development, and demographic trends, post-industrial welfare states face increasing pressures (Esping-Andersen, 1998). Social protection has become more challenging using traditional and mostly insurance-based policy tools due to the less predictable nature of new social risks. For instance, fragmented working biographies, i.e. alternating temporary and non-standard employment with periods of unemployment, make it more difficult to fulfill requirements for insurance time-based unemployment benefits and to receive adequate pensions. Moreover, sluggish economic growth, high levels of public debt and austerity measures prioritize cost-containment by cutting or recalibrating welfare expenditures and arrangements (Hemerijck, 2013). Against this background, Social Investment (SI) emerged as a policy perspective supporting the relevance of the welfare state in employing public resources to foster "productive" social policies, to combine social inclusion and economic competitiveness at the end of the 1990s (Esping- Andersen et al., 2002; Morel et al., 2012).

Despite the recognition that SI policies rely strongly on the provision of capacitating services implemented at the local level (Morel et al., 2012), research on territorial implications of SI is limited (Kazepov & Cefalo, 2022). This gap is in contrast with the local characterization of the new social risks (Ranci, 2010), which are closely linked to contextual factors. In addition, the neglect of local dimensions in debating and planning SI policies underestimates the increasing relevance of sub-national governance levels in policy provision. For this reason, our contribution attempts to understand the possibilities of adopting a territorialized SI. By doing so, we mobilize concepts such as social inclusion, territorial cohesion, and economic growth in a multi-scalar setting (Kazepov, 2010). This chapter aims at reflecting on the territorial features that affect the implementation of SI policies and, consequently, whether these policies are adaptable to territorial specificities. Approaching these issues means inevitably considering the complexity of multi-scalar governance alongside the territorial divides that characterize European countries, therefore dealing with the issue of territorial cohesion (Cordini et al., 2021).

Sections 1–2 will first describe the Social Investment (SI) approach. Beginning with the relationship between welfare states and changing societal challenges, we review the origins, policy strategies and criticisms levelled at SI. Subsequently in section 3, we reflect on the territorial dimension of these policies, arguing that this dimension emanates from the interaction between several factors, including the reliance on service provision, the process of rescaling, the persistence of spatial disparities in European territories, and the characteristics of the knowledge economy. Finally, in section 4, we explore the relationship between place-sensitive Social Investment (SI) and Territorial Cohesion (TC) (Medeiros, 2016; Marques et al., 2018) to analytically connect service provision and territories. The SI approach benefits from the TC lenses of regional specifics, and, more importantly, SI becomes more effective when there is sensitivity for regional disparities and balancing socio-economic development.

New social risks and the emergence of the social investment state in Western Europe

Western European welfare states developed to maturity during the post-war "golden age". During the "mid-century social compromise" (until the early 1970s), industrial capitalism, liberalism and citizenship achieved a balanced institutional configuration in Western Europe: favorable economic conditions allowed for mitigation of social conflicts through the increased distribution of income and services among social categories. This period resulted in expanding welfare policies and the wide diffusion of well-being (Amable, 2016). Starting from the mid-1970s, however, profound socio-economic changes and the mutating landscape of new social risks (Ranci, 2010) brought pressure to bear on the constrained traditional configuration of social protection systems. During their silver age (Taylor-Gooby, 2004), the European welfare states experienced complex reforms of recalibration and retrenchment. This period was characterized by an increase in selectivity and marginality of social policies regarding family and the market as sources of comprehensive welfare (Saraceno, 2015). Some authors also stressed the emergence of common directions of change in the process of "recalibration" (Pierson, 2002) of welfare policies: cost-containment measures aimed at limiting current and future social spending; activation policies reduced dependency on the state and increased individual responsibility; territorialization mechanisms affected different scales of governance and types of actors involved, bringing sub- and supra-national governance levels to the fore (Kazepov, 2010).

Against this background, the relationship between welfare efforts and socio-economic performance was extensively debated in sociological and economic literature. Okun (1975) shaped this relationship according to a "big trade-off" between equality and efficiency. Redistribution operated via welfare state programs to reduce inequality and poverty was viewed as potentially harmful to economic growth due to the distortions in the labor market and wages shaped by a comprehensive social provision, labor market regulation and progressive taxation. Thus, high levels of social expenditure would be linked to stagnating competitiveness due to lower labor supply, higher unemployment and less investment in training. Iversen and Wren (1998) described the relationship between welfare and economic growth as a "trilemma" between the policy goals of employment creation, wage equality and budgetary restraint. They argued that welfare states could successfully pursue at most two of these policy goals simultaneously. If priority is given to budgetary restraints and cost containment, employment growth can be accomplished mainly in the private sector but only at the cost of increasing wage inequality. The latter could be generated only in the public sector for governments pursuing wage equality and employment growth, but this would entail high public spending and taxation. Finally, welfare states committed to equality in wages but not willing to finance public employment expansion due to budgetary constraints would face the prospect of low levels of employment creation in a context of de-industrialization. The core argument lay in the tertiarization and de-industrialization processes as the engine of employment growth. However, in service sectors with a strong component of interpersonal interaction, productivity gains are meagre (Esping-Andersen, 1998). Recently, Wren (2017) reviewed her argument starting from the evidence of a significant contextual change in the economic domain, i.e. the expansion of high productivity, ICT intensive, trade service sectors that could potentially reduce the starkness of the service economy "trilemma". This economic transition to the knowledge-based or globalized learning (Lundvall & Lorenz, 2012) economy has further implications: the relevance of education and institutional formation systems in managing adaption of the workforce to navigate the dynamics of service sectors/economies.

Against this background, the SI approach emerged at the end of the 1990s as a normative approach to counterbalance neoliberal trends of austerity policies promoting retrenchment in welfare expenditure (Morel et al., 2012; European Commission, 2013). In the SI approach, the welfare state is viewed not as an obstacle but rather as an actor of coordination, promotion and stimulation of economic development (Giddens, 1998; Esping-Andersen et al., 2002). The expansion of the public service sector is argued to have direct effects on public employment creation and also indirect effects (via skill formation) on high value-added private service sectors. For example, increasing investments in tertiary education and specifically in strategic courses (like ICT) would feed the skill-intensive job demand in the service sectors, resulting in more high-skilled workers and increased economic competitiveness. Therefore, high public spending can be associated with employment and economic growth, thus assuring the sustainability of the welfare state: as more people work with good earnings, providing resources to the welfare state (see Hemerijck et al., 2016). In social-democratic welfare regimes, substantial public investment in education and protection of wages are simultaneously associated with lower levels of inequality and the pursuit of a high productivity growth strategy. In turn, the high productivity reduces the tax burden on both individuals and firms for public service provision (Hemerijck, 2017).

Early contributions, such as Esping-Andersen and colleagues (2002), refer to the SI perspective within a positive theory of the (nation) state. Herein, the state administration should assume both a redistributive function that provides social protection to citizens in need, as well as a capacitating function through services promoting human capabilities and work-life balance. From the SI perspective, the development of human capital through education and training represents the core of a policy mix that aims to prepare individuals to face new social risks, rather than only compensating them when they already have already experienced these fallouts (Hemerijck et al., 2016).

The SI approach can be viewed as a paradigmatic change in social policy research and practice. Policy interventions should shift from protection to prevention, preparing individuals to face the less predictable and changing configurations of new social risks. This shift could be achieved by adopting a life course perspective, promoting the development of skills and human capital through (lifelong) education and training, participation in the labor market in high-quality jobs, work-life balance, and female employment. However, the SI approach should not support the substituting conventional income guarantees (such as minimum income schemes and unemployment benefits). Instead, the minimization of poverty and promotion of income security is a precondition for the effectiveness of SI policies (Esping-Andersen et al., 2002).

The ambitious goals of SI have to be pursued through a comprehensive policy mix (Solga, 2014), broadly encompassing education policies, labor market policies, poverty alleviation policies and family policies. Broadly speaking, the following types of policies have been described as coherent with the SI approach (Hemerijck et al., 2016):

- Education and training policies (e.g., policies addressing coverage, quality and accessibility of Early Childhood Education and Care (ECEC); coverage, attainment and quality or achievement in primary education, secondary and vocational education and training, tertiary education, and lifelong learning)
- Selected labor market policies (e.g., generous but short-term unemployment benefits, availability and accessibility of training programs, employment services and active labor market policies directed at employment growth and avoiding the depletion of skills)
- Poverty alleviation policies (e.g. social assistance and minimum income, housing benefits and general policies aimed at equal opportunity and poverty reduction)
- Employment-centered family policies (e.g. parental leave policies and other work-family life reconciliation measures, coverage and accessibility of ECEC).

By investing in people, combined with traditional social protection, welfare systems become more sustainable as they adapt to new socio-economic developments and meet the needs of future generations (Cefalo & Kazepov, 2018). Social policies under the SI approach should both protect individuals from the perils of the labor market and prepare them to navigate an ever-shifting society in the expectation that positive results at both individual and societal levels will be achieved. In fact, by enabling individuals to participate in the labor market (individual level), these policies promote the increase of national income and reduce long-term reliance on social benefits. Accordingly, these policies could lower budgetary pressure and encourage new forms of business investment (societal level). SI strategies aim not only at creating employment but at creating high-quality jobs. These are jobs that have stable and good working conditions as well as adequate remuneration (Nelson & Stephens, 2012). Moreover, SI advocates for equal opportunities, with particular attention to gender issues: work-family reconciliation policies are needed to foster both the cognitive development of young children and the participation of mothers in paid work (Hemerijck et al., 2016). Therefore, the SI approach addresses key challenges of new labor markets and tries to tackle old and new inequalities that traditional welfare policies struggle to mitigate.

Overall, the SI approach implies a shift in the social protection focus, from the collective or assumed homogenous social group to the individual. This aspect may also mean that responsibility is put more onto the shoulders of "individuals" (Cantillon & Van Lancker, 2013). Herein, the role of social protection within the SI approach is vital, following two opposite interpretations (Morel et al., 2012). From a more liberal view, SI should replace the traditional forms of social protection. Individuals, thanks to their human capital, are considered able to cope with the downfalls of new social risks or transition periods. Or, as in the model followed by Scandinavian countries, SI and traditional forms of social protection should be implemented together since income security is a precondition for an effective SI strategy (Esping-Andersen et al., 2002).

This constitutive ambiguity of the SI perspective is also manifest in the varieties of SI reforms and trajectories displayed across countries (Garritzmann et al., 2017). Meaningful progress and innovations coherent with the SI paradigm have been identified in a broad range of countries primarily located in Western-Central Europe, for instance, in Scandinavian countries, Austria, Belgium, Germany and the Netherlands (Hemerijck, 2017). The CEE region has experienced different path-dependent or path-breaking trajectories in the development of their welfare states. This variation is also reflected in SI reforms. Important signs of progress towards SI policies have been part of welfare developments in Slovenia; catching-up trends have been identified in Hungary, Poland, and Slovakia. Conversely, according to Bouget et al. (2015), countries like Romania, Bulgaria and the Baltic States have been falling behind in several SI policy fields, mainly because of austerity-retrenchment measures enacted after 2010 (Hemerijck, 2017).

Critiques of social investment

Even though SI aims to uplift individuals and societies, some pitfalls need to be considered. Critical literature on highlights shortcomings and difficulties of SI approaches to social policies. The SI perspective has been widely debated on various levels which address its underlying principles (Saraceno, 2015); its contextual preconditions at the interface of education systems, labor markets and welfare states (Kazepov & Ranci, 2016); and the ambiguous outcomes of SI interventions in terms of reducing inequalities (Cantillon, 2011). A narrow SI focus on activation and cost-containment could potentially ignore increasing poverty (Nolan, 2013), thus leading to an approach governed by neoliberal market-driven logic. If the economic impact becomes the dominant consideration for expenditure, program design, policy targets, and social spending, it risks becoming limited to the fields that are able to demonstrate an immediate economic return. The paradoxical result can be an increase in inequalities via social policies, as following the SI approach could give less value to social sustainability goals that are not pertinent to economic rationality. In greater detail, according to Cordini et al. (2021), three main arguments arise to discuss the SI perspective critically (Cantillon & Van Lancker, 2013):

(1) Excluding less or non-productive people and people outside of labor markets (e.g. frail people, people with disabilities and/or chronic illnesses): In the SI approach, participation in the labor market is the key for social inclusion. For example, non-employed persons in charge of taking care of "family" dependent members are at risk of poverty and social exclusion even more under the SI scheme (Saraceno, 2015).
(2) The complexity of individual responsibility: Putting responsibility at the center of SI potentially fosters conditional and disciplinary policies. Given the thin line between (a lack of) effort and societal circumstances, defining individual responsibility is neither simple nor straightforward. "A narrow view of responsibility denies the context-specific nature of human agency and the unequal distribution of opportunities, which in itself shapes the range of choices open to people" (Cantillon & Van Lancker, 2013, 7).
(3) Cementing inequalities (Matthew effect[1]): Under the "Matthew effect", social groups with already high socio-economic status benefit the most from SI policies (Bonoli et al., 2017). Without careful policy design, SI would fortify social inequalities instead of re-vitalizing social mobility. Childcare policies are an explicative example of this effect: most childcare services are

1 The phenomenon that social policies might benefit middle and higher-income groups has been labeled as the Matthew Effect in reference to a verse in the gospel of Matthew; in popular discourse, it is summarized as: the rich get richer, the poor get poorer (Bonoli et al., 2017).

only available to those families with two already working parents. However, dual earner-ship is not equally dispersed. Lower-income households with only one parent working (full-time) will be more likely to be excluded from these rationed services. In these ways, investment in education and childcare may exacerbate inequalities and existing divisions between different socio-economic groups (Di Stasio & Solga, 2017) and among territories (Sabatinelli & Semprebon, 2018).

Failures of the SI approach have been usually interpreted as a consequence of faulty implementation or interpretation (Abrassart & Bonoli, 2015). However, Solga (2014) has observed that the feasibility of SI strategies depends on the specific interdependencies among the education system, the labor market and social inclusion policies. Kazepov and Ranci (2016) similarly highlight how SI policies need a set of preconditions to fulfill both economic and social inclusion goals. Their work suggests that sometimes, as in the Italian case, SI policies not only did not reach their goals but have even had perverse contradictory effects in the absence of the necessary preconditions. Some contextual preconditions identified as necessary for SI policies to work effectively are that the education system and labor market should share the same orientation towards high skill employment and work interdependently. Moreover, both households and labor markets should show relatively high levels of gender parity to avoid gendered Matthew effects in care-work conciliation and work-life balance. Labor market and social protection systems should strive to provide people with opportunities for requalification and by ensuring good quality employment, prevent social exclusion.

Territorial challenges in the provision of SI services

As noted in the previous section, Kazepov and Ranci (2016) stress the necessity to enrich the knowledge on SI impacts by looking at contextual and institutional preconditions structuring the interface between the labor market, the welfare state and the education system. Aside from a policy focus, this also calls for the adoption of territorially differentiated approaches as national, regional, and to some extent, local contexts have vital implications for SI service provision. Territorial scales and local socio-economic structures influence policy interdependencies and play a key role in strengthening differentiated patterns of TC (Hemerijck, 2017). However, despite the recognition that SI policies can only be implemented at a local level – as they strongly rely on services and in-kind benefits provision (Morel et al., 2012), research contributions specifically focused on the territorial dimension of SI are limited. This deficit calls for adopting a territorially differentiated approach to spatialize SI and its implication for economic growth and territorial cohesion. Along this line, Kazepov and Cefalo (2022) and Cordini et al. (2021) argue that the SI territorial dimension is related to the interaction of four main factors:

(a) The delivery of capacitating services

SI addresses the changing social risks that emerged in post-industrial societies through the provision of capacitating social services to equip citizens with the capabilities of orientating themselves on flexible labor markets and de-standardized life courses. This focus is the reason SI advocates for resources to be invested in, amongst other components, childcare, education and training at secondary and tertiary levels, lifelong learning and active labor market policies (Hemerijck et al., 2016). SI policies, as strongly reliant on service provision, are better managed and provided at a local level, closer to the scale at which the needs arise, as they carry the possibility of being more context-sensitive than centrally designed, nationally standardized schemes. The local level is considered the ideal dimension to recognize and meet social needs, create networks, and mobilize resources (Moulaert, 2013). Sub-national contexts can become arenas for innovative solutions to social challenges (Baines et al., 2019). On the flip side, decentralized service provision can also entail reduced accountability, public de-responsibilization and increased territorial differences (Martinelli et al., 2018). In the absence of a definition of enforceable social rights and/or minimum intervention standards, local policy innovation may further increase inequalities among citizens, depending on where they reside. Therefore, the impact of service delivery on territorial differences must be considered when looking at the outcomes of SI strategies.

(b) The process of institutional rescaling affecting European welfare states

Differences in the institutional settings exist not only between but also within countries. Specific processes of territorial reorganization of social policies began developing at the end of the 1970s (Kazepov, 2010). Overall, subsidiarization and European integration redesigned the role of the central (nation) state government and administration. At the same time, these processes attributed more relevance to supra- and sub-national scales of governance. The definition of subsidiarity implies that matters should be handled by the smallest or lowest competent authority, meaning that the central state administration should perform only those tasks that cannot be performed effectively at a lower level. The central role of local scales and cities brought about the development of local welfare systems (Andreotti et al., 2012; Ranci et al., 2014). In turn, this gave rise to different profiles of persons in need; varying mixes of actors, interventions and stakeholders involved as well as diverse approaches for social policy provision. Rescaling dynamics can create the conditions for developing effective and localized solutions to social needs, yet they entail some critical aspects. Sabatinelli and Semprebon (2018) observed that rescaling reforms have not always brought about a balanced attribution of responsibilities among the various institutional levels involved in the regulation, financing, planning and provision of social services.

Moreover, re-allocation of these functions has not always been accompanied by an adequate parallel attribution of resources. Finally, in some countries, the central state has recently regained a more prominent role in steering policies (Kröger, 2011) sometimes due to the 2008 economic crisis and following austerity measures or, most recently, the COVID-19 pandemic. Overall, cities and local welfare actors are entry points into structures of multilevel governance, which can provide investment-related interventions. Looking at local distributions of welfare in view of downward rescaling as well as re-centralization trends further stresses the need to de-construct the assumed internal homogeneity of SI approaches (Morel et al., 2012).

(c) The persistence of spatial disparities amongst sub-national territories

As stated in the 7th European report on economic, social and territorial cohesion (Dijkstra, 2017), from 2008 onwards, regional disparities in employment and unemployment rates widened, as did those in GDP per head. The divide between stagnating, industrialized, remote regions and privileged productive ones, typically metropolitan areas (Medeiros, 2016), has been complicated by the impact of the Great Recession: Several capital metropolitan regions have been severely hit, while some rural and intermediate regions have displayed more resilience (Charron et al., 2014). All in all spatial disparities in socio-economic conditions remain highly pronounced (Iammarino et al., 2018). For instance, EU regions where young people experience more difficulties entering the labor market tend to cluster close to each other (Cefalo et al. 2020). These findings have also led to the identification of low-income and low-growth regions, as well as Inner Peripheries (ESPON, 2017a), characterized by a combination of disadvantages, ranging from economic and demographic conditions to access to services and connectedness of relevant social networks. Scholars recognize that high levels of spatial disparities and economic polarization threaten general economic progress and social cohesion (Barca, 2009; Barca et al., 2012). Equal opportunities and reduced inequalities are crucial to realizing the potential of citizens and are also at the core of the SI perspective (Hemerijck, 2017). However, spatially-blind SI interventions may even produce new social inequalities or aggravate existing ones.

(d) The characteristics of the expanding knowledge economy

SI emphasizes skills development and facilitation of employment, especially in the context of expanding knowledge economies (Lundvall & Lorenz, 2012). The concept of a knowledge economy comes with particular territorial implications (Boczy et al., 2020), as it entails a high demand for specialized and highly skilled labor, such as engineering, information, and communication technologies. Knowledge economies also generate spill-over effects for creating jobs in related sectors and foster the upskilling/skill-improvement of workers, emphasizing the role of higher education and vocational training in the provision of updated and advanced competencies (ESPON, 2017b). However, technological developments (Kalleberg, 2009) and regional innovation tend to reinforce territorial divergence in remuneration and employment opportunities. In the current European context, innovation and employment growth are still concentrated in a limited number of north-western but mainly central-axis regions. There, virtuous circles of good interregional connections, a highly skilled labor force and an attractive business environment allowed neighboring regions to benefit from their/metropolitan/urban proximity. Large metropolitan areas and their suburbs are centers of agglomeration, specialization and cumulative advantages that demonstrate strong dynamism regarding income and employment creation (Medeiros & Van der Zwet, 2020). Less competitive regions are challenged by brain-drain dynamics that often depend on returning in-flow of remittances (ESPON, 2017b; Cefalo et al., 2020). Conversely, many southern and eastern EU regions are characterized by a lack of innovation, brain-drain dynamics and lack of employment opportunities, as well as high youth unemployment and NEET rates (Dijkstra, 2017). Overall, knowledge diffusion has not been strong enough to provide better opportunities for people remaining in lagging-behind regions (Iammarino et al., 2018).

Towards place-sensitive services and policies: The concept of territorial cohesion

As outlined in the previous sections, neglecting the territorial articulation of SI may lead to ineffective interventions or even the reproduction of inequalities and disadvantages, thus negatively affecting cohesion within and across territories. Without place-sensitive interventions (Barca et al., 2012), which should re-vitalize the socio-economic status of weaker places, we can assume that a socio-economic downward spiral will widen social, economic, and political disparities at a regional level. This issue correlates the debate on SI and its lack of spatial sensitivity with the literature on territorial cohesion (TC, see Cordini et al., 2021).

Locally based conditions can render investment policies effective (or ineffective), which means that deprived territories, where the positive impacts of SI services are most needed, are also those territories in which the capacity to develop effective capacitating services are likely limited/restrained. Institutional settings and economic conditions contribute to determining the capacity or the lack of it in implementing SI policies successfully. For instance, the scarcity of funds (as an institutional feature) associated with low employment rates or the lack of innovative firms, render the implementation of SI policies useless or even counterproductive.

A place-sensitive SI approach should include territorial diversity and its consequences as a highly significant trait of the analytical frame of inequalities and social policies, especially in post-industrial economies. A multi-scalar approach is needed to implement effective SI policies that adapt to the specific socio-economic conditions at local levels (Kazepov & Cefalo, 2022). The risk of neglecting the focus on the local features is widening the territorial divide within regions. On this specific point, SI is likely to intercept the TC debate.

Although TC is most often used within spatial planning contexts (Abrahams, 2013), it represents an inter-disciplinary concept of socio-economic development, especially within the EU. The EU Territorial Agenda 2020 indicates this special focus in the very beginning of the document by stating that "territorial cohesion is a common goal for a more harmonious and balanced state of Europe" (European Commission, 2011). While the overall concept of social cohesion is a broad issue for EU institutions, TC references more concrete issues of territorial inequality that aim to overcome a divergent EU. The debate on territorial cohesion and spatial inequality (Barca, 2009; Böhme et al., 2011) recognized that regional inequalities strongly influence individual well-being and opportunities to combat new social risks. Consequently, reinforcing economic and social cohesion by reducing disparities between regions is a clear objective of EU policies (Faludi, 2013; Medeiros, 2016). As part of this broader objective, TC is about ensuring people are able to mobilize the inherent features of the areas in which they reside to achieve both economic growth and social justice. According to the TC view, no European citizen should be disadvantaged regarding access to public services, housing, or employment opportunities simply by dwelling in one region rather than another. Still, there is no coherent definition of TC within the main EU documents on the topic (European Commission, 2008, 2010, 2011, 2014). Accordingly, adaptation and implementation processes of the concept into concrete strategies on national and sub-national levels differ (Marques et al., 2018).

According to Humer (2013), territorial cohesion refers to the territorialized provision of Services of General Interest (SGI). Equal access to SGIs and particularly infrastructure is crucial for a balanced economic and social resource distribution. Apart from planning perspectives, the connection between TC and spatial justice is also apparent in EU documents (European Commission, 2008, 2011). These documents describe social justice within TC presenting it almost as a means to achieve greater cohesion within the EU. Investigating regional development documents on TC in the case of Portugal, Marques et al. (2018) filtered the most relevant EU documents on the topic. They devised with four dimensions of territorial cohesion. For others, such as the ESPON KITCASP (Daly et al., 2013) project, the aim in defining TC was to point out policy indicators for measuring TC. In this work, the Espon Kitcasp identified four policy themes relevant to spatial planning and TC. Medeiros (2016), on the other hand, suggested a comprehensive definition due to the relevance of the TC to the EU cohesion policy, containing four political dimensions. The COHSMO project integrated these definitions of TC to further discussions both in terms of research and political dimensions. Even though conceptual work is currently incomplete, the discussions on TC already indicate common denominators.

A territorialized SI approach bears some similarities to the concepts of TC particularly in the way territorialized SI emphasizes inclusion (cohesion) and competitiveness (balanced and polycentric development), as well as the importance of complementarities resulting from multi-scalar interaction of public and private actors (vertical and horizontal coordination). Literature on TC suggests that an integrated approach is needed to achieve a more balanced and sustainable development – both in socio-economic and ecological terms (Daly et al., 2013; Faludi, 2013; Medeiros & Rauhut, 2018). This perspective implies better coordination between sectoral policies at horizontal and vertical levels (Marques et al., 2018). A place-sensitive SI approach can contribute to such an integrated

Table 2.1. Definitions of territorial cohesion.

Working Definitions of Territorial Cohesion						
COHSMO (2019); Cordini et al. (2021)	Balanced development & accessibility to services	Polycentric development and advancement of (urban) economic growth	Place-based approach	Empowering of regional governments with EU-multi-level governance system	Integration & coordination between policies	
			[political participation]	[vertical collaboration]	[horizontal collaboration]	
Marques et al. (2018)	Social and territorial solidarity and equity	Diversity and Specificity of territorial policies	Territorial Organization		Territorial Governance	
Daly et al. (2013)	Social Cohesion and Quality of Life	Economic Competitiveness and Resilience	Integrated Spatial Development			Environmental Resource Management
Medeiros (2016)	Social and Economic Cohesion	Polycentrism	Cooperation/Governance			Environmental Sustainability

Source: Cordini et al. (2021).

approach and increase coordination between sectoral policies (even across nation-state boundaries) due to its focus on facing new social risks both individually and collectively.

TC and SI both attempt to strengthen economic competitiveness while simultaneously increasing individual well-being. For SI, economic competitiveness and increased participation in labor markets are the means to sustain crucial welfare services. For TC, boosting welfare services is more implicit than explicit in the goals of polycentric and balanced development, the utilization of existing territorial assets, and in improving access to specific SGIs, e.g. ECEC or education facilities. Successfully implementing these goals may boost local economies, help to uplift lacking regions and equip these territories and their residents with the necessary means to provide for residents equally.

However, the TC and SI differ in their analytical levels: Where SI focuses on individual life courses and well-being for a population, looking at social policies to increase opportunities for individuals and consequently social groups, TC targets spatial units, regions and their collective (socio-economic) development, looking at infrastructure and resource distribution to provide balanced socio-economic development. Still, the two ideas meet again to thrive for more (spatial) equality in socio-economic developments. Territorializing SI means incorporating institutional specificities and territorial assets to better understand the local impacts of socio-economic policies. From a policy design standpoint, it means looking at multilevel governance arrangements and territorial specificities for implementing effective SI policies. Benefitting at first individuals, in turn, SI should affect the collective, regional socio-economic development positively. Therefore, the SI approach complements the more infrastructure-focused TC regional planning concept. Conversely, the SI approach benefits from the TC lenses of regional specifics and, more importantly, the focus on balancing socio-economic development by including a sensibility for regional disparities.

Conclusions

SI advocates claim that creating virtuous circles helps produce win-win returns in terms of social cohesion and economic growth (Hemerijck, 2017). However, the success of a comprehensive SI strategy lies in locally specific contextual conditions and multi-scalar institutional arrangements (Kazepov & Cefalo, 2022). Territorial-related variables may foster or hinder SI strategies. Hence, local specificities within multilevel governance structures should be considered in the conceptual frame of SI research and interventions by assuming context- and place-sensitive analysis. A context-sensitive SI approach aims at promoting inclusive growth across different contexts, avoiding the reproduction of existing inequality structures through one-size-fits-all policy solutions. Incorporating the SI approach, the existing lens of TC assists in becoming sensitive to territorial disparities in opportunities and access.

Notwithstanding analytical differences, TC and SI meet to strengthen economic competitiveness while simultaneously increasing social inclusion and individual well-being (Cordini et al., 2021). Research on TC suggests the need for an integrated approach to pursue a balanced and sustainable development; this requires improved coordination between sectoral policies at horizontal and vertical levels. A place-sensitive SI strategy can contribute to an integrated approach and help increase coordination between measures and policy fields. Under a territorialized SI approach, economic competitiveness and increased participation in labor markets should pave the way for sustainable welfare states in all regions to mitigate territorial imbalances. Investigating territorial divergence through the lens of territorialized SI focus opens up the debate on specific local inequalities and policies to counteract them.

References

Abrahams, G. (2013). What "Is" territorial cohesion? What does it "Do"?: Essentialist versus pragmatic approaches to using concepts. *European Planning Studies*, *22*(10), 2134–2155.

Abrassart, A., & Bonoli, G. (2015). Availability, cost or culture? Obstacles to childcare services for low income families. *Journal of Social Policy*, *44*(4), 1–20.

Amable, B. (2016). Institutional complementarities in the dynamic comparative analysis of capitalism. *Journal of Institutional Economics*, *12*(1), 71–103.

Andreotti, A., Mingione, E., & Polizzi, E. (2012). Local welfare systems. A challenge for social cohesion. *Urban Studies*, *49*(9), 1925–1940.

Baines, S., Bassi, A., Csoba, J., & Sipos, F. (Eds.). (2019). *Innovative social investment*. Bristol: Policy Press.

Barca, F. (2009). *An agenda for a reformed cohesion policy*. Independent Report, Brussels.

Barca, F., McCann, P., & Rodríguez-Pose, A. (2012). The case for regional development intervention: Place-based versus place-neutral approaches. *Journal of Regional Science*, *52*(1), 134–152.

Boczy, T., Cefalo, R., Parma, A., & Nielsen, R. S. (2020). Positioning the urban in the global knowledge economy: Increasing competitiveness or inequality. *Social Inclusion*, *8*(4), 194–207.

Böhme, K., Doucet, P., Komornicki, T., Zaucha, J., & Świątek, D. (2011). How to strengthen the territorial dimension of 'Europe 2020' and EU cohesion policy. Warsaw, checked on 5/30/2018.

Bonoli, G., Cantillon, B., & Van Lancker, W. (2017). Social investment and the Matthew effect: Limits to a strategy. In A. Hemerijck (Ed.), *Social investment uses* (pp. 66–76). Oxford: Oxford University Press.

Bouget, D., Frazer, H., Marlier, E., Sabato, S., & Vanhercke, B. (2015). Social investment in Europe: A study of national policies, European Social Policy Network (ESPN). Brussels: European Commission.

Cantillon, B. (2011). The paradox of the social investment state: Growth, employment and poverty in the Lisbon era. *Journal of European Social Policy*, *21*(5), 432–449.

Cantillon, B., & Van Lancker, W. (2013). Three shortcomings of the social investment perspective. *Social Policy and Society*, *12*(4), 553–564.

Cefalo, R., & Kazepov, Y. (2018). Investing over the life course: The role of lifelong learning in a social investment strategy. *Studies in the Education of Adults*, *50*(2), 203–218.

Cefalo, R., Scandurra, R., & Kazepov, Y. (2020). Youth labor market integration in European regions. *Sustainability, 12*, 3813.

Cefalo, R.; Boczy, T., Kazepov, Y., Arlotti, M., Cordini, M., Parma, A., Ranci, C., Sabatinelli, S. (2019). COHSMO Project report (D5.1) Literature review on Social Investment. https://cordis.europa.eu/project/id/727058/results.

Charron, N., Dijkstra, L., & Lapuente, V. (2015). Mapping the regional divide in Europe. A measure for assessing quality of government in 206 European regions. *Social Indicators Research, 122*(2), 315–346.

Cordini, M., Boczy, T., & Cefalo, R. (2021). Place-sensitive social investment and territorial cohesion: Implications for sustainability. *Sustainability, 13*(13), 7085.

Daly, G., Gonzalez, A., Gleeson, J., McCarthy, E., Adams, N., Pinch, P., et al. (2013). KITCASP key indicators for territorial cohesion and spatial planning. (Draft) Final Report Part D Appendix B. ESPON. ESPON & National University of Ireland.

Dijkstra, L. (2017). My region, my Europe, our future. Seventh report on economic, social and territorial cohesion. Luxembourg: Publications Office of the European Union.

Di Stasio, V., & Solga, H. (2017). Education as social policy: An introduction. In Journal of *European Social Policy, 27*(4), 313–319.

Esping-Andersen, G. (1998). *Social foundations of post-industrial economies.* Oxford: Oxford University Press.

Esping-Andersen, G., Gallie, D., Hemerijck, A., & Myles, J. (2002). *Why we need a new welfare state.* Oxford: Oxford University Press.

ESPON. (2017a). Inner peripheries: National territories facing challenges of access to basic services of general interest. Luxembourg: ESPON.

ESPON. (2017b). Territorial cooperation for the future of Europe. Luxembourg: ESPON.

European Commission. (2008). Green paper on territorial cohesion. Turn-ing territorial diversity into strength. Brussels.

European Commission. (2010). Investing in Europe's future. Fifth report on economic, social and territorial cohesion. European Commission. Luxembourg (Report on economic, social and territorial cohesion).

European Commission. (2011). Territorial agenda of the European Union 2020: Towards an inclusive, smart and sustainable Europe of diverse regions. Agreed at the informal ministerial meeting of ministers responsible for spatial planning and territorial development, 19 May.

European Commission. (2013). Towards social investment for growth and cohesion. COM(2013) 83 final. Bruxelles.

European Commission. (2014). Investment for jobs and growth. 6th Report on economic, social and territorial cohesion. European Commission. Luxembourg (Report on economic, social and territorial cohesion).

Faludi, A. (2013). Territorial cohesion and subsidiarity under the European union trea-ties: A critique of the 'Territorialism' underlying. *Regional Studies*, *47*(9), S. 1594–1606.

Garritzmann, J. L., Häusermann, S., Palier, B., & Zollinger, C. (2017). WoPSI – the world politics of social investment. An international research project an international research project to explain variance in social investment agendas and social investment reforms across countries and world regions. SciencePo (LIEPP Working Paper).

Giddens, A. (1998). *The third way: The renewal of social democracy*. Cambridge: Polity Press.

Hemerijck, A. (2013). *Changing Welfare States*. Oxford: Oxford University Press.

Hemerijck, A. (2017). *Social investment uses*. Oxford: Oxford University Press.

Hemerijck, A., Burgoon, B., Di Pietro, A., & Vydra, S. (2016). *Assessing social investment synergies* (ASIS). Brussels: European Commission.

Humer, A. (2013). Researching social services of general interest: An analytical framework derived from underlying policy systems. *European Spatial Research and Policy*, *21*(1), 65–82.

Iammarino, S., Rodriguez-Pose, A., & Storper, M. (2018). Regional inequality in Europe. Evidence, theory and policy implications. *Journal of Economic Geography*, *53*, 898–924.

Iversen, T., & Wren, A. (1998). Equality, employment and budgetary restraint: The trilemma of the service economy. *World Politics*, *50*(4), 507–546.

Kalleberg, A. L. (2009). Precarious work, insecure workers: Employment relations in transition. *American Sociological Review*, *74*(1), 1–22.

Kazepov, Y. (Ed.). (2010). *Rescaling social policies: Towards multilevel governance in Europe* (Vol. 38). Farnham: Ashgate Publishing, Ltd.

Kazepov, Y., & Cefalo, R. (2022). The territorial dimension of social investment. In Y. Kazepov, R. Cucca, E. Barberis, & E. Mocca (Eds.), *Handbook of urban social policy*. Cheltenham: Edward Elgar (*forthcoming*).

Kazepov, Y., & Ranci, C. (2016). Is every country fit for social investment? Italy as an adverse case. *Journal of European Social Policy*, *27*(1), 90–104.

Kröger, S. (2011). Five years down the road. An evaluation of the streamlining of the open method of coordination in the social policy field, OSE briefing paper.

Lundvall, B., & Lorenz. E. (2012). Social investment in the globalizing learning economy – A European perspective. In N. Morel, B. Palier, & J. Palme (Eds.), *Towards a social investment welfare state* (pp. 235–259). Bristol: Policy Press.

Martinelli, F., Anttonen, A., & Matzke, M. (Eds.). (2018). *Social services disrupted. Changes, challenges and policy implications for Europe in times of austerity*. Cheltenham, UK, Northampton, MA, USA: Edward Elgar Publishing.

Marques, T. S., Saraiva, M., Santinha, G., & Guerra, P. (2018). Re-thinking territorial cohesion in the European planning context. *International Journal Urban & Regional Research*, *42*(4), S. 547–572.

Medeiros, E. (2016). Territorial cohesion: An EU concept. *European Journal of Spatial Development*, *60*, 1–30.

Medeiros, E., & Rauhut, D. (2018). Territorial cohesion cities: A policy recipe for achieving territorial cohesion? *Regional Studies*, *60*(4), S. 1–9. https://doi.org/10.1080/00343404.2018.1548764.

Medeiros, E., & van der Zwet, A. (2020). Sustainable and integrated urban planning and governance in metropolitan and medium-sized cities. *Sustainability*, *12*, 5976.

Morel, N., Palier, B., & Palme, J. (Eds.). (2012). *Towards a social investment welfare state?* Bristol: Policy Press.

Moulaert, F. (Ed.). (2013). *The international handbook on social innovation: Collective action, social learning and transdisciplinary research*. Aldershot: Edward Elgar.

Nelson, M., & Stephens, J. D. (2012). Do social investment policies produce more and better jobs? In N. Morel, B. Palier, & J. Palme (Eds.), *Towards a social investment welfare state? Ideas, policies and challenges*. Bristol: The Policy Press.

Nolan, B. (2013). What use is "social investment"?. *Journal of European Social Policy*, *23*(5), 459–468.

Okun, A. M. (1975). *Equality and efficiency: The big trade-off*. Washington D.C.: Brookings Institution Press.

Pierson, P. (2002). Coping with permanent austerity: Welfare state restructuring in affluent democracies. *Revue française de sociologie*, *43*(2), 369–406.

Ranci, C. (Ed.). (2010). *Social vulnerability in Europe. The new configuration of social risks*. Basingstoke: Palgrave Macmillan.

Ranci, C., Brandsen, T., & Sabatinelli, S. (2014). *Social vulnerability in European cities. The role of local welfare in times of crisis*, New York: Springer.

Sabatinelli, S., & Semprebon, M. (2018). The vertical division of responsibility for social services within and beyond the state: issues in empowerment, participation and territorial cohesion. In M. Flavia, A. Anneli, & M. Margitta

(Eds.), *Social services disrupted. Changes, challenges and policy implications for Europe in times of austerity* (pp. 114–133). Cheltenham, UK, Northampton, MA, USA: Edward Elgar Publishing.

Saraceno, C. (2015). A critical look to the social investment approach from a gender perspective. *Social Politics*, *22*(2), 257–269.

Solga, H. (2014). Education, economic inequality and the promises of the social investment 'state'. *Socio-Economic Review*, *12*(2), 269–297.

Taylor-Gooby, P. (2004). *New risks, new welfare*. Oxford: Oxford University Press.

Wren, A. (2017). Social investment and the service economy trilemma. In A. Hemerijck (Ed.), *Social investment uses* (pp. 97–107). Oxford: Oxford University Press.

Part II Social investment policy challenge in a small-scale country: Interventions, governance and services provision in the Lithuanian case

The second part of this book elaborates the framework for implementing a social investment policy approach in Lithuania. The chapters discuss the appropriate policy interventions at municipal level, policy design, and governance mechanisms citing the cases of three social investment policy intervention fields: vocational education and training (VET), early childhood education and care (ECEC) and active labor market policy (ALMP). Firstly, the assessment of territorial inequalities and related socio-economic and demographic indicators is important to identify the contextual framework that enables the implementation of territorially fitted social policy tools and measures (Chapter 3). The second part of the book elaborates in detail the selected social investment policy interventions and designs that are aligned with the local context in selected Lithuanian urban, suburban, and rural municipal cases (Chapters 4–6). The chapters ask if the place-based approaches are feasible apropos coordination across governance levels, policy goals, service provision and different stakeholder involvement in territorial governance. Unsurprisingly, the analysis of institutional design and governance options remains imperfect due to the ongoing country level debates on welfare state provisions, institutional complementary and adaption to crucial changes to solve demographic decline, enhance the role of family and gender, and foster economic development, amongst other external factors. A social investment paradigm as an emerging political framework requires strong compromise between political interests and socio-economic development in territories.

Artūras Tereškinas, Viktorija Baranauskienė, Jurga Bučaitė-Vilkė

Chapter 3 Territorial profiles: Spatial inequalities and the importance of socio-economic differences

Abstract: This chapter examines the national body of literature on territorial inequalities and spatial differentiation in terms of socio-economic development in rural and urban regions. The assessment of regional development should be premised on a robust methodical framework that grasps the dynamics of several inter-related indicators such as demographic change, economic performance and labor productivity, public health, education and social exclusion and other quality of life parameters. In this chapter, we focus on the territorial inequalities in Lithuanian urban and rural regions and provide an overview of the socio-economic differentiation at municipal level. In addition, the chapter reveals that focus on economic parameters and demographic indicators might limit the options to re-arrange the territorial development notion along the lines of social investment policies. The critical argument stretches the limits of bridging territorial development indicators and welfare policy instruments for more sustainable regional growth. Finally, we present the methodological notes on case study selection for researching diverse urban, suburban, and rural municipalities as empirical background for social investment policy analysis.

Keywords: territorial inequalities, territorial development, spatial differentiation, social investment policies, municipalities, Lithuania.

Introduction: Talking over territorial development policy in Lithuania

In the heated debate on the territorial differences and territorial sensitivity in relation to social investment strategy, various political positions feature in the case of Lithuania. On the one hand, the national regional development policies tend to focus on economic growth and regional competitiveness. On the other hand, questions arise as to the contextual local-based conditions for social investment policies, and possible progress registered in identifying territorial differences. Although territorial diversification assessment is important to enable social investment (SI) policies as an effective welfare provision mechanism, it mostly remains silent in public discourse.

A review of Lithuanian academic bibliographies uncovers the specificity of the national political tradition which conceptualizes territorial development policy as part of economic growth policy rather than linking it to welfare state provisions. Therefore, the multilevel conception of territorial cohesion that combines economic growth, spatial justice and democratic capacities, is beyond the scope of national policy discourse. Territorial cohesion policies, as they are defined in contemporary political and academic discourse, only recently became the subject of investigation. Spatial dimensions of the socio-economic development in territories and regions receive relatively more attention in the academic field and at the policy-making level. The rather delayed advancement is obviously determined by the broader socio-political changes the country experienced in the past decades. Some Lithuanian scholars argue that regional policy emerged as the by-product of the EU accession processes, and thus was a reaction to the external pressures, but not an integral political response to the discrepancies in socio-economic development (Česonis, 2012; Puidokas & Daukaitė, 2013). Others argue that regional policies existed long before the accession, however the institutional integration into the EU catalyzed the advancement of the conceptual foundations, legislation, institutional system and monitoring of the regional policies (Burneika, 2013).

The lack of a comprehensive methodology underpinning the calculation and assessment of the regional territorial inequality over the last two decades, is one of the main issues in conducting this type of investigation. In the case of Lithuania, the conceptualization and measurement of territorial development at regional level are closely related to relatively new national regional policy which became an issue on the political agenda since 1989. Emerging from this period, the social and economic disparities between regions began to increase extensively, stimulating the necessity for a coordinated regional national policy. One of the first strategic documents was approved in 2005 and aimed to increase territorial, social, and economic cohesion within the country regions (Lithuanian Regional Policy Strategy until the year 2013). The most important goal emphasized the imperative to reduce disparities focusing on territorial economic development and economic performance indicators, such as employment, labor productivity and high labor quality. However, the other related social indicators (health, education, subjective well-being, etc.) were not carefully considered.

One of the priorities of the national strategic document on progress strategy adopted by Seimas of the Republic of Lithuania on 15 May 2012, is to ensure a high quality of life and employment opportunities for all citizens regardless of the area in which they live, the upgrading and development of infrastructure and the promotion of small and medium business development in different regions of the country (Lithuania Progress Strategy 2030, approved in 2012). As the most important precondition, sustainable economic performance should positively affect common regional welfare. The national strategic regional policy documents introduce mainly the neo-classical economic approach based on regional economic capital and competitiveness rather than measuring social capital dimensions. Following this approach (Solow, 1956; Swan, 1956), the regions with similar technological progress and social indicators will follow the convergence path of aggregating per-capita incomes. One could summarize that this approach which supports economic competitiveness of regions dominates the national regional politics emphasizing economic infrastructure and economic performance indicators rather than investing in social policies. Even though regional income and consumption derive from the economic assets, investments and diversified economic activities, there is a significant absence of an understanding of comprehensive territorial development.

Specifically, in this chapter we focus on the territorial inequalities profile in Lithuanian regions. We provide an overview of the socio-economic differentiation covering also urban/rural variability on LAU level (as for municipalities). Lithuania represents the case of a consolidated regional development system with a relatively low level of municipal autonomy in fiscal, functional and discretion terms. We focus on the main trends and processes of territorial inequalities, for example, demographic processes, migration, employment, economic development and selected educational indicators. The statistical data reveals the evolution of socio-spatial segregation and differentiation in rural and urban territories in the last decade (from 2008 to 2019). It should be noted that the national research competencies both in theoretical conceptualization and empirically based evidence are relatively inexperienced when compared to the European territorial development studies tradition. Despite the underdevelopment of national research on territorial cohesion and territorial policies, we suggest a framework for identifying contextual indicators important for social investment policy instruments and tools. Finally, the chapter offers methodological remarks on empirical research for selected urban, suburban, and rural localities (municipalities). The empirical research represents a repertoire of diverse social investment policy experiences, practices and tools across territories and multiscale governance levels.

Linking contextual indicators: National experience in measurement of territorial development

In Lithuania, the most common approach to conceptualizing territorial development is based on the reduction of regional disparities seeking to sustain basic infrastructure investments, for example, encouraging economic growth and attracting foreign investments. The measurement approach monitors the changes of economic indicators and economic competitiveness at the regional (counties) level. For example, research on regional growth by Česonis who measured the economic and social development of Lithuanian regions, relied mostly on economic performance indicators (regional GDP, employment rate, labor productivity, material investments and a number of business entities). The evaluation of regional economic potential becomes the most necessary and exceptional argument for national regional policy implementation and planning agenda (Česonis, 2012). Other researchers (Snieška & Bruneckienė, 2009; Bruneckienė, 2010) provide a more complex regional competitiveness index comprising multiple indicators such as (1) factors of production conditions (human resources and human capita, physical infrastructure, and geographical position), (2) regional demand (size of local demand, size of export market) and (3) factors increasing the competitiveness of regionally based companies. The competitiveness assessment results of Lithuanian regions demonstrate that the demographic structure, infrastructure and availability of education, and the extent of export markets exert the predominant influence on such competitiveness (Snieška & Bruneckienė, 2009). However, the proposed national regional competitiveness index does not directly indicate the extent of territorial inequality measuring economic and social outcomes, such as education, labor market participation, health and well-being. The White Paper of 2017–2030, proposes ideas for the development of balanced regional development, which state that every inhabitant of the country, regardless of their place of residence, must be guaranteed high-quality access to public services not more than a half hour's journey from home (The White Paper on Lithuanian Regional Policy, 2017, p. 6–7). However, the concept of sustainable development raised in the above-mentioned document raises many debatable questions for example whether all services should be distributed evenly throughout the country, because the population, density of the territory, etc. should be carefully considered, and even regional development is not appropriate (Baranauskienė, 2021).

A further section of the national research investigates economic and social development in rural areas, focusing on measuring multiple human and social capital indicators (demographics, migration, ageing, health, level of education, unemployment, and average gross monthly earnings) (Pareigienė & Kuliešis, 2011a, 2011b). Researchers argue that the combination of various social and human capital indicators may potentially reveal disparities in Lithuanian rural, semi-urban and urban areas. Social geographers focus extensively on measuring demographic structure and changes in separate urban and rural regions emphasizing intensive depopulation and de-urbanization trends. Sparsely populated territories are considered one of the greatest threats to both sustainable economic performance and quality of life parameters (Kriaučiūnas & Ribokas, 2012; Kriaučiūnas & Daugirdas, 2013; Ubarevičienė et al., 2016). For example, a combination of parameters of social segregation, dissimilarity, and isolation from the 2001 to 2011 censuses were used in a study by Burneika, Ubarevičienė and Valatka (2015). The researchers attempted to reveal different aspects of socio-spatial segregation in the Lithuanian urban regions experiencing the predominant occupational changes. The greatest difference in distribution of household income and wages was observed in a capital area of Vilnius region which generates more intense economic compared to other regions (Burneika, Ubarevičienė, & Valatka, 2015).

In addition, Lithuanian social geographers are attentive to the spatial differentiation of the population in the three metropolitan regions of Lithuania (Vilnius, Kaunas and Klaipėda), where the analysis of population segregation (spatial residence differentiation) of these three metropoles is presented in detail and includes: demographic, socio-economic, national territorial differentiation, electoral residency differentiation (Burneika et al., 2017). There is in addition, a newly formed typology of the level of Lithuanian urbanization at the level of elderships (LAU-2) (Baranauskienė, 2019), where urbanized, suburban territories or territories are closely connected with the city (strongly dependent on the city administrative center) and non-urban areas. The methodology for determining the level of urbanization is based on three exclusion principles: according to the predominant type of settlement (city or village), according to population change in the analyzed period (positive population change is attributed to urban areas) and according to the location of the administrative center (the administrative center operates in an urban or rural type area). The typology of the level of urbanization reveals a more realistic accounting of the country's rural and urban population, compared to the methodology used by Lithuanian Department of Statistics, where only urban residents and suburban residents are classified as rural residents (Baranauskienė, 2019, 2021).

The development of rural regions contributes to ongoing methodological debates on how to measure the spatial differentiation and whether there is a linkage with welfare policy provision on a multiscale level. Based on the typology of the level of urbanization, more detailed studies of sparsely populated areas are developed (Baranauskienė, 2021). Researchers in this field are especially cognizant of the problems of uneven regional development in Lithuania, where aspects of socio-economic well-being were analyzed not only in the whole country, but also detail urban and rural (peripheral) problems (Daugirdas et al., 2019). For example, Pociūtė-Sereikienė et al. (2019a; 2019b) have comprehensively assessed the spatial exclusion of Lithuanian municipalities including demographic, social and economic indicators and evaluated which municipalities experience high, medium, and non-spatial exclusion (Pociūtė-Sereikienė et al., 2019a, 2019b). Referring to Baranauskienė (2021), it is important to focus on the socio-territorial segregation of sparsely populated areas in Lithuania. Her assessment covers the change in the number of public and private institutions and their distribution (network) at the level of municipalities and elderships in sparsely populated and non-urbanized areas were analyzed according to population change and density. The analysis demonstrates that socio-spatial exclusion affects peripheral and non-urban areas (the largest number of institutions are concentrated in cities and larger settlements, and peripheral areas are difficult to reach, especially for the elderly), but there are cases (at the eldership level) where in some areas, local authorities are influencing the development of the network of public service bodies, as population indicators are not always considered.

In summary, the indicators of urban and rural disparities are used as a most appropriate tool for understanding spatial inequality at inter-regional and intra-regional level. Empirical efforts to measure spatial inequalities eventually lead to more comprehensive and integrated approaches on developing national territorial policy design. However, we can also observe the focus on economic parameters and demographic indicators that limit the opportunity to reconfigure understanding of territorial development along the lines of social investment policies. We must admit a deficiency of more comprehensive methodological instruments for measuring territorial inequality over time.

Demographic change and (de)urbanization: Different perspective to spatial differentiation

Encompassed in the indicators that reflect the national picture of territorial differentiation and spatial inequalities is a variety of demographic change evidence. The long-term academic experience in research on demographic changes at state and regional level contributes significantly to the development of national territorial policies tradition. Overall, demographic change in Lithuanian scholarship received considerable interest during the decades after the 1990s. The change in population size, composition, and trends in demographic processes were actively analyzed based on various data sources and by applying more conventional and innovative techniques (Lietuvos gyventojų politikos strategijos metmenys, 2004; Jasilionis et al., 2015; Stankūnienė et al., 2016). Much of the research is focused on revealing radical developments in demographic processes – fertility and family change (Stankūnienė, 1997; Stankūnienė & Jasilionienė, 2008; Stankūnienė, Baublytė & Maslauskaitė, 2013; Stankūnienė & Maslauskaitė,

2008, 2012; Maslauskaitė & Baublytė, 2012; Stankūnienė et al., 2013), mortality (Jasilionis et al., 2011; Jasilionis et al., 2012) and migration (Sipavičienė, 2006, 2014; Sipavičienė & Stankūnienė, 2013), which the country has experienced since the 1990s.

The socio-economic differentiation of the demographic processes is comprehensively covered in Lithuanian scholarship. More recent research based on the 2011 census linked population register datasets focused on socio-economic differentiation of fertility (Jasilioniene, Stankuniene, & Jasilionis, 2014; Jasilionis, Stankūnienė, Maslauskaitė, & Stumbrys, 2015), family formation and dissolution (Maslauskaitė, 2014; Maslauskaitė & Jasilionis, 2015; Maslauskaitė et al., 2015), migration (Klüsener et al., 2015), and mortality (Jasilionis et al., 2014; Stumbrys et al., 2014; Jasilionis et al., 2015; Grigoriev et al., 2017) and applied advanced methods of statistical analysis. It uncovered the disparities linked to education, employment status, gender, urban-rural place of residence, and some life course characteristics.

However, despite significant advancement in the field, the research on the inter- and intra-regional inequalities of demographic process remains the underdeveloped area in Lithuania, thus the knowledge is sparse and far from comprehensive. Overall, it could be stated that the number of studies which apply the spatial perspective is very limited. Moreover, in most cases spatial analysis is used as a tool for the visualization of data, thus the deeper underlying mechanisms of the inter- and intra-regional inequalities remain unreported and under-reflected. To date there exist only several studies (on migration see Klüsener et al., 2015; Ubarevičienė, 2016; Ubarevičienė, 2016, 2018a, 2018b; Ubarevičienė & van Ham, 2017; on male mortality – Grigorjev et al., 2015, 2017; Stumbrys, 2016), which are based on more advanced methods of spatial analysis and accordingly overcome the methodological limitations.

The studies which include the component of territorial analysis present a framework for methodological underpinning and principal results. In talking about the demographic research into population decline, it is necessary to remember that Lithuania is an EU country with the largest relative decrease in population. However, the existing evidence suggests that there is significant spatial variation in population decline. The descriptive analysis of the 2001 and 2011 Census data conducted at the LAU 2 level demonstrates that positive population change was experienced only in suburban zones of the major cities – Vilnius, Kaunas and Klaipėda, while in the other areas it is negative, particularly in the rural and peripheral areas of the country most remote from the largest cities (Burneika et al., 2014; Ubarevičienė et al., 2016; Lietuvos Respublikos Vidaus, 2017; Baranauskienė, 2019, 2021). While similar processes are observed in other post-communist countries, some scholars suggest that the distinct variation of population change in Lithuania is more profound because of the specific settlement structure developed in the Soviet period during which the largest cities were relatively underdeveloped due to the planning policy oriented towards an equitable distribution of settlements and service institutions (Ubarevičienė, van Ham, Burneika 2016; Baranauskienė, 2019, 2021). Depopulation of the country and the expansion of the sparsely populated areas was also covered by national scholarship. Analysis conducted at the LAU 2 level indicates a 40.4 % increase in the sparsely populated areas in Lithuania from 2001 to 2011 (Daugirdas et al., 2013). In addition to the growth of the sparsely populated areas in the Northeast of the country, this tendency was also noted in the South and West of the country (ibid).

Sparsely populated areas (hereinafter - SPA) are a rapidly spreading problem that is receiving increasing attention, therefore the number and speed of spread have been adjusted based on a new exclusion methodology (exclusion was based on Baranauskienė's (2019) typology of urbanization level) (Baranauskienė, 2021), which revealed a more realistic picture of the country, as the previous exclusion methodology estimated only the density of the rural population, regardless of the level of urbanization of the area. According to this new methodology, it was determined that at the eldership level (LAU 2) in 2018, 37.2 % of the whole territory of the country was occupied and 41.6 % of non-urban areas. Comparing the different methodologies for the exclusion of sparsely populated areas, it was found that according to the methodology developed by Baranauskienė (2021), the mentioned areas are not as widespread as previously thought. In the period 2001–2011, the area occupied by the SPA increased by 16.3 percentage points, and according to Baranauskienė – from 2001 to 2018 – it occupied only 13.7 percentage points more of the country's area. In this case, it can be said that it is difficult to compare the trends in sparsely populated areas using two different methods, because different periods are analyzed, for example, social geographer Daugirdas et al. (2013) refers to the period 2001–2011. While Baranauskienė (2021) distinguishes sparsely populated territories based on data from 2001 to 2018. Although the actual prevalence of territories in the case of her work is lower, it is clear that territorial dispersion and its trends are similar. However, both the number of sparsely populated areas and the occupied areas of the country are still increasing, especially in the North-Eastern, Southern Lithuania and Žemaitija regions. It was also found that there remain only a few rural territories in North-Eastern Lithuania, which are not classified as sparsely populated. Their rapid spread indicates that in the near future (over a period of 10–15 years), this will be the case for almost all non-urbanized areas. Analysis of the components of depopulation and their territorial variation also received some interest and the indication is that the positive population change in the three areas around the largest cities could be accounted for by internal migration (Lietuvos Respublikos Vidaus, 2017).

Change in the population structure and its spatial variation also attracts research interest. Daugirdas et al. (2013), Baltoji knyga (2017) and Stankūnienė and Baublytė (2016) proffer the territorial distribution of the aged population (65 and over, old age dependency ratio, index of demographic ageing) on the LAU2 level and map the change in age structure of the population at several points in the period between 2001 and 2011. Based on the individual level 2011 Census data, Stankūnienė and Baublytė (2016) analyze the sex-gender pyramids in various cities and locations of Lithuania. With regard to population structures, descriptive spatial analysis was employed to demonstrate the educational discrepancies by gender and age on the LAU 2 level (Stumbrys, 2016). Baranauskienė (2021), based on the data provided by the State Enterprise Centre of Registers on the declared place of residence of the population, suggests a detailed analysis of changes in the spatial age structure at the eldership level (LAU 2) from 2001 to 2018. The conclusions assist in the assessment of the socio-spatial exclusion experienced by the population of various age groups in the regions. Spatial analysis of mortality processes has attracted relatively more research interest compared to fertility and migration. The studies have been conducted using innovative detailed datasets and advanced methodologies. However, the research relates solely to male mortality. The spatial pattern of female mortality remains an under-researched area. Grigoriev et al. (2015) refer to spatial patterns of alcohol-related male mortality and concludes that most problematic are districts along the Lithuanian–Belorussian border. Stumbrys (2016) similarly focuses on male mortality, but in addition to that which is alcohol related, he analyzed the spatial patterns pertaining to suicidal behavior and revealed the primary contributing problematic areas at individual and area-level.

With regard to the demographic processes, very few studies covered the issues of inter- and intra-regional variation. Fertility, family processes and household structures have been thus far very sparsely covered. Some recent attempts to analyze the distinctive variation of fertility trends are based on the mapping of the crude fertility rate at the LAU 2 levels (Baltoji knyga, 2017), however, bearing in mind the limitations of this coefficient, additional research predicated on more advanced methodologies and techniques is necessary. Territorial variation of non-marital fertility and trends over time was also covered in the literature (Maslauskaite, 2014) and reveals some spatial patterns of non-marital fertility.

The other question associated with measuring spatial differentiation includes the indicators on migration. The studies cover the territorial disparities linked with migration using individual level census data and applying more sophisticated methods of spatial analysis thus overcoming the limitations of the descriptive methods. Klüsener et al. (2015), based on the 2011 Census and population register, linked data analyzed the entire working age Lithuanian population from 2011 to 2012 and concluded that along with the individual level characteristics, the spatial international outmigration varies considerably. Employing the 2001 and 2011 individual level data and multilevel methods, Ubarevičienė and Van Ham (2017) analyze the internal migration and reveal the spatial patterns of selective migration. They determined that individuals with higher education, who are both younger and not married are more likely to leave the depopulating areas and to move to the regions. Generalizing their findings, the researchers also pointed to the relevance of the advancement in local self-governance and community initiatives to improve the life quality in the peripheral regions.

Urbanization and suburbanization processes supplement the picture of Lithuanian spatial differentiation. Using the 2001 and 2011 Censuses and applying multilevel methods, Ubarevičienė, Van Ham, and Burneika (2016) conclude that areas surrounding the three biggest cities are increasing in population, while the opposite trend is observable in peripheral and rural areas. Burneika et al. (2017) explore the process of metropolization and social segregation in the three largest cities and predicate their research on the 2001 and 2011 Censuses. Further, as mentioned earlier, Baranauskienė (2019), forms a typology of the level of urbanization based on 2001–2018 data. In this typology, suburban areas are distinguished according to the positive population change of the areas analyzed, and non-urban areas are classified as "purely" rural peripheral areas with a negative population change with no connection to urban settlements.

Spatial perspective and regional socio-economic development: Turning back to spatial injustice

The concept of spatial justice is almost absent from Lithuanian scholarship. There are almost no works that would utilize that particular concept to analyze the empirical data. It is difficult to find any research that employs the concept to demonstrate how space is actively involved in "sustaining inequality, injustice, economic exploitation, racism, sexism, and other forms of oppression and discrimination" (Soja, 2010, p. 4). That is to say, that the concept of spatial justice is neither operationalized nor used as a research strategy in the sociological, economic, political, or geographic analyses. Research into spatial cohesion and spatial justice has been underdeveloped and often limited to generalized speculations about urban space transformations and urban discourse, unsubstantiated by any empirical data (Samalavičius, 2005; Burneika, Kriaučiūnas, & Ubarevičienė, 2010; Lavrinec, 2011) or general reflections on urban culture (Samalavičius, 2010). Lately, the most thoroughly analyzed aspects have been discursively constructed identities of particular cities (Maniukaitė et al., 2014), urban subcultures (Kraniauskas, 2012a, 2012b), safety and sustainability in Lithuanian cities (Ceccato & Lukyte, 2010; Acus, 2011), and housing policies (Aidukaitė, 2013; Aidukaitė et al., 2014). Hardly any attempt has been made to scrutinize empirically based processes of spatial justice, socio-spatial segregation and differentiation in the post-Soviet Lithuanian cities and countryside. In general, there is a marked dearth of statistical data on social justice and social inequality in Lithuanian regions including cities (Žilys, 2013; Tereškinas & Žilys, 2013).

When the issue of justice is addressed from a spatial perspective, other terms are typically used, such as social inequality, social differentiation, sustainable development, criminalization, and segregation. Thus, the works that are marginally related to spatial justice can be divided into three parts briefly summarized thereafter: social differentiation and segregation in Lithuanian cities; the rising levels of marginalization and criminalization in different Lithuanian localities; and territorial or regional allocation of resources and sustainable development of different regions.

The most comprehensive research that can be attributed to spatial justice is related to empirical description of the geographical patterning of social inequality and social exclusion. Here the studies by scholars of Vytautas Magnus University in the field of sociology, social stratification, social geography, and urban studies are most prominent. In their research project "Social Exclusion in Lithuanian Cities: Forms of Spatial Segregation and Polarization" (2011–2012), the researchers systematically identified social exclusion, its processes and relation to the spatial zones of social tensions in the cities. The scholars uncovered multi-dimensional and dynamic social exclusion that differed according to different urban spaces. Differences in socio-demographic and socio-economic composition of three Lithuanian cities – Vilnius, Kaunas and Klaipėda – demonstrate an increasing level of social differentiation and social exclusion: it is possible to notice specific socio-demographic segregation according to age and education in these cities: the oldest and least educated respondents usually reside in so-called old working-class neighborhoods in Lithuania. These features of socio-spatial segregation correspond to the general context and trends of a post-Soviet city in which income is less important as a factor of socio-spatial segregation. A further important variable of social exclusion, which is characteristic of societies with market economies, is spatial polarization: significantly more economically well-to-do families live in the Lithuanian suburbs than in old working-class neighborhoods. It can be argued, although with some reservations, that urban spaces in post-Soviet Lithuania increasingly become agents of complex social exclusion (Žilys, 2013; Tereškinas & Žilys, 2013).

This research by Tereškinas and Žilys (2013) also demonstrates how the urban population's passivity, insecurity, mistrust in their abilities to influence local change, and local government decisions affect socio-spatial segregation and spatial inequality. These weighty emotions and experiences create social barriers and distances. They prevent the emergence of positive, socially bonding collective practices and provoke some collective urban experience (for instance, feeling unsafe and "disposable") that contribute to socio-spatial segregation of some neighborhoods in the cities, particularly those that are at the lowest end of social hierarchies (working-class and Soviet style neighborhoods). They divide and fragment these neighborhoods and communities instead of drawing them closer together and create the so-called places of marginality marred by growing urban inequality and social antagonisms (Tereškinas & Žilys, 2013). Certain researchers investigating segregation processes in the metropolitan areas from 2001 to 2011, argued that spatial segregation remained low in the most urban core and suburban areas. The capital city and its richest groups of the population experienced the most rapid increase in segregation (Burneika, Ubarevičienė & Valatka, 2015). In a similar vein, Sawers argues that "Lithuania's transition from socialism to a market economy was accompanied by an unusually large jump in income inequality and that a major but neglected dimension of that growing inequality reflects the very diverse ways that the different regions of the country have been affected by the economy's restructuring" (Sawers, 2006, p. 49). His research demonstrates that spatial inequality and injustice largely affected the country's towns, villages, and rural areas while the capital city and the second and third largest cities have survived the economic transition reasonably well.

An additional related method of analyzing spatial (in)justice is to document the process of peripheralization conditioned by historical circumstances and political, economic, and demographic tendencies. Analyzing demographic and socioeconomic indicators, Gintarė Pociūtė (2014) demonstrated similar trends to the research of Juška, Johnstone, and Pozzuto (2004) and Sawers (2006). According to her (Pociūtė, 2014), while cities and municipalities close to the largest cities experience relative demographic and socio-economic stability, peripheralization is characteristic of some municipalities of Lithuania (Vilkaviškis, Alytus, Prienai and Šiauliai districts and others) but the regions of Northeast, North, South, Central and Southwest Lithuania – half of all the municipalities of the country – are marked by the deepest peripheralization processes. Another related recent work is similarly devoted to the analysis of socio-spatial exclusion in peripheral sparsely populated areas, where Baranauskienė (2021) performed an analysis of the network of public service institutions in comparison with population change and population density at the municipal and eldership levels. The analysis of socio-spatial exclusion demonstrated that the uniform settlement system that was created during the Soviet period, as well as the concomitant infrastructure of public services that was adapted to this system, began to change rapidly, yet unequally, with the establishment of free market forces (Baranauskienė, 2021, p. 218). The assessment of socio-spatial exclusion also revealed that although "the concentration of the networks of public institutions in the cities covered all areas, except for cultural institutions, the decline of these services is not as rapid as the official data sources alone suggest. The greatest problem is that the lowest concentration of the customer services is typical of most peripheral municipal LAU 2 regions where the inhabitants find it most difficult to access services in the municipal centres" (Baranauskienė, 2021, p. 222). Similar studies reveal how the principle of the "center-periphery" model works; where the largest cities experience the least territorial isolation and act as overall centers of attraction, whereas the peripheral areas experience high territorial isolation (Pociūtė-Sereikienė, Baranauskienė, & Daugirdas, 2019a, 2019b).

The third component of research related to spatial (in)justice deals with territorial or regional allocation of resources and sustainable development. In this type of research, the strengthening of the competitiveness of rural areas via entrepreneurship in local community organizations is discussed. It has been argued that community-based entrepreneurship could increase investments and guarantee the future of rural areas in Lithuania (Pilipavičius, 2011, p. 177). However, more comprehensive research on the everyday operation of housing, patterns of financial investment, public expenditure, and spatial planning in the different regions is necessary to demonstrate the working of spatial (in)justice. Further, it is necessary to identify sustainable growth policies promoting spatial justice that has not to date been covered by Lithuanian research.

To sum up, the issue of spatial justice has been neglected in both theoretical and empirical research in Lithuania. The concept of spatial justice must be considered critically in the studies on regional, urban, and rural development. However, spatial justice is implied in the described research on socio-spatial segregation and differentiation in Lithuanian cities, marginalization, and peripheralization of some regions and increasing levels of social inequality in both urban and rural areas. Supplementary empirical research on the geographical patterning of social justice is crucial to design strategies for emerging social and spatial injustices and inequalities.

Indicators revealing territorial inequality: Shrinking regions and growing urban zones

The effects of population emergency in regions

Subsequent to Lithuania regaining independence, significant processes involving transformation of the population and settlement system, and differentiation of economic development began to take place becoming even more pronounced after 2004, when Lithuania joined the EU (Burneika et al., 2013, 2017; Ubarevičienė, 2018a, 2018b; Baranauskienė, 2019, 2021). At that point, due to intensified migration processes (both internal and external), the socio-spatial structure changed dramatically as the population began to concentrate in larger cities and affiliated suburbs thus creating problematic peripheral territories which continue to be accompanied by intensive depopulation processes (Ubarevičienė, 2017, 2018a; 2018b; Baranauskienė, 2021). Population density in Lithuania has been persistently decreasing for more than two decades. In 1990, the population density rate was 55.4 inhabitants/km^2, in 2000 – 53.8 inhabitants/km^2, in 2010 – 48.1 inhabitants/km^2 and in 2019 it reached the level of 42.8 inhabitants/km^2 (Statistics Lithuania, 2021).

Recent research determines that the least populated areas are north-eastern and southern Lithuania, and the trend is beginning to spread quite rapidly in Žemaitija (Baranauskienė, 2021). Baranauskienė's research on rural sparsely populated territories (further as SPT) revealed that such territories were distinguished according to the newly formed typology of urbanization and only from the type of non-urbanized areas (the rural population density was $\leq$ 12.5 inhabitants/km^2). In 2018, there were 166 sparsely populated territories (in LAU 2 regions of all 556 LAU 2 regions in the country) and more than half – 53.2 % – of non-urban LAU 2 areas which covered 58.4 %of area of the rural territories were classified as SPT. SPT covered 37.2 % of the entire territory of Lithuania, 42.2 % of the total rural population and 7.0 % of the population of the country. The distribution of SPT is very uneven – in the North-East they cover almost all rural spaces while in the West there remain very few such territories. The analysis of alterations in the distribution of SPT clearly indicate that in the 21st century, there has been a very rapid decline in population density. In 2001, such territories were still more prevalent in Eastern Lithuania, but from 2001 to 2018 the number increased from 101 to 166 (Baranauskienė, 2021, p. 98). In addition, during the same period, the number of municipalities (LAU 1) where the rural population density was ≤ 12.5 inhabitants/km^2 increased from 7 (the total rural population – 113,167) to 23 (the total rural population – 272,678), which accounted for 16.6 % and 46.4 % of the country respectively. The development of sparsely populated municipalities (LAU 1) is characterized by similar territorial trends in the spread of sparsely populated territories (LAU 2). Currently these territories are concentrated in the North-East and South, as well as Žemaitija, but the pace of spread also suggests that the rural territories in all municipalities not affected by metropolization will soon become sparsely populated (Baranauskienė, 2021, p. 110).

According to Statistics Lithuania, in 2018 about 67 % of the population lived in the city and about 33 % in rural areas. The typology of urbanization reveals a different picture. According to the newly formed typology of urbanization, urban and suburban areas cover about 36 % of the country and are home to about 83 % of the urban and suburban population, while the non-urbanized population covers 64 % of the country's territory in which about 17 % of the rural population live. According to the new typology of urbanization for the period 2001–2018, the population increased by 1.8 % in the urbanized type elderships and decreased by 17.6 % in the non-urbanized type (Baranauskienė, 2019). These figures differ radically from the trends in the rural and urban population presented in official statistics, which suggest an unchanged balance. The figures obtained clearly illustrate the country's ongoing urbanization, which is "disappearing" when a formal classification of territories is employed. According to the data provided by Statistics Lithuania, from 2001 to 2018 the population decreased by 19.3 % in urban areas and 19.8 % in rural areas (Baranauskienė, 2021, p. 97). Thus, it can be said that the newly formed typology of urbanization reveals a more realistic picture of the country, where the rapid urbanization processes taking place in the country are clearly visible and the population is concentrated in cities and suburban areas.

The population change indicator not only illustrates the rapid depopulation processes in the country (especially in peripheral rural areas), but also demonstrates the rapid urbanization processes around the three major cities (Vilnius, Kaunas and Klaipėda) (Figure 3.1). The analysis of 2008–2019 indicate that the population of the country decreased by 13.0 %. The greatest decrease was in Pagėgiai (by 27.9 %) and Visaginas (by 27.0 %) municipalities, while positive change occurred only around the three largest cities and in Vilnius city and Neringa municipality itself. Thus, it can be argued that metropolitan regions are growing at the expense of peripheral rural areas (Figure 3.2).

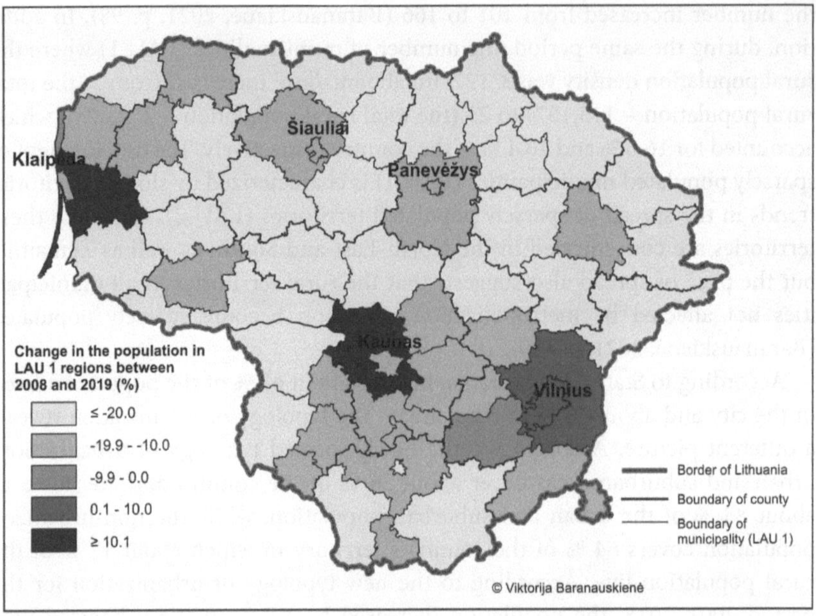

Figure 3.1. Changes in the population in LAU 2 regions between 2008 and 2019. Source: Statistics Lithuania, own calculations by V. Baranauskienė (2021), https://www.stat.gov.lt/.

The analysis of migration data from Statistics Lithuania in 2008 and 2019 demonstrates that the migration of the country's population is territorially differentiated and the intensity of migration processes in 2008 and 2019 is very different (Figure 3.3). It is necessary to mention that the data which reflects solely the two years selected for the analysis, does not illustrate the actual situation in the country, but it is still possible to detect the principal trends. The analysis of the data indicated that in 2008 migration processes were not intensive (proportion of arrivals 2.1 %, proportion of departures 2.6 %) compared to 2019 (proportion of arrivals 4.1 %, proportion of departures 3.7 %). It can be expected that this was influenced not only by Lithuania's accession to the EU, but also by the growing processes of metropolization, as metropolitan regions attract not only residents of peripheral regions, but also those coming from abroad (Burneika et al., 2017; Baranauskienė, 2019, 2021).

Further analysis of the data indicated that the fewest number of settlers in 2008 were in Alytus and Panevėžys (1.3 % in both) and Pasvalys district municipalities

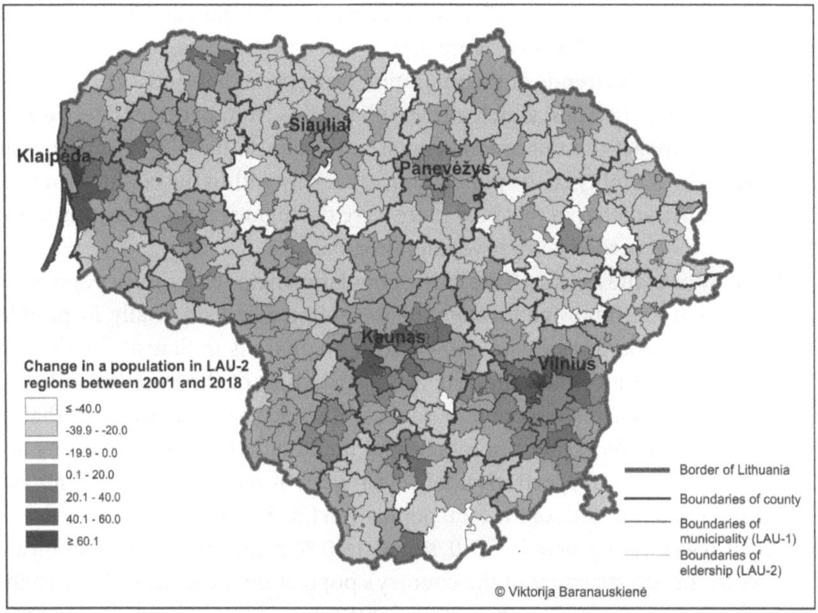

Figure 3.2. Changes in the population in LAU 2 regions (administrative municipal level) between 2001 and 2018. Source: State Enterprise Centre of Registers, own calculations by V. Baranauskienė (2019, 2021), https://www.registrucentras.lt/.

(1.4 %), as well as large Lithuanian cities, were among the least populated Kaunas district however, boasted the greatest number (4.7 %) with Klaipėda district (5.4 %) municipality and Neringa municipality (15.0 %).[1] The majority of emigrants and emigrants lived in the municipalities of Neringa (7.3 %), Akmenė (5.1 %), Visaginas (4.2 %) and Rietavas (4.1 %). Data from 2008 data and a cartoscheme (Figure 3.3) illustrate that suburban development continues to take place and the population is mostly settling in areas near major cities. In 2019, the least number of settlers were in the municipalities of Šilalė district (2.0 %), Panevėžys city (2.3 %), Pasvalys district (2.5 %). Meanwhile, the cities of Vilnius (2.4 %) and Kaunas (3.0 %) received the lowest proportion of those who left and emigrated in 2019; while the greatest proportion of immigrants was recorded in

1 Neringa municipality is an exceptional territory, which is difficult to assess by all assessment indicators, because residents in this municipality declare their place of residence with reference to the exceptional benefits granted to them.

the municipalities of Neringa (7.1 %), Pagėgiai (5.9 %), Kaunas district (5.6 %) and Klaipėda district (5.1 %) (Figure 3.4).

Summarizing the trends of the migration process in 2008 and 2019, it can be asserted that the big cities, which attract inhabitants from peripheral territories, significantly impact the migration processes. It can also be said that there is an increase in the mobility of the population, especially within the country, and the 2008 data illustrate that in that year there were the highest number exiting as the whole country recorded a negative migration balance.

An analysis of the age structure of the population helps to assess depopulation processes that are intensive throughout the country and especially in peripheral rural areas (Baranauskienė, 2021). Such an analysis in Statistics Lithuania in 2008 and 2019 indicated that the age distribution of the population in the country is very uneven (Figure 3.5). Data at the national level suggests that in both those years, the greatest proportion of the population was of working age (62.2 % and 61.6 %, respectively), far fewer were of retirement age, which accounts for about one-fifth of the total population (20.8 % and 21.5 %respectively) and even fewer young people (17.0 % and 16.0 % respectively). No significant changes in the age structure of the country's population are observed due to the relatively short period between 2008 and 2019, but general population is aging rapidly. The presented cartoschemes (Figures 3.5 and 3.6) clearly reveal that the retirement age population has increased throughout the country, and especially in the North-East, Central Lithuania and Žemaitija. In 2019, they accounted for the smallest proportion of the population in the suburban municipalities of the largest cities and in Western Lithuania, where there is a larger proportion of youth.

The data from 2008 to 2019 indicates that the proportion of the working age population increased in the North-East and South and decreased in the largest cities of the country. During the same period, the proportion of young people decreased in almost all territories of the country, except for the three largest cities and several municipalities, where it increased slightly in Kaunas city and in the Neringa municipalities it remained stable (15.9 % and 14.8 %). In the municipalities of Klaipėda city (from 15.1 % to 17.4 %), Visaginas (from 13.7 % to 16.0 %) and Vilnius city (from 15.2 % to 17.8 %) the proportion of young people increased.

Summarizing the territorial differentiation in terms of change in the population age structure, it can be stated that the population is unevenly distributed in the country and this distribution was uneven from 2008 to 2019. The largest proportion of the country's population was of working age and this group experienced very little change (decreased by 0.6 percentage points in the analyzed

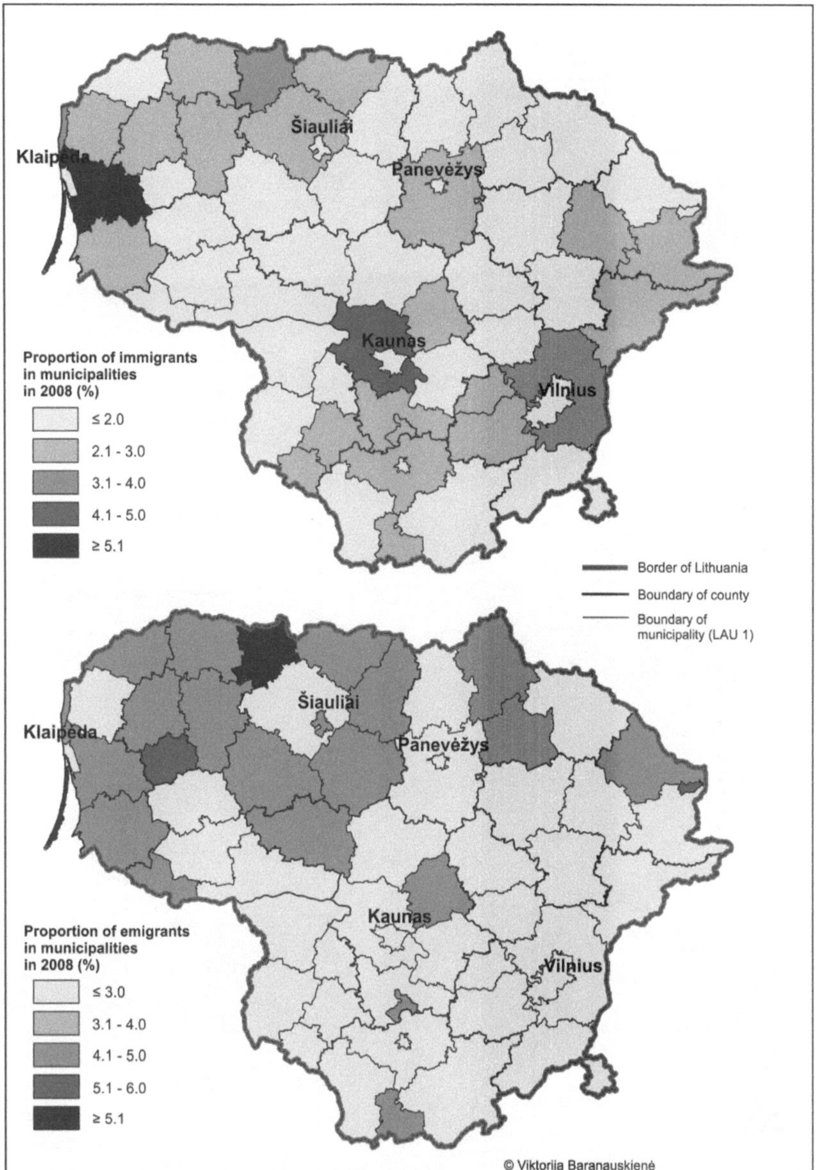

Figure 3.3. Population migration in Lithuanian municipalities in 2008.
Source: Statistics Lithuania, calculations by V. Baranauskienė (2021), https://www.stat.gov.lt/.

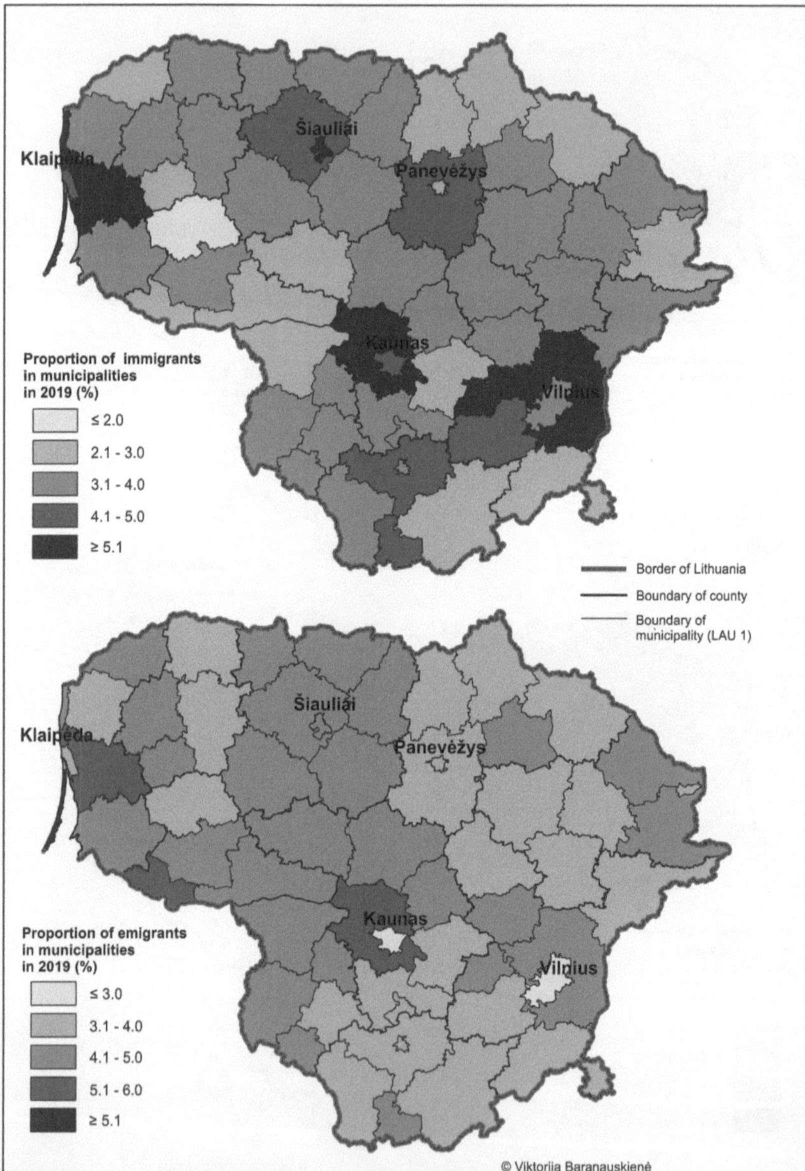

Figure 3.4. Population migration in Lithuanian municipalities in 2019.
Source: Statistics Lithuania, calculations by V. Baranauskienė (2021), https://www.stat.gov.lt/.

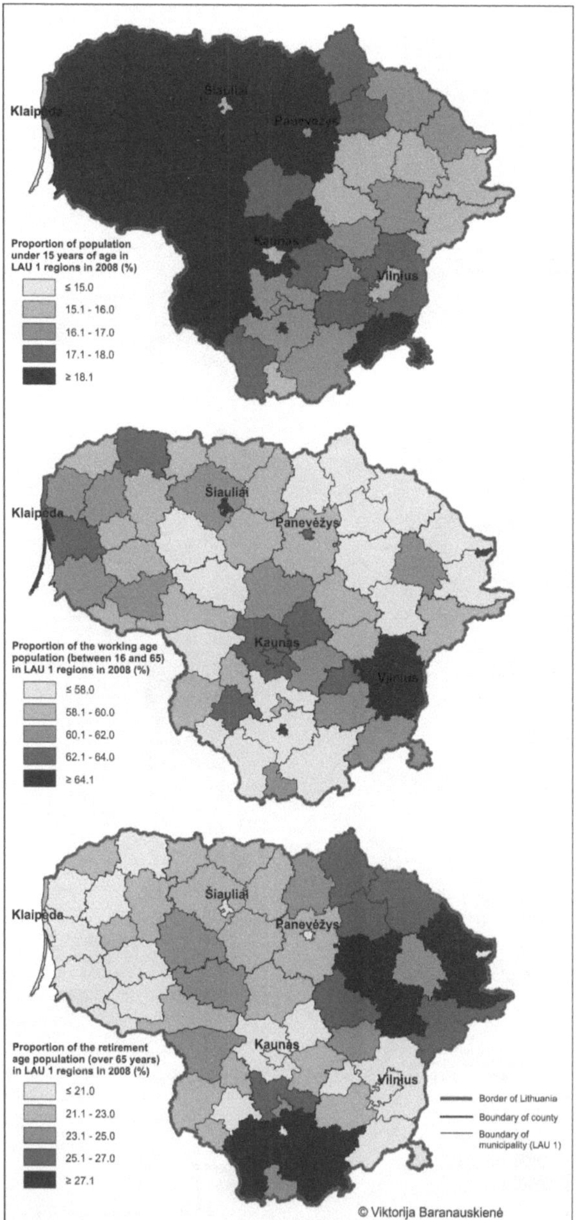

Figure 3.5. The age structure of the population in municipalities (LAU 1 level) in 2008. Source: Statistics Lithuania, calculations by V. Baranauskienė (2021), https://www.stat.gov.lt/.

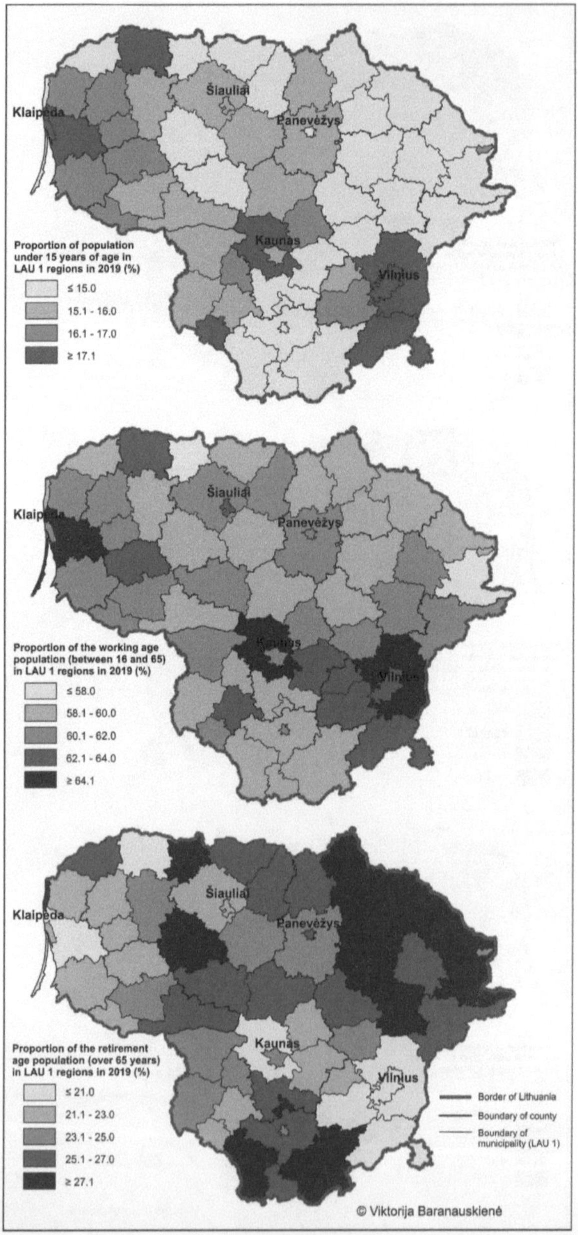

Figure 3.6. The age structure changes of the population in municipalities (LAU 1 level) in 2019. Source: Statistics Lithuania, calculations by V. Baranauskienė (2021), https://www.stat.gov.lt/.

period from 2008 to 2019). There were marginally more young people (decreased by 1.0 percentage points), but this category reflected the least growth. The greatest changes were experienced in the retirement age population, which increased by 1.6 %. The number of people of retirement age increased in North-Eastern, Central Lithuania and Žemaitija, the number of young people decreased especially in Western, Central, South-Western and North-Eastern Lithuania, and the working-age population increased almost across the country, although slightly less in Žemaitija. Thus, it can be said that the country's population is aging, especially in peripheral rural areas. The situation is slightly better in the largest cities and their related suburban municipalities which function as economic vitality centers and comprise younger families with kids (the same trends are observed in the three selected municipalities).

Summarizing the demographic and urbanization indicators of the analyzed period 2008–2019, it can be stated that the naturally occurring settlement processes will continue; three metropolitan regions (urban Vilnius, Kaunas and Klaipėda municipalities) will continue to grow, which will attract residents both from the country's peripheral regions and from abroad – rather intensive migration processes. Analyzing the level of urbanization in the country, it is difficult to assess the data provided by the Lithuanian Department of Statistics on urban and rural population, as the population of suburban areas is classified as rural (Baranauskienė, 2019, 2021). It can also be assumed that the country's population will continue to decline, especially in peripheral rural areas, due to an aging population, and the country's major cities and their suburbs will continue to expand as populations grow, increase in working age and remain stable.

The Labor market: Between economic dynamics and need for employment

Regarding possible alternatives in the expansion of welfare state provision at regional level and considering the enactment of social investment policy design, economic growth indicators represent the wider picture of the household situation. The total number of employed persons has undergone drastic changes and employment rates fluctuate due to structural economic transitions from a command economy without formal unemployment data to a market economy, as well as factors such as emigration, negative natural population growth and other causes.

Comparing the period from 2008 to 2019, the employment rate in Lithuania increased from 64.4 % to 73.0 % in the presented carto scheme (Figure 3.7) it is clear that the employment rate is unevenly distributed in the country, where the in North-West Lithuania and the country's metropolitan regions and adjacent municipalities it has clearly increased in recent years.

The most substantial positive change in the employment rate was observed in the municipalities of Zarasai district (23.9 %), Rietavas (29.9 %) and Šilalė district (30.4 %), the least change (negative) – in Kalvarija (−13.1 percentage points) and in the municipalities of Ignalina district (−11.4 %) The largest proportion of the employed working age population in 2019 was in Trakai district municipality (80.9 %) and the municipalities of Vilnius city (82.5 %), Druskininkai (83.2 %) and Neringa (89.5 %). The lowest rate of employment is observed in Ignalina district (51.8 %), also in Biržai district and Kelmė district municipalities (by 57.3 % respectively). During the analyzed period, the employment rate of the working age population remained relatively stable in Biržai district (56.7 % and 57.3 % respectively), Marijampolė (67.2 % and 67.6 %), Kelmė district (57.6 % and 57.3 %), and the municipalities of Panevėžys district (63.8 % and 63.4 %) and Alytus city (69.5 % and 68.9 %) (Figure 3.7).

Summarizing the available data on the employment rate of the population for the period 2008–2019, it can be stated that the employment rate of the working age population is increasing in the country. The highest level of employment is typical of the largest cities of the country and their suburban territories, the lowest – the peripheral and remote municipalities. The increase in the working age employment rate in large cities and neighboring suburban municipalities indicates that more working age people are settling in these areas (employed people are recorded according to their permanent declared place of residence). The change symbolizes the intensive expansion of suburban areas, and metropolitan cities that have become the growth points and centers for accumulating economic competitiveness and productivity.

A more detailed labor market perspective reveals significant regional disparities in unemployment. The analysis of the data on the ratio of the unemployed from 2008 to 2019 demonstrates that the proportion of registered unemployed persons in the country has dramatically increased (from 3.7 % in 2008 to 8.4 % in 2019). Such a remarkable shift is explained as follows, "the growth of labour supply has been caused by unfavorable economic conditions, workers made redundant due to corporate bankruptcies and reorganization" (Užimtumo tarnyba, 2010, p. 3), as a result of the global economic crisis which began in 2008 reaching Lithuania in 2009.

As can be seen from the cartoscheme (Figure 3.8), in 2019, only the Western part of Lithuania, Northern Lithuania (only Pakruojis district municipality) the two large cities (Šiauliai and Panevėžys) and the municipalities of (Vilnius city, Trakai district, Elektrėnai, Kaunas district, Birštonas, Prienai district,

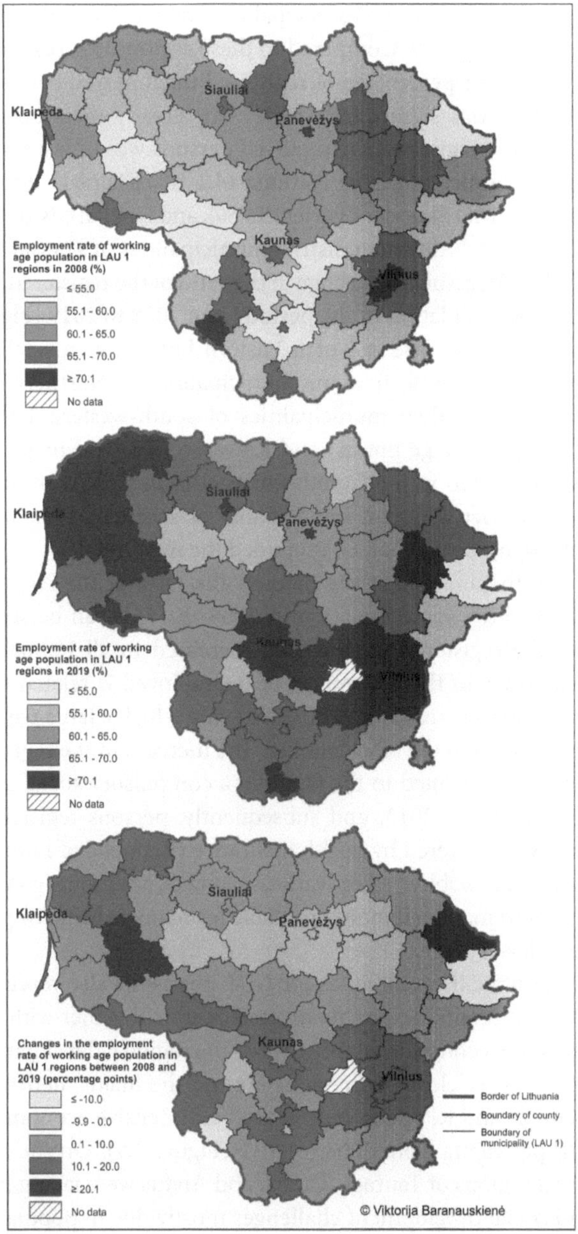

Figure 3.7. Changes in the employment rate of working age population in municipalities (LAU 1 level) between 2008 and 2019. Source: Statistics Lithuania, calculations by V. Baranauskienė (2021), https://www.stat.gov.lt/.

Marijampolė and Šakiai district municipalities) had a lower percentage of registered unemployed in 2009. Compared to these regions, the rest of the country saw a relatively greater percentage of registered unemployed compared to 2008 when the situation was significantly better. As already mentioned above, the lowest proportion of registered unemployed persons was in Western Lithuania, especially in the municipalities of Neringa (4.1 %), Klaipėda district (4.7 %), Kretinga district (5.1 %) Skuodas district (5.7 %), and Šiauliai city (6.0 %), and the highest in the Eastern Lithuanian district municipalities of Zarasai (14.4 %) and Ignalina (14.1 %). Assessing the change in the ratio of the registered unemployed to the working age population in the period from 2008 to 2019 (Figure 3.8), the indicator showed an increase in North-Eastern Lithuania especially in Zarasai district municipality (9.3 %) in some municipalities in Northern and Central Lithuania and in individual municipalities of south-western Lithuania (e.g., Kazlų Rūda (9.6 percentage points) and Kalvarija (9.8 percentage points). The least alteration occurred in the Skuodas district municipality of north-western Lithuania and the Druskininkai municipality of southern Lithuania (1.0 percentage points each), both of which remained the most stable.

Summarizing the analysis of the data on the ratio of the registered unemployed to the working age population in 2008–2019, it can be stated that the proportion of the registered unemployed increased in all Lithuanian regions equally. The increase in the percentage of unemployed is related to the global and national economic crisis from 2008 following which a large part of the population did not return to the labor market. The increase in the registered unemployed can also be attributed to the fact that a compulsory social insurance tax had been introduced in 2013, and subsequently, persons registered with the labor exchange were covered by health insurance (Republic of Lithuania, 1991), thereby creating a favorable system (various benefits, additional guarantees, etc.) for the unemployed making it more profitable for many to be unemployed rather than work for a lower wage.

Regional economic inequalities as for GDP per capita also represent a heterogenous picture of economic activity diversification. Together with the employment indicators, the economic vitality reveals the regional development patterns in Lithuania. It is very clear that regions around the major metropolitan areas of Vilnius, Kaunas and Klaipėda experienced an intensive economic growth in terms of GDP per capita from 2008 to 2019 (Figure 3.9). On the contrary, the rural peripheral regions of Tauragė, Utena, and Alytus were facing more intense economic and social development challenges mostly due to population decline, out-migration and less diversified economic sectors.

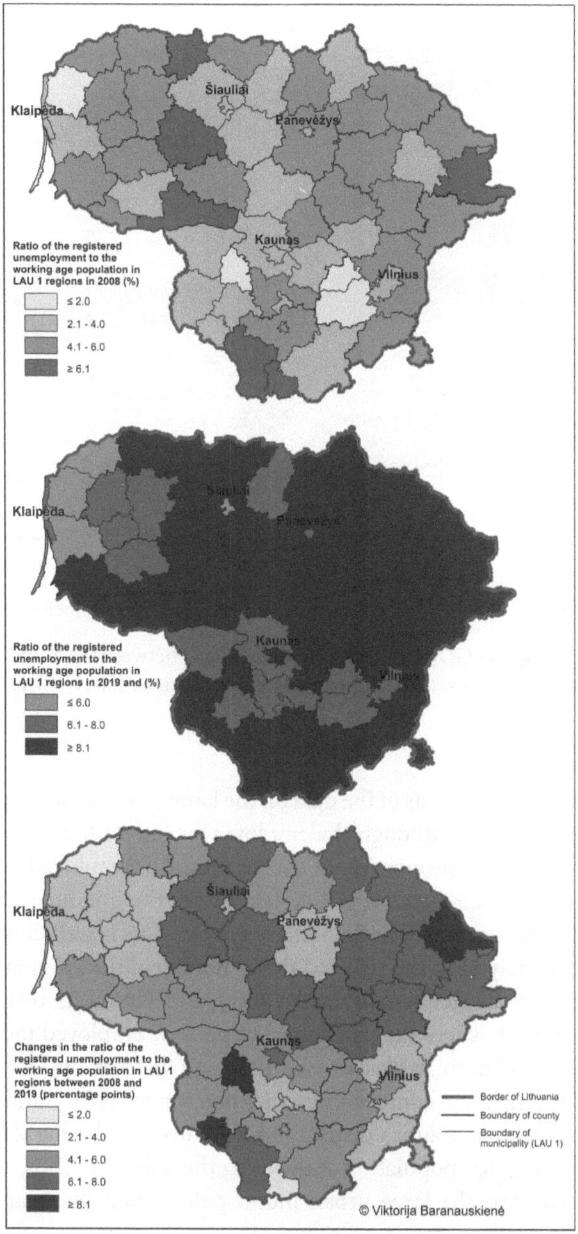

Figure 3.8. Changes in the ratio of the registered unemployment to the working age population in municipalities (LAU 1 level) between 2008 and 2019. Source: Statistics Lithuania, calculations by V. Baranauskienė (2021), https://www.stat.gov.lt/.

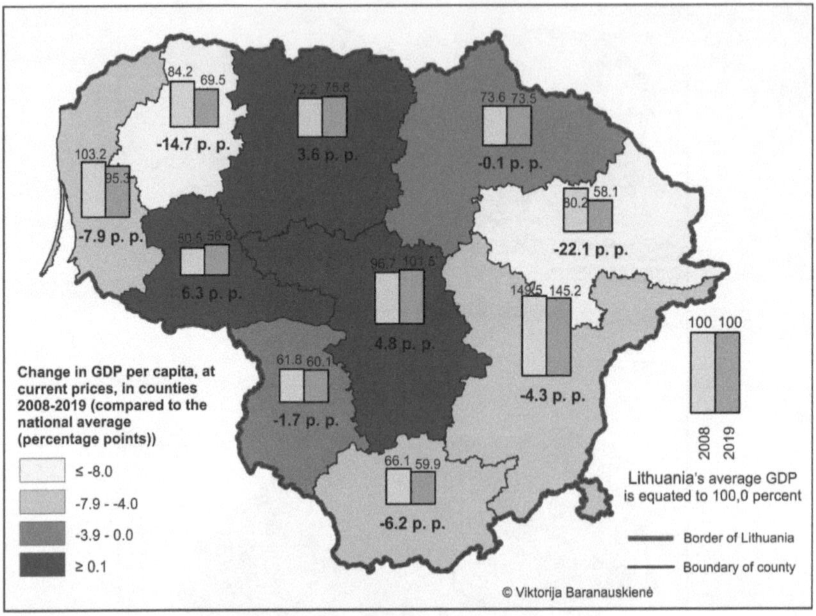

Figure 3.9. Changes in GDP per capita (regional level) between 2008 and 2019. Source: Statistics Lithuania, calculations by V. Baranauskienė (2021), https://www.stat.gov.lt/.

Summarizing the analysis of the data on the labor market for the period 2008–2019, it can affirm that although the employment rate of the country's population has increased, the proportion of the registered unemployed remains at the highest point as the country's social system favors the unemployed persons by encouraging them to remain in the welfare system. This is well illustrated by the statistical data analysis in the selected three municipalities (Kaunas city (urban locality), Kaunas district (suburban locality) and Pakruojis district (peripheral rural locality)), where the percentage of persons employed increases as the working age population decreases (see next sub-chapter on "Methodological remarks on linking local context and social investment policy indicators"). The exception is suburban Kaunas district municipality that is characterized by an intensive working age population moving to the suburbs. Thus, we can summarize that whereas the large urban municipalities and the nearby suburban municipalities perform better on economic growth indicators, the situation is significantly different in the peripheral rural municipalities of the country. Thus, the intensive growth of urban poles faces challenges such as housing, public infrastructure, and transportation costs, whereas rural areas face intensive depopulation and de-urbanization streaming including a decline in tax collection, quality of educational and health care provision all of which should guarantee the sustaining of stable household income.

Spatial inequalities and educational services provision

While analysing spatial inequalities, it is obvious that educational accomplishment and educational infrastructure level is important in determining the differences between urban and rural areas. In other words, the dynamics of inequality depend on the level of educational services provided in different municipalities. Therefore, we consider a few selected educational indicators that reflect our discussion on social investment policies development, such as vocational education and training (VET), and early childhood care and education (ECEC). The more detailed analysis of VET and ECEC policies design, institutional framework, allocation of responsibilities across multiscale governance levels, beneficiaries' groups and services provision can be found in Chapters 4 and 6.

Regional disparities in terms of educational accomplishment indicators reflects the general welfare state diffusion. As is observed in the research, the highest education inequality as GINI sub-indicator is observable in smaller regions of Lithuania (Tauragė, Telšiai regions) and the lowest in the largest metropolitan areas of Kaunas and Vilnius. Therefore, is comes as no surprise that the greatest educational inequality is detected among women, rural and small regions compared to larger metropolitan Lithuanian regions (Maksvytienė & Polgrimaitė, 2015). As for all Lithuanian educational institutions, vocational education and the network of vocational training institutions have undergone many different institutional mergers in terms of consolidation of the school network, educational service delivery, and financial budgeting schemes. However, the reforms had less downward effect for VET schools network compared to the other educational institutions (e.g., the network of general education or preschool education institutions) (Baranauskienė, 2021). The slower decrease in the number of institutions is explained due to the relatively small number of vocational schools in the country (according to the Lithuanian Department of Statistics, there were 71 institutions in 2019), but major institutional network transformations (reorganizations, mergers, liquidations, etc.) are expected as a part of the central government agenda for educational services consolidation. For example, "it is proposed to transform VET units in small areas into VET departments of general education schools or to join forces with general education schools by concluding joint activity agreements under which general education schools would provide general education to students and VET institutions would teach professions" (Šileikytė, 2020; Statistic Lithuania, 2021).

The number of vocational schools depends on the admitted number of students (Figures 3.10 and 3.11). In general, the number of vocational education institutions in the country decreased slightly, for example, in the period 2008–2020 the total number of institutions decreased by 11.3 % (from 80 to 71, respectively). On the contrary, the decrease in the number of students was rather significant in the period from 2012/2013 to 2019/2020 the total number of admitted students decreased by 37.9 % (from 44797 to 27824 students respectively) (Figures 3.10 and 3.11).

Analyzing the change in the number of vocational training institutions, the cartoscheme (Figure 3.10) demonstrates that some municipalities have no vocational training institutions in their territories (in total 14 municipalities). In the analysed period from 2008/2009 to 2019/2020 a positive uptick of institutions

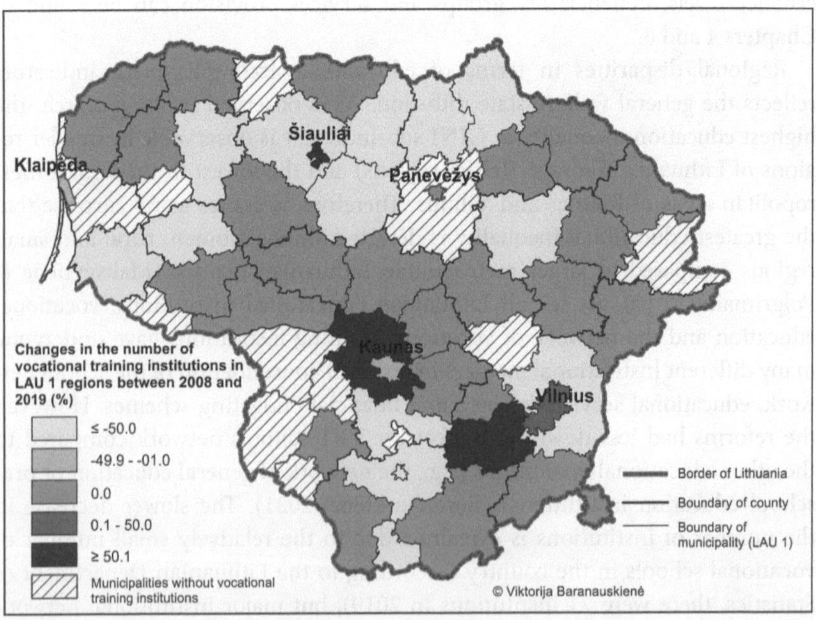

Figure 3.10. Changes in the number of vocational training institutions between 2008/2009 and 2019/2020 academic years. Source: Statistics Lithuania, calculations by V. Baranauskienė (2021), https://www.stat.gov.lt/.

is visible in only a few municipalities (in Vilnius city, Šiauliai city, Kaunas district (increased from 1 to 2 institutions), and Trakai district). The increase in institutions is usually associated with geographical relocation and mergers with the neighboring schools. The decrease in institutions was observed in 17 municipalities, and 6 of them were closed down (Druskininkai, Anykščiai district, Pakruojis district, Pasvalys district, Prienai district and Šilalė district municipalities). Referring to Baranauskienė's (2021) analysis of the network of vocational education institutions in regions, "the decrease in the number of vocational education institutions is related to the fact that it is not popular to choose vocational schools among young people in Lithuania, many study at universities or go abroad to work abroad. There has been a recent shortage of various professions in labor market. Also, the strongly declining network of professional institutions is explained by the fact that there are usually only one or two institutions in the municipal territory, therefore when one is closed or institutions are merged, a large change in the numbers is observed" (Baranauskienė, 2021, p. 149).

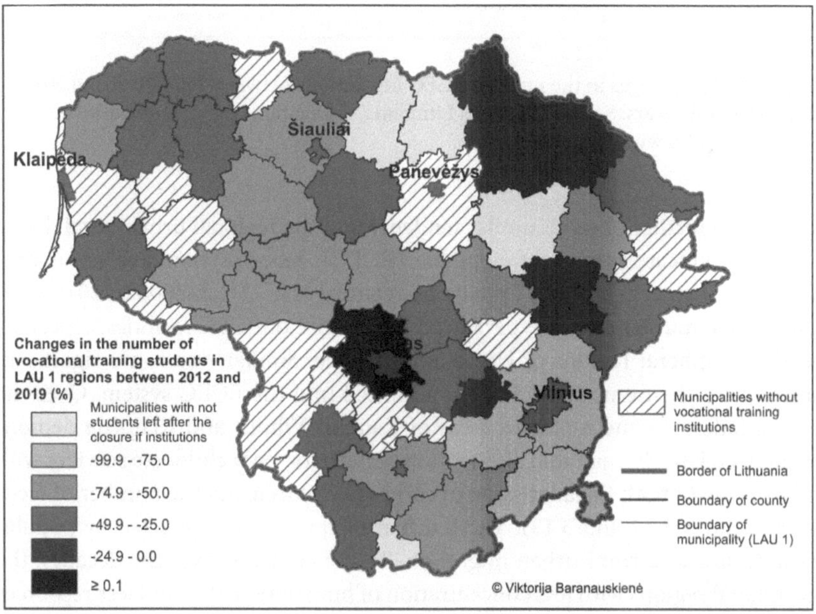

Figure 3.11. Changes in the number of vocational training students between 2012/2013 and 2019/2020 academic years. Source: Statistics Lithuania, calculations by V. Baranauskienė (2021), https://www.stat.gov.lt/.

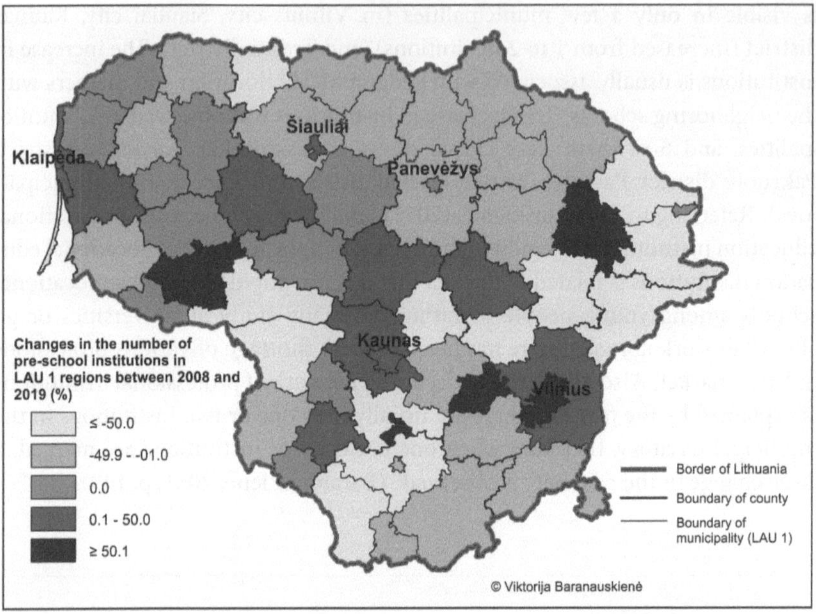

Figure 3.12. Changes in the number ECEC institutions between 2008/2009 and 2019/2020 academic years. Source: Statistics Lithuania, calculations by V. Baranauskienė (2021), https://www.stat.gov.lt/.

We can further observe similar tendencies in the regional urban-rural divide in early childcare system development (ECEC). More detailed analysis is provided in Chapter 5 on ECEC policy on regional level. From 2008 to 2019 most Lithuanian municipalities experienced the closure of ECEC facilities, especially in the peripheral regions of Utena and Tauragė. Similar trends are significant in terms of the number of children admitted into the ECEC system. Over the last decades, the metropolitan areas of Kaunas, Vilnius and Klaipėda demonstrated a relatively equitable distribution pattern for early childcare services with an increase in both the admission of early age children and the number of facilities (Figures 3.12 and 3.13). These urban regions are less affected by population decline and rural-urban migration. To the contrary, over the decades, the peripheral regions with less concentration of human potential and less resources continue to face sustainable economic and social growth challenges.

Summing up the changes in the number of VET and ECEC institutions and admission numbers, it can be affirmed that both selected educational field

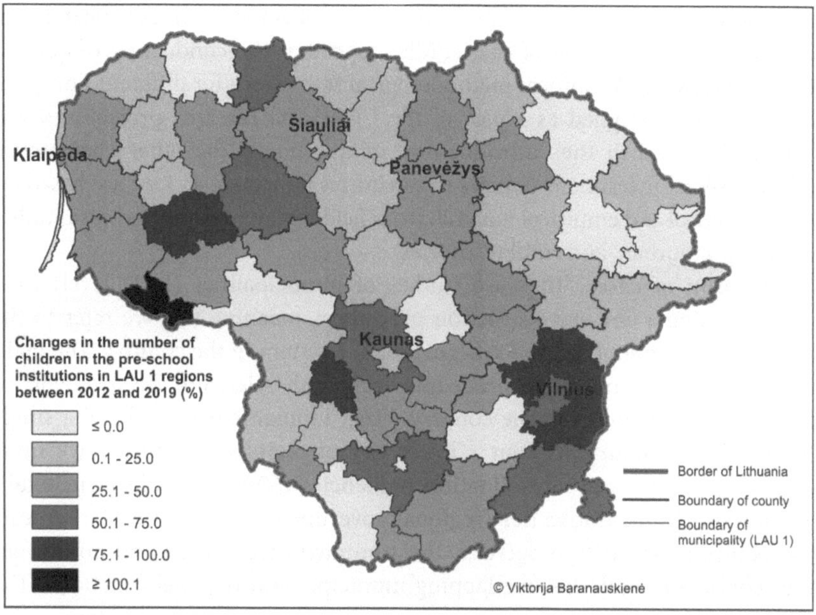

Figure 3.13. Changes in the number of children in ECEC institutions between 2012/2013 and 2019/2020 academic years. Source: Statistics Lithuania, calculations by V. Baranauskienė (2021), https://www.stat.gov.lt/.

indicators reflect the heterogenous patterns of service provision within regions. An Urban-rural pattern for educational provision is observable. However, much depends on the centralized policy approach in equalizing access to different educational services despite the area size and other external factors, as the percentage of young population declines. For example, the VET institutional network is constantly affected by various reorganizations, mostly due to the rapidly declining number of students. The greatest losses for both the network and the number of pupils is observed in the most problematic peripheral territories, where the population is declining, especially the proportion of young people.

Methodological remarks on investigating local context and social investment policy

Regarding our empirical investigation on territorially driven social investment policies, we have selected three municipalities in Lithuania: urban, suburban, and rural (Figure 3.14). This sub-chapter introduces the methodological design that defines the selection of case studies as well as the conducting of qualitative interviewing. A uniform methodological framework for different European countries was designed as a part of the COHSMO research project and was briefly presented in the "Introduction" of this book. The other chapters on selected social investment policies in territories (Chapters 4, 5, 6) are based on the theoretical and empirical material from field research in selected case studies of urban, suburban, and rural territories.

Selection of cases. The case studies of municipalities (LAU level) were selected using a one-stage selection procedure, meaning that we refer to the administrative boundaries of self-governance system in the country. The main arguments for the one-stage procedure are mainly related to the specificity of administrative systems in the country. First, Lithuania is considered a single NUT 2 level country without a lower tier of regional administrative units with strong territorial consolidation tendencies (60 municipalities in total). The upper administrative tier (regional government level, former "counties") was abolished in 2010 to decrease the administrative burden and implement the economy of scale for overlapping municipal and regional functions. The absence of a strong regional governmental tier tends to increase the tendencies towards centralization where central governmental actors play an important role in territorial development policies. Secondly, the allocation of municipal tasks and financial resources is based on centralized state policies, including planning of vocational training, pre-school childcare, secondary education, labor market, area regeneration policies, health care, etc. However, the areas of economic growth and urban development strategies remain at municipal discretion. Thirdly, the size of the population in a single municipality is also important. In Lithuania, the population size in municipalities varies significantly from 3,530 in the smallest municipality of Neringa to 562,030 in the capital area of Vilnius in 2020. For suburban we have selected the so called "ring" municipality of Kaunas district that exceeds 96,441 thousand inhabitants. As for a rural municipality, Pakruojis district municipality represents one of the smallest municipalities with a population of 18,606 thousand in 2020. Kaunas city municipality represents the metropolitan case with 289,380 thousand inhabitants (Statistics Lithuania, 2020).

Fourthly, the strong internal socio-economic variations between different territorial units are also important in selected municipalities. As administrative subdivisions of municipal administrations, so-called *elderships or wards* do not have decision-making power or financial autonomy other than social

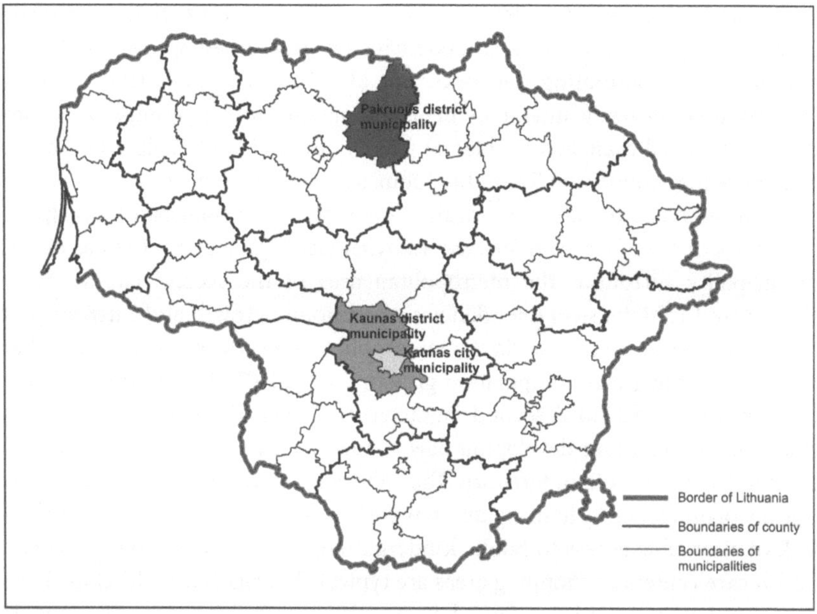

Figure 3.14. Selected case studies: urban, suburban and rural localities in Lithuanian administrative system.

care, social welfare and public infrastructure maintenance. The elderships are strictly controlled by the intra-municipal coordination mechanism and cannot define their own agenda. Finally, we refer to the results from the ESPON 2007 study on metropolitan areas and functional urban areas (ESPON report, 2007). According to the study, the current state of the socio-economic development of the municipality, including economic growth indicators, labor market dynamics and demographic change (particularly, the size of population) should be seriously considered when defining the status of urban territories. The policy coordination mechanisms and the potential to develop innovative economic growth and territorial cohesion strategies in the urban territory eventually provide rich empirical material.

In greater detail, the main arguments for the selection of the metropolitan area of **Kaunas city municipality** (Lith. *Kauno miesto savivaldybė*) represents the structure of monocentric agglomeration (ESPON 2007 report). Kaunas city municipality is characteristic of the majority of metropolitan area features including high population density, economic growth accumulation, intensive private and public investments, tendencies towards urban sprawl, established and intensive commuting networks, but also "unexpected" social outcomes (for example, growing unemployment among specific age groups or income dynamics, social exclusion problems) (see Figure 3.15 and Table 3.1). 52 % of Kaunas region population live in the Kaunas metropolitan area.

With reference to suburban locality, we analyze the suburban municipality of Kaunas district (*Kauno rajono savivaldybė*) (see Figure 3.16). Kaunas district municipality surrounds the metropolitan area of the second largest city of Kaunas and exhibits strong tendencies of economic growth and intensive outwards commuting networks via the metropolitan area. The municipality is characterized by the greatest population growth (around 17.42 %) in the territories between 1996 and 2020. A second characteristic is related to comprehensive land resources strategies for developing new residential areas, especially in the areas close to the metropolitan territory. The suburban sprawl is surrounded by chaotically planned family housing districts with poor public infrastructure and the lack of affordable access to public kindergarten, secondary schooling, primary health care centers or shopping areas are typical. The rigorously developed economic and urban interdependence between the metropolitan area of Kaunas city and Kaunas district municipalities further creates policy coordination problems, especially in public services delivery (for example, public transportation, childcare, and access to secondary schools).

Finally, the central arguments for the selection of the borderland rural locality of Pakruojis district (*Pakruojo rajono savivaldybė*) emphasize the criteria of low population density, tendency for out-migration and the significant role of agricultural activities (see Figure 3.17). The selected municipality is characterized by significant de-population trends over the past two decades that affected the primary and secondary education system, student enrolment in vocational schools and labor market supply. The Municipality mostly relies on agricultural activities; among these 71.4 % of the territory are specifically used for productive field farming. Due to continuous de-population and the lack of diversified economic activities, the municipality has developed a local cultural tourism strategy together with other local stakeholders to strengthen the local economic potential, for example, to renew Pakruojis manor ensemble for cultural tourism purposes.

The selected cases studies of municipalities represent different territorial development patterns including social-demographic indicators and economic growth. The main demographic and social indicators of population change in urban, suburban and rural municipalities provided in Table 3.1 demonstrate the

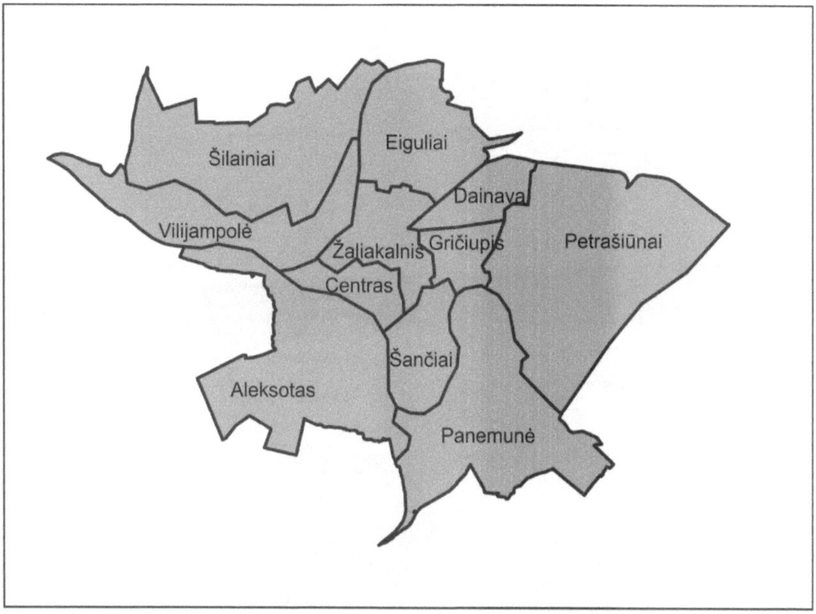

Figure 3.15. Administration structure of urban Kaunas city municipality.

different development variations. The statistical indicators demonstrate that the population of Pakruojis district municipality, like many other peripheral municipalities, decreased considerably by 26.5 % Kaunas city population decreased by 15.5 % while Kaunas district municipality population increased by 13.3 %. Suburban Kaunas district municipality attracts residents from peripheral territories and a large proportion probably not only of Kaunas city residents, but also others, moved to suburban territories, which perform the functions of "sleep over" districts (Burneika et al., 2017; Baranauskienė, 2021). Thus, it can be stated that the naturally functioning transformations of population settlement will continue, and both Kaunas and the other two metropolitan regions will continue to be the centers of attraction for peripheral territories and foreign population. With regard to migration tendencies, the data shows that the most intensive positive migration processes are observed in urban and suburban municipalities. The peripheral rural municipality of Pakruojis district experienced the largest negative annual net migration indicators. Kaunas city and Kaunas district municipalities are characterized by the features of a metropolitan region, while the suburban territory of Kaunas district municipality is expanding due to new

Figure 3.16. Administration structure of suburban Kaunas district "ring" municipality.

incoming settlers (arrivals and immigrants in 2008 accounted for 4.7 %, and in 2019 as for 6.7 %).

As for the working age population (compared to the whole country) decreases were only observed in Kaunas city, while the indicator points to slow grows in Kaunas district and Pakruojis district municipalities. The percentage of the population of retirement age, as in the whole country, increased in Kaunas city and Pakruojis district municipalities, only decreasing in Kaunas district municipality. Thus, as can be seen from the data, in suburban Kaunas district municipality the working age population is increasing, which indicates more intensive inner workforce migration for economic reasons. Pakruojis district municipality corresponds to "purely" rural areas, where the population is declining, the working age and retirement age are increasing, and the population is aging.

The analysis of the data on the ratio of the registered unemployed to the working age population of the three municipalities (Kaunas city, Kaunas district and Pakruojis district) from 2008 to 2019 shows that the proportion of unemployed increased mostly in Kaunas (from 2.8 % to 8.8 % respectively), and slightly less in Kaunas district municipality (from 2.6 % to 7.7 %). Thus, it can be

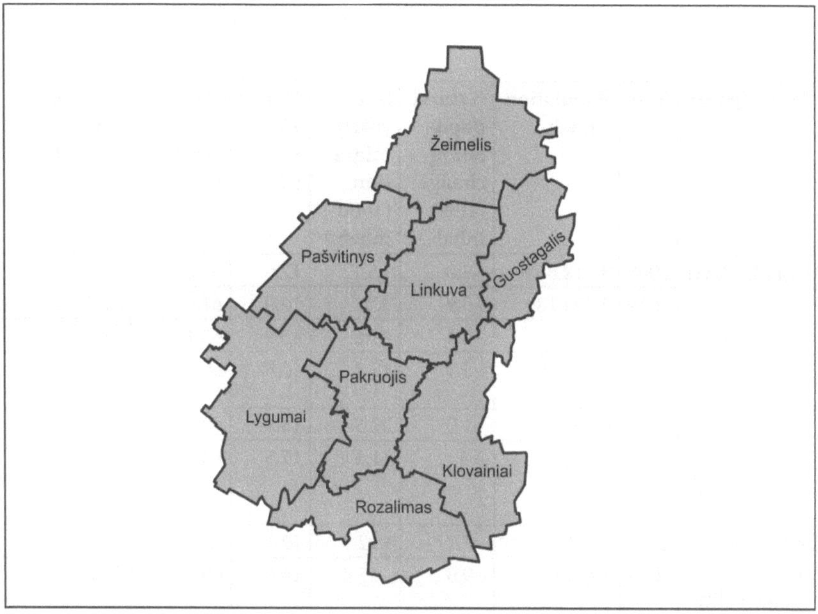

Figure 3.17. Administration structure of rural Pakruojis district municipality.

assumed that following the economic crisis from 2008, the urban and suburban territories suffered the most, losing jobs and, very likely, a large part of the population either did not return to the labor market or migrated abroad. Although in the analyzed peripheral municipality of Pakruojis district the proportion of unemployed did not increase as much as in urban and suburban municipalities (Pakruojis municipality already had a greater proportion of unemployed in 2008 compared to the others), the increase was also significant. The analysis of the employment rate data of the selected three municipalities shows that Pakruojis district municipality enjoys the most stable proportion of working population, but remains low compared with Kaunas city (68.0 % in 2008 and 77.0 % in 2019 respectively) and Kaunas district (59.4 % and 70.8 % respectively). The employment rate has experienced the significant rise in Kaunas district municipality as for 11.4 % during the last decade. Such a significant increase can be explained by the fact that young and working-age residents have moved to newly built housing in the suburban areas (Burneika et al., 2017).

Empirical data. For the next chapters we use the empirical data from the qualitative interview in selected localities in Lithuania. The list of interview

Table 3.1. Indicators of population change in selected case study municipalities in 2008 and 2019.

Municipality	Year	Population (inhab.)	Natural population change (1000 inhab.)	Net yearly migration (1000 inhab.)	Under 15 years (%)	Working age (16–65) (%)	Retirement (over 65 years) (%)
Country level	2008	3,212,605	−3.8	−5.1	17.0	62.2	20.8
	2019	2,794,184	−3.9	3.9	16.0	61.6	21.5
Kaunas city municipality (urban)	2008	339,535	−2.4	−9.8	15.9	63.1	21.0
	2019	286,754	−3.3	12.4	15.8	60.8	23.4
Kaunas district municipality (suburban)	2008	83,946	−1.0	22.5	18.5	62.7	18.8
	2019	95,120	2.3	11.5	17,5	64.6	17.9
Pakruojis district municipality (rural)	2008	25,953	−7.7	−12.3	19.1	59.0	21.9
	2019	19,071	−9.0	−15.4	14.6	60.2	25.2

Data source: *Calculations based on 2008 and 2019 data of Statistics Lithuania*, https://www.stat.gov.lt/.

questions addresses three main topics, including (1) the level of territorial disadvantages and advantages related to locality, (2) the level of collective efficacy related to local life opportunities and (3) mechanisms and arrangements of territorial governance, collaborations, and coordination to mobilize territorial capital and implement the policies of pre-school childcare, active labor market, urban area regeneration, VET and economic growth. Three different groups of local stakeholders were identified as following: (1) community stakeholders (representatives from community organizations, local NGOs), (2) business stakeholders (business associations and enterprises with strong interconnectedness to local government) and (3) public authorities (municipal officials involved in planning, business relations, municipal officials and state institution representatives from childcare, labor market, VET policy fields). As for community interviewees, we analyze the involvement and experiences of local community organizations and NGOs in territorial activation projects, inquiring about the efficiency of collective mobilization efforts and improving access to local welfare. The perspective of public authority actors uncovers how different institutions coordinate their actions and interests in territorial-driven policies, what kind of deliberative practices are used to integrate different policies and practices. The third group of business actors is advantageous in analysing business involvement in territorial growth and development policies. The interviews were performed in three urban, suburban, and rural localities (20 interviews in each municipality, 60 in total) during the period July-November 2018. The snowballing sampling strategy was used as an effective tool for identifying the most important experts in the field and excluding the irrelevant ones. The list of interviewees represents different fields of expertise, social and professional background, and different degrees of public engagement in social investment policy fields. Finally, the transcriptions of the interviews were prepared as well as interview notes summarizing interview data on territorial problems and advantages, level of collective efficacy, and place-based approaches in territorial governance and policies, coordination across governance levels and different stakeholder involvement.

Conclusion: National territorial inequalities profiles

The national input related to the multi-level conception of territorial inequality and spatial justice has advanced over the past decade but still lacks more empirically based evidence on socio-economic and demographic dynamics of inequality patterns at the regional and municipal level. Although the term territorial cohesion points to a variety of socio-economic dimensions directed at reducing territorial socio-economic imbalances, the conceptual confusion around the territorial cohesion and methodological limitations remains one of the biggest challenges. Firstly, the Lithuanian national tradition still lacks coherent empirical studies based both on qualitative and quantitative regional and municipal level data and, secondly, the research remains primarily descriptive.

Generally, the picture of territorial development in Lithuania represents the analytical attempts to combine the territorial demographic changes, urbanization processes, economic productivity of regions, and socio-spatial segregation and differentiation. It is possible to distinguish few main research directions related to territorial issues. The first one focuses on regional competitiveness and indicators of economic wealth to describe the economic productivity processes in both rural and urban territories. The second direction examines territorial differentiation of the demographic processes. The third direction related to the conception of spatial justice is limited to studies on the transformations of urban space, urban discourses, and empirically based evaluation of socio-spatial segregation in different size territories and localities. Although territorial development policy and spatial justice is premised on the idea of merging economic productivity and local welfare, there is a need to apply a complex framework for analyzing the phenomenon. On the one hand, the previous studies cover the level of urban and rural disparities focusing exclusively on economic parameters (economic productivity and economic performance indicators), socio-demographic changes (natural population change, ageing and migration indicators) and urban socio-spatial segregation and differentiation. On the other hand, national research lacks systemic territorial patterning which could define the dynamics of territorial inequality in terms of socio-demographic change, scope of urbanization, economic productivity, and social-economic outcomes for households (for example, household income, social exclusion, material deprivation, and availability to public services).

Summarizing existing patterns of territorial inequality in the Lithuanian case, we can define classical dual rural/urban differentiation. The variation between different social and economic indicators demonstrates that the capital area of Vilnius together with the second and third largest cities of Kaunas and Klaipėda, signify intensive multi-centered economic development compared with the rest of the rural regions. Three urban areas, including the Capital generate the largest proportion of economic effectiveness resulting in higher labor force productivity, growing power of household income, and a higher quality of educational and social services infrastructure. On the other hand, the imbalance of economic productivity growth in the more rural regions of Tauragė, Utena, Telšiai is linked to significant changes in demographic, social and economic indicators (for example, labor market fluctuations, growing social inequality, high disposable income dispersion, limited consumption of households and dependency on social welfare system). The trends in social and economic outcome indicators demonstrate that disparities in income inequality in urban and rural counties remain very high. The income distribution level is significantly lower in the sparsely populated counties of Telšiai, Tauragė, Utena compared to the capital area. The disparities in other indicators of human capital (education level and employment) are less significant in urban and rural territories. The analysis of territorial inequality trends in Lithuania suggests that the most significant spatial diversification is observed between the capital area as well as two other urban areas of Kaunas and Klaipėda, and the rest of the country. The recent trends in economic development from 2008 to 2020 indicate a still greater imbalanced concentration of economic growth in the capital area of Vilnius which also aggregates the highest levels of income, social welfare, and high-value workplaces.

Finally, the national academic advancement demonstrates the focus on territorial disparities in terms of migration, natural population changes and demographic ageing. Most previous studies are lacking the dimension of spatial justice and territorial patterning and only cover the issues of urban socio-spatial segregation and differentiation, social inequality, marginalization, and criminalization in both urban and rural areas. However, the concept of territorial cohesion and territorial development is rarely used to define inter-regional and intra-regional variations and their impact on welfare provisions and well-being of inhabitants from different socio-economic backgrounds. Some findings indicate the imperative to discuss the capacities of municipal authorities and institutions to provide public services. Nevertheless, the role of local communities in co-production and their relation to the territorially driven policy would be a good starting point. Further political and analytical efforts should concentrate on the inter- and intra-regional variations leading to new social investment policy instruments and tools.

References

Acus, A. (2011). Nusikalstamumo raida Klaipėdoje 1990–2000 metais: kultūros ir nusižengimų santykis. *Tiltai*, *57*(4), 13–28.

Aidukaitė, J. (2013). Būsto politika skirtinguose gerovės modeliuose. *Sociologija: mintis ir veiksmas*, *33*(2), 304–20.

Aidukaitė, J., Lipnevič, A., Nefas, S. Narkevičiūtė, A., & Anulytė, F. (2014). *Būsto politika ir visuomenės iniciatyvos mieste*. Vilnius, LSTC.

Baranauskienė, V. (2019). Kaimiškų teritorijų identifikavimo problema: Lietuvos seniūnijų atvejis. *Geografijos metraštis*, *52*, 55–72.

Baranauskienė, V. (2021). Socioteritorinė atskirtis Lietuvos retai apgyventose teritorijose. /Daktaro disertacija/. Vilnius: Lietuvos socialinių mokslų centras.

Bruneckienė, J. (2010). Šalies regionų konkurencingumo vertinimas įvairiais metodais: rezultatų analizė ir vertinimas. *Ekonomika ir vadyba – Economics & Management*, *15*, 25–31. Ryga: Riga Technical University.

Burneika, D. (2013). *Regioninė politika Europoje*. Vilnius: Vilniaus universitetas.

Burneika, D., Kriaučiūnas, E., & Ubarevičienė, R. (2010). The problem of research of actors of urban change in post-soviet cities – Vilnius case. *Annales Geographicae*, *43–44*, 42–53.

Burneika, D., Daugirdas, V., Kriaučiūnas, E., Ribokas, G., & Ubarevičienė, R. (2013). Socioeconomical aspects of depopulation in eastem EU border region – case of eastem Lithuania. *Region and regionalism*, *11*(2), 195–215.

Burneika, D., Ubarevičienė, R., & Valatka, V. (2015). Socio-economic segregation in growing urban regions of Lithuania. *Filosofija. Sociologija*, *26*(4), 277–292.

Burneika D., Daugirdas V., & Ubarevičienė R. (2014). Role of migrations in depopulation processes of rural areas in East EU – The case of Lithuania. EUROPA XXI, 27. Warszawa. ISSN 1429-7132.

Burneika, D., Ubarevičienė, R., Valatka, V., Baranauskaitė, A., Pociūtė-Sereikienė, G., Daugirdas, V., & Krupickaitė, D. (2017). Lietuvos metropoliniai regionai. Gyventojų erdvinė diferenciacija XXI a. pradžioje. Vilnius: Lietuvos Socialinių Tyrimų Centras.

Ceccato, V., & Lukyte, N. (2010). Safety and sustainability in a city in transition: The case of Vilnius, Lithuania. *Cities*, *28*, 83–94.

Česonis, G. (2012). *Lietuvos regioninės politikos tobulinimo kryptys*. PhD thesis. Vilnius: Mykolas Romeris University.

Daugirdas, V., Baranauskienė, V., Burneika, D., Kriaučiūnas, E., Mačiulytė, J., Pocius, A., Pociūtė-Sereikienė, G., & Ribokas, G. (2019). *Netolygaus regioninio vystymosi problema Lietuvoje: socio-ekonominiai gerovės aspektai*. Vilnius: LSTC.

Daugirdas, V., Burneika, D., Kriaučiūnas, E., Ribokas, G., Stanaitis, S., & Ubarevičienė, R. (2013). *Lietuvos retai apgyventos teritorijos*. /Monografija/. Vilnius: Lietuvos socialinių tyrimų centras.

Grigoriev, P., Jasilionis, D., Shkolnikov, V. M., Meslé, F., & Vallin, J. (2015). Spatial variation of male alcohol-related mortality in Belarus and Lithuania. *The European Journal of Public Health*, *26*(1), 95–101.

Grigoriev, P., Jasilionis, D., Stumbrys, D., Stankūnienė, V., & Shkolnikov, V. M. (2017). Individual-and area-level characteristics associated with alcohol-related mortality among adult Lithuanian males: A multilevel analysis based on census-linked data. *PloS One*, *12*(7), e0181622. https://doi.org/10.1371/journal.pone.0181622

Jasilionienė, A., Stankūnienė, V., & Jasilionis, D. (2014). Census-linked study on ethnic fertility differentials in Lithuania. *Studies of Transition States and Societies*, *6*(2), 57–67.

Jasilionis, D., Meslé, F., Shkolnikov, V. M., & Vallin, J. (2011). Recent life expectancy divergence in Baltic countries. *European Journal of Population/Revue européenne de Démographie*, *27*(4), 403–431.

Jasilionis, D., Shkolnikov, V. M., Andreev, E. M., Jdanov, D. A., Vågerö, D., Meslé, F., & Vallin, J. (2014). Do vanguard populations pave the way towards higher life expectancy for other population groups?. *Population*, *69*(4), 531–556.

Jasilionis, D., Stankuniene, V., Ambrozaitiene, D., Jdanov, D. A., & Shkolnikov, V. M. (2012). Ethnic mortality differentials in Lithuania: Contradictory evidence from census-linked and unlinked mortality estimates. *Journal of Epidemiology and Community Health*, *66*(6), e7.

Jasilionis, D., Stankūnienė, V., Maslauskaitė, A., & Stumbrys, D. (2015). *Lietuvos demografinių procesų diferenciacija*. Vilnius: LSTC.

Juška, A., Johnstone, P., & Pozzuto, R. (2004). The changing character of criminality and policing in post-socialist Lithuania: From fighting organized crime to policing marginal populations? *Crime, Law & Social Change, 41*, 161–177.

Klüsener, S., Stankūnienė, V., Grigoriev, P., & Jasilionis, D. (2015). The mass emigration context of Lithuania: Patterns and policy options. *International Migration, 53*(5), 179–193.

Kraniauskas, L. (2012a). Miesto erdvė ir subkultūrų dinamika Klaipėdoje 1991–2010 m. (1). *Sociologija: Mintis ir veiksmas, 30*(1), 165–209.

Kraniauskas, L. (2012b). Miesto erdvė ir subkultūrų dinamika Klaipėdoje 1991–2010 m. (2). *Sociologija: Mintis ir veiksmas, 31*(2), 153–186.

Kriaučiūnas, E., Daugirdas, V. (2013). Rečiausiai apgyventų Lietuvos teritorijų gyvenviečių tinklo ypatumai. *Geografijos metraštis, 46*, 32–45.

Kuliešis G., Pareigienė L. (2011a). *Lietuvos kaimo raidos tendencija: mokslo studija*. Vilnius: Lietuvos agrarinės ekonomikos institutas.

Kuliešis G., Pareigienė L. (2011b). Lietuvos regionų depopuliacijos prielaidų tyrimas. *Management theory and studies for rural business and infrastructure development, 5*(29), 116–125.

Lavrinec, J. (2011). Revitalization of public space: From 'Non-places' to creative playgrounds. *Santalka, 19*(2), 70–75.

Lietuvos gyventojų politikos strategijos metmenys. (2004). Vilnius: Socialinių tyrimų institutas.

Lietuvos pažangos strategija "Lietuva 2030" (Lithuania Progress Strategy 2030) (2012). Parliament of Republic of Lithuania, approved 2012 May 15, No. XI-2015.

Lietuvos Respublikos valstybinio socialinio draudimo įstatymas. *Lietuvos Aidas*, 1991-05-31, Nr. 107-0.

Lietuvos Respublikos. *švietimo, mokslo ir sporto ministro 2018 m. kovo 29 d., įsakymo Nr. V-305 „Dėl valstybinių profesinio mokymo įstaigų, kuriose švietimo, mokslo ir sporto ministerija įgyvendina savininko (dalininko) teises ir pareigas, tinklo vystymo 2018–2020 metų bendrojo plano patvirtinimo" pakeitimo*. 2020 m. kovo 17 d. Nr. V-378.

Lietuvos Respublikos Vidaus reikalų ministerija. (2017). *Lietuvos regioninės politikos Baltoji knyga darniai ir tvariai plėtrai 2017–2030 (The White Paper on Lithuanian Regional Policy for Sustainable Development for the Period of 2017 to 2030)*. https://vrm.lrv.lt/uploads/vrm/documents/files/LT_versija/Naujienos/Regionines_politikos_baltoji_knyga_20171215.pdf.

Maksvytienė, I., & Polgrimaitė, S. (2015). Išsilavinimo nelygybės Lietuvoje vertinimas. *Taikomoji ekonomika: sisteminiai tyrimai, 9*(1), 143–156.

Maniukaitė, G., Matulionis, A. V., Kasparavičienė, V., Krukauskienė, E., Kublickienė, L., Sviklas, E. K., Trinkūnienė, I., & Žilinskaitė-Vytienė, V. (2014). Vilniečių kultūrinis tapatumas: 1993–2013 metai. Vilnius: LSTC.

Maslauskaitė, A. (2014). Nesantuokinis gimstamumas Lietuvoje: raida ir erdvinė diferenciacija. *Lietuvos socialinė raida*, *3*, 54–66.

Maslauskaitė, A., & Baublytė, M. (2012). *Skyrybų visuomenė. Ištuokų raida, veiksniai, pasekmės*. Vilnius: LSTC.

Maslauskaitė, A., & Jasilionis, D. (2015). Vyrų išsilavinimas ir pirmos santuokos kūrimas: ar universitetas suteikia pranašumų. *Kultūra ir visuomenė*, *6*(2), 11–26.

Maslauskaite, A., Jasilioniene, A., Jasilionis, D., Stankuniene, V., & Shkolnikov, V. M. (2015). Socio-economic determinants of divorce in Lithuania: Evidence from register-based census-linked data. *Demographic Research*, *33*, 871–908.

Pilipavičius, V. (2011). Bendruomeninio verslumo formavimas ir kaimo vietovių konkurencingumo stiprinimas. *Ekonomika ir vadyba: aktualijos ir perspektyvos*, *4*(24), 169–178.

Pociūtė, G. (2014). Trends of imbalances of demographic and socioeconomic development in the post-reform period in Lithuania. In P. Churski (Ed.), *The social and economic growth vs. the emergence of economic growth and stagnation areas* (pp. 129–150). Poznań: Bogucki Wydawnictwo Naukowe.

Pociūtė-Sereikienė, G., Baranauskienė, V., & Daugirdas, V. (2019a). Lietuvos savivaldybių teritorinės atskirties kompleksinis vertinimas. *Netolygaus regioninio vystymosi problema Lietuvoje: socio-ekonominiai gerovės aspektai* (red. V. Daugirdas ir D. Burneika) (pp. 53–76). Vilnius: LSTC.

Pociūtė-Sereikienė, G., Baranauskienė, V., Daugirdas, V. (2019b). Spatial exclusion in Lithuania: Peripheries as „losers“, metropolitan areas as „winners“. *Przegląd Geograficzny [Polish Geographical Review]*, *91*(2), 5–19.

Population and Population Change statistics (2017). Eurostat.

Samalavičius, A. (2005). Miestas: erdvė ir vieta. *Urbanistika ir architektūra*, *29*(1), 18–21.

Samalavičius, A. (2010). Vilnius city: Urbanism driven by consumption. *Lituanus*, *56*(2), 43–52.

Sawers, L. (2006). Inequality and the transition: Regional development in Lithuania. *Baltic Journal of Economics*, *6*(1), 37–51.

Šileikytė, D. (2020). Siūloma pertvarkyti profesinio mokymo įstaigų tinklą. *Švietimo naujienos*. http://www.svietimonaujienos.lt/siuloma-pertvarkyti-profesinio-mokymo-istaigu-tinkla/ (accessed 11 August 2021).

Sipavičienė, A. (2014). *Recent developments in international migration and migration policy in Lithuania*. Paris: OECD.

Sipavičienė, A., & Stankūnienė, V. (2013). The social and economic impact of emigration on Lithuania. *Coping with Emigration in Baltic and East European Countries*, OECD Publishing. http://dx.doi.org/10.1787/9789264204928-en.

Snieška, V., & Bruneckienė, J. (2009). Measurement of Lithuanian regions by regional competitiveness index. *Inzinerinė ekonomika – Engineering Economics*, *1*, 45–57.

Soja, E. W. (2010). *Seeking spatial justice*. Minneapolis: University of Minnesota Press.

Solow, R. M. (1956). A contribution to the theory of economic growth. *The Quarterly Journal of Economics*, *70*(1), 65–94.

Stankūnienė, V. (1997). Nauji Lietuvos šeimos bruožai: tradicinių ir modernių šeimos formavimo strategijų sandūra. In V. Stankūnienė & A. Mitrikas (Eds.), *Šeima ir gimstamumas Lietuvoje* (pp. 18–33). Vilnius: LFSI.

Stankūnienė, V., & Baublytė, M. (2016). Gyventojų struktūros senėjimo ilgalaikė trajektorija. In V. Stankūnienė, M. Baublytė, K. Žibas, & D. Stumbrys (Eds.), *Lietuvos demografinė kaita. Ką atskleidžia gyventojų surašymai* (pp. 15–48). Kaunas: VDU.

Stankūnienė, V., Baublytė, M., Žibas, K., & Stumbrys, D. (2016). *Lietuvos demografinė kaita. Ką atskleidžia gyventojų surašymai*. Kaunas: VDU.

Stankūnienė, V. & Jasilionienė, A. (2008). Lithuania: Fertility decline and its determinants. *Demographic Research*, *19*, 705–718.

Stankūnienė, V. & Jasilionienė, A. (2008). Family transformations in the post-communist countries: Attitudes toward changes. In C. H. Hoen, D. Avramova, & I. Kotowska (Eds.), *People, population change and policies* (pp. 113–138). Berlin: Springer.

Statistic Lithuania. (2021). *Database of indicators*. https://osp.stat.gov.lt/statistiniu-rodikliu-analize#/ (accessed 28 July 2021).

Stumbrys, D. (2016). *Lietuvos vyrų mirtingumo diferenciacijos sociologiniai demografiniai veiksniai*. PhD Thesis Manuscript. Vilnius: LSTC.

Swan, T. W. (1956). Economic growth and capital accumulation. *Economic Record*, *32*(2), 334–361.

Tereškinas, A., & Žilys, A. (2013). Emocijos ir socioerdvinė segregacija Lietuvos didmiesčiuose: ar aš galiu ką nors pakeisti? *Kultūra ir visuomenė: socialinių tyrimų žurnalas*, *4*(2), 11–35.

Ubarevičienė R. (2017). *Socio-spatial change in Lithuania – Depopuliation and increasing spatial inequalities*. Delft: Delft University of Technology.

Ubarevičienė, R. (2018a). *Baltijos šalių gyvenviečių sistemų teritorinės organizacijos kaitos sociodemografinė analizė.* Daktaro disertacija. Vilnius: Lietuvos socialinių tyrimų centras.

Ubarevičienė, R. (2018b). City systems in the Baltic states: The Soviet legacy and current paths of change. *Europa Regional*, *25*(2), 15–29.

Ubarevičienė, R., & van Ham, M. (2017). Population decline in Lithuania: Who lives in declining regions and who leaves?. *Regional Studies, Regional Science*, *4*(1), 57–79.

Ubarevičienė, R., van Ham, M., & Burneika, D. (2016). Shrinking regions in a shrinking country: The geography of population decline in Lithuania 2001–2011. *Urban Studies Research*, http://dx.doi.org/10.1155/2016/5395379.

Užimtumo Tarnyba. (2010). *2009 m. veiklos ataskaita.* https://uzt.lt/wp-content/uploads/2019/03/2009-m.-veiklos-ataskaita.pdf (accessed 10 August 2021).

Žilys, A. (2013). Rezidencinė diferenciacija ir skirtumai Lietuvos moderniajame mieste: (po)sovietinis ar Vakarų miestas? *Kultūra ir visuomenė*, *4*(2), 67–102.

Aušra Maslauskaitė

Chapter 4 Promoting social investment policy through the development of early childhood education and care policy. The Lithuanian case[1]

Abstract: Since the 1990s, the development of the early childcare and education (ECEC) system in Lithuania has undergone dynamic shifts. Supply and demand for these services which decreased at the beginning of the 1990s, was followed by recovery, but also by significant urban-rural differentiation of the trend. The childcare provision is acknowledged as the goal of both national and local level policy, but the institutional system in Lithuania is very decentralized which exacerbates territorial diversity. Currently, the ECEC system is expanding in urban areas and the role of private actors is growing. This results in contradictory social investment outcomes: growing participation yet unequal educational opportunities.

Keywords: early childhood education and care, territorial diversity, local policies on early childhood education and care, social investment

Introduction

Formal childcare provision is at the center of the social investment policies and a central part of any policy for social inclusion (Esping-Andersen, 2002). The high quality of the childcare signals the investment of the welfare state in the children as future human capital, a labor force, and a source of productivity. In addition, the ready accessibility and typical high standards of early education and care provision should mitigate the effect of social background on the child's development, uplift children from disadvantaged families and work as the equalizer of educational opportunities. ECEC services also stimulate the return and participation of mothers in the labor market assisting them to balance work and family duties, and thus contribute to productivity and gender equality. Thus, ECEC as a social investment strategy is aimed at current and future human capital, social inclusion and equal opportunities, reduction of poverty and gender equality.

1 During the various stages of the research, the help in collecting the material was provided by Jurga Bučaitė-Vilkė, Ieva Dryžaitė, Viktorija Baranauskienė. The author acknowledges their input and assistance.

This chapter is dedicated to the analysis of the ECEC policies, and their implementation mechanisms among different governmental tiers. It focuses on responsibility at central administrative and municipal levels, policy goals, planning, beneficiaries, expenditures, and the role of community and private actors. It aims to reveal the institutional context of the ECEC, to discuss the various level actors and policy discourses, uncover the shifts in the ECEC policies as well as the territorial variations in the development and implementation of the ECEC policies. The chapter provides an in-depth analysis of three localities: urban (Kaunas city), suburban (Kaunas district), and rural municipality (Pakruojis district) and demonstrates the territorial diversity of ECEC policies.

Like all policies, the ECEC policies are path-dependent and shaped within the broader framework of historical legacies. The system of institutionalized childcare in Lithuania began developing between the 1920s and 1930s. However, although there was a growing demand, the coverage was marginal. The system predominantly targeted the poor working mothers employed in the industry, which represented only a very small part of this period's economy. The services were primarily delivered by charitable or religious bodies and the role of the state was very limited. Only in the second half of the 1930s did the state take a more active role in delineating the legal norms and regulations for childcare (Bukelevičiūtė, 2016). Overall, in the political discourse, the care of both young and old was allocated to the family which impacted the development of the welfare policies (Aidukaite, Bogdanova, & Guogis, 2012). The Soviet period brought an expansion of childcare services; the crèche and kindergarten system were established in rural and urban areas along with the implementation of full-employment policies for men and women. However, despite the official ideology which now removed the onus of early childcare from the family, the demand for formal childcare was never met (Leinarte, 2021). In 1980, 40 % of children under 3 years and 53 % of children 3–6 years of age attended the nurseries and kindergartens (Stankūnienė, Maslauskaitė, & Baublytė, 2013). The services provided were of poor quality and many families relied on the care provided by grandparents. Following the regaining of independence in the early 1990s, many formal childcare institutions, particularly in the rural areas, were closed.

Research on the ECEC in Lithuania is prolific but primarily focuses on the quality of the services (Liukinevičienė & Paulauskienė, 2019), the qualifications of the pedagogical personnel or the issues related to the management of the childcare institutions (Martišauskienė, 2010, 2011). The ECEC policies and services were previously analyzed within the broader framework of the family-work balance and family policies (Purvaneckienė, 2005; Stankūnienė, Jasilionienė,

& Jančaitytė, 2005; Bučaitė-Vilkė et al., 2012; Stankūnienė, Maslauskaitė, & Baublytė, 2013). Čižauskaitė and Gruževskis (2018) based on the EU-SILC data, suggest that the low attendance of children in the ECEC system accounts for the low participation of mothers in the labor market. The territorial aspect of the ECEC system did not attract much scholarly interest. Baranauskienė (2021) revealed the territorial disparities in the development of the ECEC system based on the socio-spatial analysis of the statistical data for the period 2001–2018. However, research on the implementation of the national ECEC policy on the municipal level remains insubstantial.

In this chapter, we discuss the national institutional context of the ECEC policies and thereafter present the changes in the policy from 2010 to 2020. In the next step, an overview of the participation trends in the ECEC in Lithuania is presented and the supply of services by public and private actors is discussed. In the following, we analyze the local governance systems and subsequently present the results of three case analyses from different municipalities. The chapter closes with a summary of results and policy recommendations.

National institutional context: Between centralization and municipal autonomy

Lithuania is a country in which the ECEC provision is split between national and local policy actors. The general legal framework is defined by the Law on Education (Lietuvos Respublikos švietimo įstatymas, 2011), which states the general aims, mechanisms, and policy actors responsible for the ECEC. Strategic goals of Education are defined in the National Strategy of Education, which is prepared by the Government for a ten-year period and approved by the Parliament (Nacionalinė švietimo strategija 2013–2020, 2013). At national level, the Ministry of Education, Science and Sport is responsible for the policy formation, quality, and coordination of educational policies. Along with the national level actors, municipalities are independently responsible for the network of ECEC institutions and quality of the services. Municipalities are also responsible for the procedures of enrollment, discounts, and fee policies. Municipalities might partially reimburse the costs of the private child-care services to the families. Thus, in Lithuania, the responsibilities for ECEC are decentralized.

General goals defined in the policy documents of the ECEC are: the provision of high-quality services, accessibility of the services, high-quality personnel, efficient systems for monitoring and evaluation of the ECEC services, sufficient financing, and effective governance (Nacionalinė švietimo strategija 2013–2020, 2013). Currently, there are several policy goals set up as the priority in the development of the ECEC. Firstly, the expansion of participation in childcare and educational institutions in the rural areas, which is expected to continue to evolve. Expansion in urban areas is expected to be implemented by creating "sustainable and equitable funding models" (OECD, 2017; Švietimas Lietuvoje, 2019). Secondly, the development of a comprehensive quality control system at two levels – internal, executed by the municipalities, and external implemented by the National Agency for School Evaluation. Thirdly, the standardization of the services for children with special needs is set as a further policy goal in Lithuania. Fourthly, the goals linked with uplifting professional competency levels of the ECEC personnel are also prioritized.

Lithuania spends 0,7 % of the GDP on the ECEC, which is close to the OECD average (OECD, 2017) and this amount has not increased. Public institutions of the ECEC are free of charge, however, parents pay for the meals. Private expenditures comprise 15 % of the total expenditures on ECEC. EU funds are allocated for the development of early childhood education programs, training of the personnel, inter-sectoral cooperation, creating the multifunctional centers, modernization of the infrastructure, availability of the educational tools aimed at the development of child creativity, and self-regulation. The "Yellow bus" program is also partially financed from EU funds and is aimed at increasing the accessibility of services for children from remote areas, for example, the EU funding of €6 mln was allocated for a centralized purchase of 140 school buses for the period of 2014–2020 (Dėl mokyklų aprūpinimo geltonaisiais autobusais, 2017).

The standardization and equalization of the ECEC policies in the territories are established through national-level financing mechanisms. The ECEC is funded jointly by governmental funds and municipalities. The government provides basic funds for the 20 hours per week for each child and municipalities might supplement the funding. There are no additional special policies for the standardization and equalization of ECEC.

In 2011, the financing model for a "student basket" was introduced, meaning that each child is entitled to the "student basket" which is 100 % funded by the state subsidies regardless of the type of ECEC institution they attend (public or private). Children with special needs are offered a more substantial "student basket" to promote inclusion. Yet, the level of the centralized funding is too low to secure high-quality services in all territorial units, thus, the responsibility for the supply and the quality of the ECEC is transferred to the municipalities. This results in great spatial variation in the securing of ECEC services. Some municipalities subsidize family expenses in the private ECEC institutions, but the size of the subsidy and proportion of families receiving it differ. Only some municipalities provide free transportation services.

The role of the private sector in the ECEC has escalated in recent years as the result of the reforms related to the liberalization of the hygiene norms and the introduction of the "student basket" financing mechanism. The liberalization of the hygiene norms allowed for the provision of ECEC services in various establishments and thus positively affected the supply of services. Since 2011, the number of private institutions particularly in urban areas has grown (OECD, 2017). However, the private sector comprises only a very small part of the ECEC system. In 2017, only 6 % of children were enrolled in private institutions, a similar proportion to other Eastern European countries (OECD, 2019). The private actors are also eligible for the "student basket", however, parents have to cover additional expenses related to the service provider and the overall price for childcare in private institutions is high.

The responsibility for the curricula of the ECEC and the quality of the services is decentralized and thus there is no comprehensive system of quality control. The internal and external evaluations are conducted by the institution and the municipality respectively, however, municipalities lack clear guidelines and instruments for quality control and in many cases also lack the competence for the assessment (an exception could be the large urban municipalities). Thus, the level of quality of the services might vary between the municipalities. As was previously mentioned, recent policy developments additionally stress the role of external control. It is expected that external quality assurance could be implemented by the National Agency for School Evaluation (OECD, 2019). This legal entity is responsible for quality control at the primary and secondary school levels. It is also expected that the implementation of this measure will ensure "that municipalities do not experience conflicting interests that arise from being founder, funder and quality monitor" (OECD, 2019).

Currently, the parents as the stakeholders are involved to a very limited extent in the governance and supervision of the service quality of the ECEC. Although this is a common problem, in urban areas, where the parental formal and informal associations have overall higher capacities, the involvement is stronger. We will discuss this in more detail later.

Shifts in the ECEC national policies

The ECEC policy development in the past decade included several reforms. Overall, during the period, the field was dominated by policies targeting the expansion of access to the ECEC. Several factors contributed to this process.

The ECEC services are formally part of the educational policy, however, they are also central to family policy measures. Within family policy discourse, the ECEC services are positioned as the key element in the pursuit of the pro-natalist goals and very high on the political agenda of all political parties or ruling coalitions reflecting the political response to fertility decline and depopulation. As in many other post-communist countries, fertility in Lithuania began radically decreasing in the early 1990s, reaching the lowest low in 2002 when the total fertility rate was 1.23 (Demographic Yearbook, 2017). Recovery began in the middle of the 2000s and from 2012 until 2019 fluctuated at around 1,6 (Statistics Lithuania, 2021a). Together with negative trends in other demographic processes – migration and mortality – fertility decline resulted in the substantial shrinkage of population size, unfavorable trends in population structure, and rapid demographic aging. As a reaction, all strategic population and/or family policy documents emphasized the need to boost investment in the ECEC. Moreover, by the 2000s, the negative consequences of the closures of the kindergartens, which took place in the 1990s, became evident and was recognized as problematic.

A significant policy shift related to the expansion of the ECEC system was implemented in 2011. The policy reform eased the hygiene norms for the premises that provide childcare services and education. Subsequently, childcare institutions could be established in private homes, multi-functional centers, and other multipurpose housings (Aidukienė, 2014). The new legislation changed the norms which had existed since the Soviet period. The lifting of the hygiene restrictions created the pre-conditions for the establishment of childcare institutions by the private sector but also created more favorable conditions for the municipalities to adapt the existing infrastructure to childcare.

In the same year, the new model for financing the ECEC was introduced, the so-called "student basket" model. Accordingly, each child is entitled to an amount of money for care and education and the principle of "money follows the child" was introduced and implemented. As previously mentioned, state subsidy follows the child regardless of the type of ECEC institution attended, i.e. public or private. Children with special needs are offered a more substantial "student basket" in order to increase the inclusion of this group. The methodology for setting the amount of the student basket is updated from time to time.

The policies aimed at the expansion of the ECEC education also include obligatory pre-school education which previously was optional. In 2012, several financial incentives were introduced to the families to promote this type of early education. The measures targeted disadvantaged families and offered discounts for pre-school education for children from single parent families, children from families with three and more children, and families receiving social benefits (Aidukienė, 2014). The next step in the expansion of pre-school education was taken in 2015 when amendments were made to the Law on Education. The changes introduced an obligatory one-year pre-school education for all children from the age of 6 years. One of the implicit goals of the amendment was to increase participation in the formal pre-school education of children from rural areas and to improve the educational chances of more deprived children from rural areas. The most recent amendment to the Law on Education passed in 2020 anticipates that children will begin mandatory early education earlier than 6 years, and children from socially disadvantaged families even earlier.

Accessibility of the ECEC was also increased by the introduction of smaller scale policy initiatives. For example, in rural areas, the existing infrastructure was adapted to the changing needs of the population by constructing/renovating the multi-functional centers, and co-funding these activities from municipal and EU Structural funds. In addition, municipalities introduced the "yellow bus" services and preschoolers from remote areas are now able to reach the ECEC institutions or schools. To increase accessibility, many municipalities also introduced the e-queuing system, in which enrollment in the public institutions is possible only through the e-system and the progression of enrollment is monitored by the municipality. This measure served to make access to the ECEC services more transparent and to limit the cases of misuse in securing a place at the institution. The accessibility of ECEC is additionally promoted by partial coverage of the childcare services fee for the families if the municipalities do not have the capacity to provide the publicly funded facility placement. It means that the municipality decides to cover a part of ECEC fees for the private service providers if the supply is not covered by the municipal services infrastructure. The level of municipal subsidies for the families varies in different municipalities.

With regard to quality control of the ECEC services, Lithuania introduced legislation which decentralized the quality control of childcare and pre-school education services in 2007 (OECD, 2017). Both the child education curricula and quality control responsibilities were assigned to the institutions. The Ministry of Education, Science and Sport assumed a non-directive role and provided only guidance and methodological advice. Revision of the curricula also became part of the municipal responsibilities. Thus, municipalities became the founder, partial funder and the provider of the services and this condition in some cases mitigated the quality standards. After a decade in 2016 the Ministry of Education, Science and Sport initiated discussions around quality control in the ECEC services. The process was also backed by external experts and international organizations (for example OECD). There has been discussion around quality control being implemented by activating the role of the Ministry of Education,

Science, and Sport and also by delegating part of the quality assurance functions to national level institutions. The Ministry could prepare the guiding templates, which could be used by the municipality officials in the quality evaluation process. The National Agency of School Evaluation could be also included in the process and become the external evaluator. The policy discussions also stress that parents are not included in the quality assurance, and this also calls for action.

The inclusion of children with special needs into the ECEC system also becomes a policy issue. It has been recognized that there are problems related not only to the use of facilities and infrastructure, but also to the shortages of specially trained personnel (OECD, 2016). The problems are particularly relevant in the rural areas, where there is a shortage of specialists but on the other hand, more children are exposed to disadvantageous conditions. The discussions are ongoing about the creation of a more intense collaboration between the health specialists and the ECEC.

Active policy discussions about the workforce in the educational system in Lithuania, including the ECEC subsector are ongoing. The aging of the ECEC teachers is seen as one of the critical problems. Due to the low salaries offered teachers in the subsector, the profession is not attractive and young people do not enroll in the studies related to the ECEC. In addition, growing demand for the ECEC services also increases the demand for teaching staff, however, young, qualified personnel do not enter the subsector. Although the shortage of personnel is especially high in rural areas, this scarcity is experienced even by the large urban centers (Siarova & Buinauskas, 2017). Although the high-quality ECEC services are set as a priority, the system of competence development of the ECEC teachers still has room for improvement. According to the legislation, the ECEC teachers are "entitled to five days per year for their professional development, but they are not obliged to make use of this opportunity" (Siarova & Buinauskas, 2017).

Participation and supply of ECEC services: Spatial dispersion

Participation in early childhood education and care for children from 3 to 6 years of age, 6 being the start of compulsory schooling in Lithuania, is close to the EU average and in 2020 was 90.3 % (EU target – 95 %) (Education and Training Monitor, 2017). However, the attendance of children from 1 to 2 years of age is 44.2 % (Figure 4.1). Figure 4.1 portrays the long-term trend in the ECEC participation and places the current trend in a broader perspective. The shift away from family responsibility for childcare began during the Soviet period, yet, in 1960 the proportion of children in the crèches and kindergartens was minor and comprised less than 10 %. In 1987, more than two and a half-decades later, about half of the children aged 1–2 and around 70 % aged 3–6 attended formal childcare institutions.

Significant changes occurred after the 1990s with the economic downturn which resulted in massive job losses for men and women, ideological retraditionalization of the gender roles, and massive deterioration of the formal childcare system especially in the rural areas. In the early 1990s, participation more than halved and the proportion of children aged 3–6 attending the kindergartens was 30 %. For children aged 1–2 years, the decline was even more dramatic and fell from 50 % to 10 %. However, since the middle of the 1990s, the participation rates have increased again. In 2012 the proportion of children aged 3–6 attending kindergarten even exceeded the highest level of the Soviet period and since then has been continuously on the increase. A similar trend of rising participation is also observed in the age group 1–2 years; however, the level is substantially lower. The much lower participation rate of this group is related to parental leave policies, which encourage parents to take care of the child in the family.

Long and generous parental leave policies entitle parents to up to three years of leave with the choice of selecting one or two years of paid leave. One-year paid leave is compensated by a benefit equal to approximately 77 % of the previous wage, two years leave – with 54 % the first year and 31 % the second year with working also a possibility (Norgėlaitė, 2020). Parental leave of three years was introduced in 1989, but until 2008 only one year was remunerated although the share of the benefit varied from 60 to 100 % of previous wages (Stankūnienė, Maslauskaitė, & Baublytė, 2013). The two-year paid leave was introduced in 2008 with a record high level of benefits: 100 % the first year, 85 % in the second. Later, the size of the benefits was reduced and the option of employment during the second year was introduced. Thus, the parental leave policies overall support a family orientation towards early child care and contribute to the long periods of withdrawal of parents – usually mothers – from the labor market.

Although the participation rates are increasing, there is a significant urban-rural difference, which reflects the main territorial policy challenge (see Figure 4.2). The participation rate for children 1–2 years of age is 20 % in rural areas and 53 % in urban areas, while for 3–6 years of age 49 % and 107 % respectively (Statistics Lithuania, 2021b). Figure 4.2 also demonstrates that the urban-rural gap is consistent and there are no indications of convergence.

There are spatial disparities in the dispersion of children's participation in ECEC in rural and urban municipalities. In some rural municipalities (Pagėgiai, Kalvarija) the proportion of children aged 5 years and under attending childcare

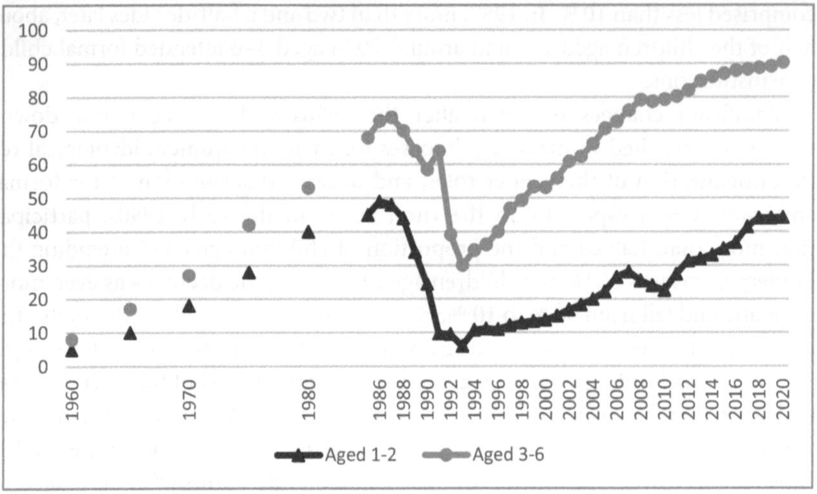

Figure 4.1. Participation in ECEC by child's age, 1960—2020. Source: For years 2000–2020 data provided by the Statistics Lithuania (2021), https://osp.stat.gov.lt/statistiniu-rodikliu-analize?hash=d909e7c3-6c3c-40ea-8739-9af95163d203#/; for the earlier years Stankūnienė, Jasilionienė 2008.

institutions is approximately 30 %, while in the large urban areas the participation rate iš approximately 75–80 % (Švietimo būklės apžvalga, 2019). The mean rate of attendance in large urban municipalities for the age group 5 years and under is 67 %, in so-called "ring" municipalities (those bordering the large cities) 58 %, in large rural municipalities – 59 % and 55 % in small municipalities (Švietimo problemų analizė, 2020).

According to some estimations, the gap in enrollment of children from socially and economically vulnerable families and children from a more advantaged background is 15.7 % (Education and Training Monitor, 2019). However, the educational statistics in Lithuania do not record whether the child is from a socially vulnerable family (Švietimo problemų analizė, 2020). Yet, based on survey results from the municipality representatives, parents from such families do not enroll children in the ECEC institutions for the following reasons: because they face transportation problems, municipalities could not provide services for children with special needs, parents have economic motives to organize childcare at home if there are younger children, parents do not want to enroll children

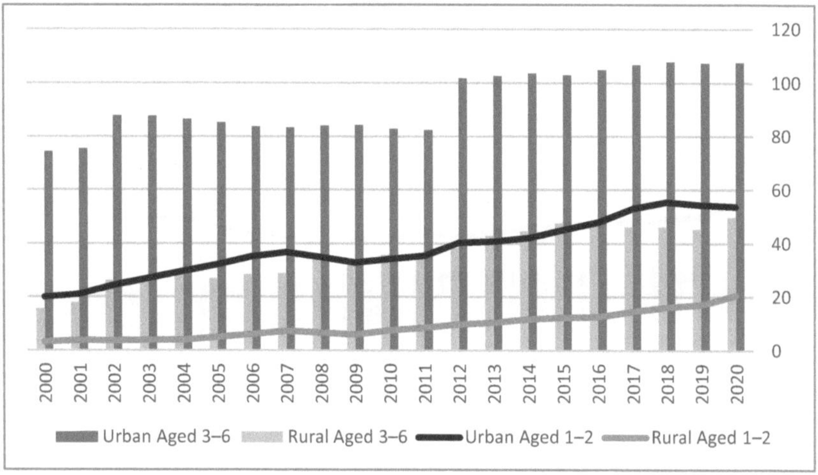

Figure 4.2. Participation in ECEC of children aged 1–2 and 3–6 years, 2000–2020. Source: Statistics Lithuania (2021), https://osp.stat.gov.lt/statistiniu-rodikliu-analize?hash=d909e7c3-6c3c-40ea-8739-9af95163d203#/.

in ECEC if the service is provided only for 4 hours per day (Švietimo problemų analizė, 2020).

From the perspective of supply, the total number of ECEC institutions dramatically decreased in the early 1990s falling from 1422 in 1991 to 748 in 1994 (Figure 4.3). Thus, the reduction over three years was 50 %. In the later years, the number of institutions slightly decreased further reaching its lowermost point in 2010 (626), but subsequently a very moderate upward trend with 716 institutions in 2020 could be observed. However, the trends are different in urban and rural areas. In urban areas, the number of ECEC institutions is growing, while in rural areas they are declining. Since 2010, when there were 499 institutions in urban areas, the number increased and in the current year there are 635 (Figure 4.3). The contrary trend is characteristic for the rural areas, where in the same period the number declined from 127 to 81.

An increase in the proportion of children attending the ECEC and a decrease in the number of institutions leads to an unmet demand. Overall, there are on average approximately 106 places for 100 children in the ECEC establishments (Švietimo problemų analizė, 2020), but a shortage of places in urban areas. Most urbanized municipalities and the surrounding large urban

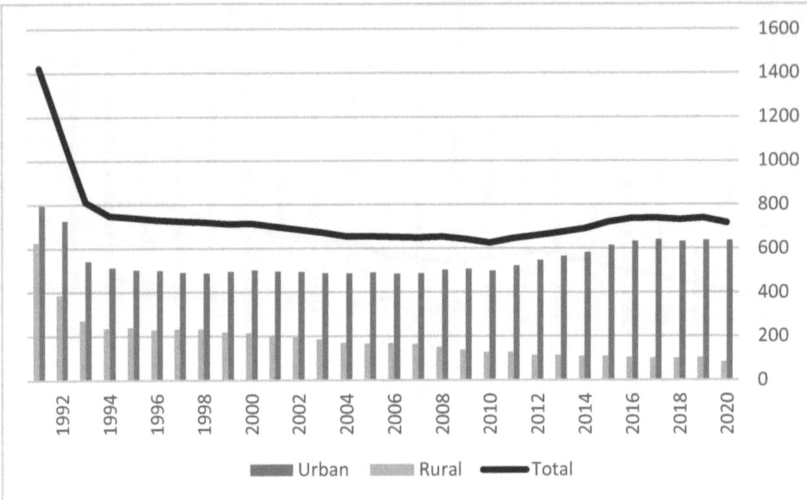

Figure 4.3. The number of the ECEC institutions in urban and rural areas, 1991–2020. Source: https://osp.stat.gov.lt/statistiniu-rodikliu-analize?indicator=S3R195#/.

center municipalities are faced with an insufficiency of places. In most rural demographically aged regions, availability of the places at ECEC institutions is the highest.

The number of private institutions is rising, but this is the trend in the largest urban cities (Vilnius, Kaunas, Klaipėda) (Figure 4.3). For example, in 2011 there were only 25 private ECEC institutions, in 2015, 115, and in 2018, 138 (Lithuania. Organization of Private Education, 2018). The private institutions offer more diverse educational programs, might have better-equipped premises, and enroll smaller groups. Admission to the private institution is managed by the service provider. Even though the private institutions receive a "class basket" for education from the state budget, they also charge fees for covering other education-related costs. The amount for this additional contribution is determined by the private ECEC institution founder and paid on a contractual basis by parents. The tuition fees range from 120 to 500 euros, while in the public establishment approximately 50–60 euros (Ikimokyklinis ugdymas, 2021). Thus, the private ECEC institutions are accessible only to the more affluent parents. In some municipalities, the costs of a privately provided ECEC might be reimbursed through public subsidies, but the size of the subsidy the family receives varies by municipality.

Local governance system: Different cases, different solutions

This chapter analyzes the local governance system including assignment of responsibilities and bodies within the ECEC policy area, the question of local autonomy, funding mechanisms, the role of private actors, and forms of public/ private partnership. The main territorial policy goals for the ECEC system are related to accessibility in urban and rural areas, educational quality and greater inclusion of children from families at risk of economic hardship and poverty. The diversity at the level of the localities will be discussed by presenting a case study of each.

As was noted previously, the central authorities provide partial funding for the ECEC system and regulate the teaching provisions and the qualifications of the ECEC teachers. The municipalities can regulate the institutional network of ECEC institutions, are responsible for the network of pre-school child-care institutions, the quality of the childcare services, and for the procedures of enrollment, discounts, and fee policies. The municipalities are also the founders of all public ECEC institutions which operate at municipal level. The private child-care providers within the administrative borders of the municipality operate in accordance with the order established by the Minister for Education, Science and Sports. The municipalities also decide the operational hours of preschool groups, and these may vary a great deal. Some preschool institutions operate for from 3 to 12 hours on weekdays and others (weekly kindergartens) operate for 24 hours a day. Some ECEC institutions decide the operational hours in accordance with parental needs (earlier opening and later closing). In all groups where educational activities last for more than four hours per day, children are provided with facilities for hot meals and nap time (bedrooms). The responsibilities of the municipalities increased after pre-primary education became compulsory in 2016 and the municipalities were obligated to establish and maintain pre-primary classes.

The ECEC is funded jointly by governmental funds and municipalities. Standardization and equalization of the ECEC policies in the territories are established through the financing mechanism within the "pupil basket" principle. This is a purposive state subsidy – a basket (firstly introduced in 2008), part of which is directly allocated to the ECEC school, while municipalities receive a smaller amount for further reallocation. In 2018, a **mixed funding method** replaced the "student's basket" with the so-called "class basket". Most of the funds are calculated for the kindergarten group and some costs according to the number of children. The government provides basic funds for 20 hours per week for each child. Municipalities might also supplement the funding for the extra personnel, for example, the social care employees, speech specialists and psychologists. As municipal councils are the founders of public ECEC institutions, it is the municipal council that decides the fees for a childcare service. Parents must pay for the provision of meals for children. Municipalities might partially reimburse the costs of the private child-care services to families at risk.

Additionally, through different programs, the state can allocate investment funds for the development of education, for example, for the construction, renovation, or restructuring of facilities, or the development of human resources. EU funds are allocated for the development of early childhood education programs, training of the personnel, inter-sectoral cooperation, the creation of multifunctional centers, modernization of the infrastructure, availability of the educational tools aimed at the development of creativity and self-regulation. The "Yellow bus" program is also partially financed from EU funds and aims to increase the accessibility of services for children from remote areas.

Local cases

In the following, we will present the three municipalities and their territorial level policies related to the ECEC. The demographic and economic context of each municipality has been previously discussed in the introductory section of this book. In this section of the chapter, we will analyze the local policy discourse and social investment strategies in developing the ECEC at the locality level.

Urban case: Kaunas city municipality

In the Kaunas city municipality, ECEC services are provided by both public and private institutions. There are institutions, which provide only pre-school childcare services and others that provide ECEC services together with primary education. In total, in the municipality, there are 97 public early childcare and pre-school institutions (kindergartens or crèches-kindergartens), and 19 private ECEC institutions (which equates to around 16 %). Between 2014 and 2018 an additional 400 places were created in various ECEC institutions (see Table 4.1).

Issues related to the development of the ECEC receive considerable attention in the main policy documents of the municipality. They are discussed in the *Strategic Plan of the Kaunas municipality development* (2013–2022) (Kauno miesto savivaldybės strateginis plėtros planas, 2013) and *Kaunas city municipality Advancement of* Education Report (2017) (Kauno miesto savivaldybės švietimo pažangos ataskaita, 2017). The development of the ECEC as a social investment is recognized and broadly supported in the policy discourse.

Table 4.1. Kaunas city municipality ECEC institutions (only for the public).

Year	Enrolment of children to ECEC, thousands	Number of ECEC establishments
2018	14800	97
2017	14672	100
2016	14657	98
2015	14769	97
2014	14403	93

Source: Statistics Lithuania (2021b).

Several themes are emerging in this policy discourse: *accessibility, quality of the infrastructure, and capacity building of ECEC providers*. Each theme has an internal dynamic of representation. The themes appear in different periods and are developed to a varying extent. As defined in the Amendment of *Smart and Civic Society Development Program* within the *Strategic action plan of the Kaunas municipality* 2019–2021, one of the main goals is to develop an effective network of formal and informal (for extra-curriculum activities) educational institutions. The narrative of delivering ECEC services is defined using the keywords of public-private partnerships: "*to ensure access to pre-school education by smartly combining initiatives of municipal and private preschool initiatives*" (Kauno miesto savivaldybės strateginis 2019–2021 metų veiklos planas, 2019). The public-private partnerships are considered an important precondition to guarantee a higher level of services availability. The indicators of parental requests for entering ECEC institutions and number of children in pre-school classes are used as the main monitoring criteria of the municipal childcare policy achievements.

The theme of accessibility of the ECEC experienced the most obvious shift overtime. In policy documents from the earlier period, the issue of accessibility was more pressing, and expansion of the infrastructure was acknowledged as the strategic goal of the municipality. The Strategic Action Plan of 2013–2015 identifies some elderships (Šilainiai and Centras) with the highest shortage of places (Kauno miesto savivaldybės 2013–2015 metų strateginis veiklos planas, 2013). The later Plan for the period 2016–2018 aims to establish additional ECEC places in the kindergartens or multifunctional centers (Kauno miesto savivaldybės 2016–2018 metų strateginis veiklos planas, 2016). Along with the municipality's institutions, private ECEC institutions are recognized as relevant actors in the provision of the ECEC services. Moreover, the shift towards the re-distribution of the municipal responsibilities between public and private sectors is institutionalized through the introduction of the financial support mechanism (partial compensation of the private ECEC costs for the families).

The second theme – the quality of the ECEC infrastructure – emerges in the current local policy discourse. The Strategic Action Plan for the period 2019–2021 is directed towards the renovation of the buildings, heating, and drainage systems, as well as reconstruction and maintenance (Kauno miesto savivaldybės strateginis 2019–2021 metų veiklos planas, 2019). The financial mechanism also includes the use of EU Structural Funds.

The third theme – capacity building of ECEC personnel – is marginally developed in the policy documents, but is, however, more oriented towards the development of managerial capacities and skills. The activities are mostly linked to the projects implemented by the municipality. The adaptation of the local community participation approach and cooperation with the other social stakeholders, especially private kindergarten developers or parental councils is undetectable in the documents. In general, the idea of civic initiatives and local participation is marginal in strategic planning documents, allowing municipal administration and Council the leading role in project policy interventions.

With reference to the problem of availability and accessibility to ECEC institutions, Kaunas city municipality has developed an initiative to secure more transparent admission to the ECEC institutions. It was among the first to introduce the e-system, which enables parents to submit online applications. The personnel of the municipality administration are responsible for the ranking of the applications based on the submission time and place of residence, for evaluating whether families are socially vulnerable or poverty stricken as well as other ranking criteria. The e-system changed the existing admission rules applied at the institution, which were not previously transparent.

The ongoing conflict between Kaunas city and Kaunas district municipality around territorial amalgamation initiatives has triggered the changes in fees policy for ECEC institutions. Kaunas city municipality has decided to increase the fees for families not registered in Kaunas city territory. The recent changes triggered wide public discontent in terms of a child's right to attend public ECEC institutions, family status and other issues. With reference to national recommendations in *the Pre-School and Pre-Primary Education Development Programme for 2011–2013* (Dėl ikimokyklinio ir priešmokyklinio ugdymo plėtros programos, 2011), the municipality has also approved the guidelines of the content of education for the ECEC institutions. Guidelines also set the rules for the size of the groups, and number of hours dedicated to the educational content, etc.

As was previously mentioned, overall, at national level, the stakeholder's involvement in the ECEC is marginal. However, Kaunas city municipality represents to some extent the exception to the rule. The involvement of communities in the governance of ECEC services is more strongly voiced in the Kaunas city municipality, where various legal bodies, for example; Family Council, Educational Council, Teachers' Union, councils of the educational institutions, etc. take an active role in setting the agenda and making decisions. As was recognized by the local community leaders, the voluntary organizations bring additional perspective and assist all stakeholders in making the most suitable decision in multiple areas (a network of educational institutions or ECEC institutions, renovation, etc.). Parent groups (parental committees) are also recognized as important players in setting the municipal agenda, and advancing the implementation of ECEC policies (Local authority actors, Kaunas city municipality). The involvement of parental organizations and committees was very apparent in 2018 when the municipality planned to change the nutrition system and centralize it. The introduction of the system was fiercely criticized by the stakeholders because the implementation had not been discussed with the parents and ECEC institutions.

The role of private actors in providing ECEC expanded in Kaunas city municipality over time as an outcome of the unmet demand for public childcare provision and general national policy trends which fostered the involvement and encouragement of private actors in the provision of such education. As mentioned earlier, the private ECEC institutions are recognized as relevant actors in the provision of the ECEC services in the local policy discourse. Moreover, the shift towards the redistribution of the municipal responsibilities between public and private sectors is institutionalized through the introduction of the financial support mechanism (partial compensation of the private ECEC costs for the families). Thus, the strategy of social investment in the ECEC involves the private actors, and private initiatives are financially supported by the municipality. Though this social investment strategy solves the issues related to accessibility to the ECEC services, it does not contribute to the equalizing of the educational opportunities for children from different backgrounds. The childcare costs in the public institutions are high as already discussed, and even with the subsidy from the municipality is affordable only to affluent families. Private establishments provide a greater diversity of educational programs, offer additional educational approaches (for example outdoor kindergarten), have smaller groups of children, and better-equipped establishments. Consequently, the private institutions provide a more favorable environment for the cognitive, emotional, and social development of the children compared to the public institutions.

Suburban case: Kaunas district municipality

Kaunas district municipality provides childcare services in 26 public institutions (17 kindergartens and primary schools-kindergartens) and 9 private institutions (see Table 4.2). Thus, almost a quarter of the ECEC institutions are private. The ECEC system in Kaunas district municipality experienced an annual growth of almost 26 % in the period from 2013 to 2017 primarily due to the growing population (young families with small children) in suburban areas. The sustained increase in the child population challenges the local ECEC system in terms of availability and accessibility of vacancies. The number of children is also the highest compared to other "ring" municipalities of the two biggest cities – Klaipeda and Vilnius. Since 2014, the total number of children enrolled in the ECEC system has consistently increased. Compared to the other so-called "ring" municipalities, Kaunas district municipality has the highest record of enrollment rate of children in ECEC (Kauno rajono savivaldybės strateginis 2021–2027 metų plėtros planas, 2019). During the last 9 years, 75 new groups in municipal kindergartens have been established in Kaunas district municipality; about 1,500 children have been admitted to subsidized childcare. However, a significant number of early-age children are on the waiting list. For example, according to Kaunas district municipality data, in September 2019, 681 children of pre-school age (1.5–2.5 years) who did not attend an educational institution were on the waiting list for kindergartens, the longest waiting list in the urban elderships of the municipality (Kaunas district municipality information, 2020).

The territorial distribution is very important for the ECEC system in the suburban locality to secure access to childcare vacancies for all parents. The highest demand for ECEC places is apparent in the urban elderships, closer to Kaunas city municipality. Based on the needs of local communities and adapting the existing school buildings in more remote territories of the municipality, new types of institutions have been established – school-multifunctional centers.

The general guidelines for the ECEC policy are set out in the *Strategic Plan of the Kaunas district municipality from 2013 to 2020* (Kauno rajono savivaldybės strateginis 2013–2020 metų plėtros planas, 2013). These guidelines encompass two aims directly connected to the ECEC. One focuses on the infrastructure and is defined as "rationally planned development of the educational institutions and modernization of the existing educational infrastructure". The second, which specifies the need to improve the quality of the educational process in the institutions of the Kaunas district municipality, is a priority. This theme notes the quality of the childcare and pre-school education (Kauno rajono savivaldybės švietimo pažangos ataskaita, 2017) but is however, covered very sporadically, and

Table 4.2. Kaunas district municipality ECEC institutions (public and private).

Year	Enrolment of children to ECEC, thousands	Number of ECEC establishments
2018	3228	26
2017	3119	27
2016	2949	26
2015	2734	25
2014	2508	24

Source: Statistics Lithuania (2021b).

the document mainly discusses the quality of primary and secondary education. The report provides statistics on the various qualification courses for the teachers and numbers of participants, yet it is not explicit about the teachers from ECEC institutions. Overall, both above-mentioned documents which shape the local ECEC policy discourse, are more focused on the latter stages of formal education (primary, secondary) or opportunities for life-long learning.

The issue of accessibility was also voiced in the Report on the Advancement of Education (Kauno rajono savivaldybės švietimo pažangos ataskaita, 2017). The Reports are prepared based on the Strategic Plans of the municipalities however, they are not issued regularly and at the time of this research, the latest available was dated 2017. In the realm of the ECEC, the focus of the Report was the accessibility of childcare services. Uneven demographic development of the different localities in the municipality produced diverse demands related to access to the ECEC institutions. Consequently, in some areas, educational institutions are restructured and adapted to the wider educational and social needs of the population (multi-functional centers created in place of the former schools). In other areas, which are closer to Kaunas city municipality, demand for the ECEC places is greater than supply. Policy documents acknowledge the growing role of private enterprise in securing the accessibility of ECEC and generally, this development is evaluated positively. Kaunas district municipality was the first in Lithuania to implement partial coverage of the family expenses related to formal childcare for children not accepted by the public ECEC institutions and was among the first in the country, which introduced reimbursement of fees for families. The measure was later replicated in other municipalities, where the private providers are part of the local ECEC system.

The development of the infrastructure is restricted by the intensive marketing tendencies in private land and limited opportunities to build new public ECEC institutions. According to the Kaunas District mayor: "The territorial development is very intensive, we are trying to keep up with it, but we are facing a problem - there is no more vacant state land in suburban settlements, all land is private, and we cannot afford to build new kindergartens" (Interview with the mayor, 2020, the official website of the municipality). For this reason, the municipality had to accommodate kindergartens in other buildings, adapting them for childcare education, (for example, student dormitories, former police station), or expand the premises of the old kindergartens. The idea of increasing the number of places in existing kindergartens by building additional container modules nearby is currently being considered.

Municipal funds allocated to the ECEC are growing over time (Kaunas district municipality, 2018). The state subsidies are mostly used for the development and reconstruction of the infrastructure of educational institutions (reconstructing outdated buildings, establishing the modular building kindergarten groups). More than 4 million EUR was planned for investment in the overall development of pre-school infrastructure. "*Creating new places in kindergartens is one of our strategic goals. We are determined to create about 1000 new places in Kaunas district this year*", states the Mayor of Kaunas District (Kaunas district municipality information, 2020).

The recent innovation in ECEC services provision is "family kindergartens" that allow childcare services to be organized in private homes for small groups of children. Home-based early age (0–2 years old) childcare provision refers to a specific childcare regime that demonstrates the extent of government-subsidized service provisions and national preferences vis-à-vis maternity leave. This type of social innovation is new in countries in which the conservative family policy model that assigns the primary role of childcare to the mother is prevalent (Sekeráková Búriková, 2019). In general, only several European countries provide regulated home-based childcare for early-age children. Home-based regulated provision varies from country to country but in general, the early-age children from 2 to 5 years old are eligible for childcare services. The home-based model is based on the notion that small groups and a home environment is convenient for small infants. For example, in France, around 57 % of childcare services for children under 3 years old are provided by private providers at home (European Commission/EACEA/Eurydice, 2019). In Denmark, 33.8 % of 0–2-year-old children attending ECEC were in home-based kindergartens (*dagpleje*).

No regulated home-based childcare regime has previously been in place in Lithuania and therefore this is a countrywide innovation in the ECEC policy field. Kaunas District municipal council approved the decision to establish and promote a family-based childcare model in September 2019. The Council has also approved the detailing of the procedure (rules and quality standards) for establishing and subsidizing home-based childcare services in private homes or rented premises. The so-called "Family-based Kindergarten" model is designed for the urban elderships close to the metropolitan area of Kaunas city. By April 2020, 10 home-based establishments had begun their operations. The specificity of these elderships close to the Kaunas city is defined by increasing numbers of working-age middle-class families with small children within a suburban sprawl. The territories report the continuing problem of a shortage of early-age childcare provision services subsidized by the municipality.

According to the legal regulations, one person will be able to care for up to 5 children in their home or rented accommodation. Children will be able to stay in the family kindergarten as needed – up to 10 hours during the working day. The family kindergartens will become branches of the municipal kindergartens, the founders will officially be employees of pre-school institutions, the municipality will pay them a salary and provide all social guarantees. The service providers do not need any specified professional qualification other than enrollment in specialized pedagogy and psychology programs (180 hours) and compulsory first aid and hygiene skills training. The regulation also stipulates the eligibility criteria for the children accepted to this type of ECEC. Firstly, the child's place of residence must be officially registered in the Kaunas district territory. Secondly, the child is registered in the Municipal Centralized Child Admission Information system database and is not being admitted to the municipal financed ECEC educational institution. Thirdly, the child does not attend any other non-governmental ECEC educational institution providing pre-school education services and does not receive a refund of part of the fee.

In general, the Kaunas district childcare innovation signifies the enhancement and mobilization of territorial capital to enable private initiatives to solve the supply and demand problems in the territorial childcare system. The municipality carries out assessments of the demand and supply for ECEC services searching for new options. It is also an example of how municipal authorities seek to implement and experiment with an innovative approach to resolve the territorial issue of how to reconcile family-work needs. In terms of territorial capacity mobilization, the innovation of the "family-based kindergartens" fulfills several functions.

Firstly, it enables the mobilization of private (parental) efforts and knowledge in providing a "mixed" type of childcare. The socio-demographics of suburban Kaunas district municipality are characterized by a growing number of young families with under-aged children. Accordingly, the municipal solution for home-based childcare provision suggests mobilizing both interested parties: private households and municipal administration. The growth of the private sector in childcare is seen as a bid to meet growing parental needs. However, private childcare is a costly service not affordable for all families. Families are treated as informed consumers of childcare whose purchasing can regulate the costs of services and quality in the private market. "Family-based Kindergarten" is a hybrid option for early-age childcare services that combine both parental interest and a subsidized regulated childcare market. Secondly, the "family-based kindergartens" employ territorial assets such as young home-based mothers and their entrepreneurial and educational skills. These proposed home-based care solutions meet the care needs of the working day of parents. It also integrates the educative and social skills of young mothers who can apply to become service providers in their private homes. Thirdly, by introducing the innovation, the municipality overcomes the problems related to its limited infrastructural and financial resources to secure the availability of center-based ECEC places. For the majority of family households, childcare is a costly service in the private sector. However, the financial and infrastructural resources of Kaunas district municipality are limited to establishing a network of affordable center-based services for all families in need. The proposed "family-based kindergarten" model attempts to fill the gap between insufficient municipal administrative skills and financial resources by providing a diverse patchwork of childcare services provision. However, the innovation does not expand the involvement of the stakeholders. The model focuses on the involvement of parents and municipal administration as a "top-down" initiative. The involvement of other social stakeholders (local community or NGOs) is very limited and not represented. The municipal administration consolidated efforts to recognize local needs in available and affordable ECEC services and combined this with foreign experiences in the field.

In terms of territorial problems, the analyzed ECEC provision innovation seeks to address several territorial problems in relation to service provision infrastructure (introduction of new service provision models), supply and demand of services and social welfare for local families. As the family-based childcare model is a new trajectory in suburban localities introduced in 2020, it is too early to evaluate the effects and outcomes of the home-based model provisions for the local families. However, the introduction of this new model is innovative in the way it deals with the limited availability of formal ECEC places in the locality. The innovation covers only parental interest in affording formal childcare and more actively participating in the labor market. Municipal interests include political intervention to subsidize ECEC services and maintain the affordable infrastructure that is a state-delegated function. Because of the limited infrastructural resources for ECEC services (e.g., lack of affordable buildings), Kaunas district municipality is being reoriented towards new models of childcare provision for early-age children.

In conclusion, the municipality subsidized family-based childcare model is an example of top-down social innovation that responds to the shortage of places in the formal ECEC system for children 0–2 years old. The child-care model case is deeply embedded in the municipal ECEC system policy in terms of service accessibility, availability, infrastructural development in all rural and urban elderships. The suburban municipality benefits from the growing number of young middle-class families, however, it also challenges the supply and demand of the availability of the ECEC system. Our family-based childcare model is an example of an innovative process that develops novel solutions for childcare combining municipal administrative and organizational knowledge, financial resources and the entrepreneurial skills of mothers.

Rural case: Pakruojis district municipality

Pakruojis district municipality is one of the smallest municipalities in the country and additionally is peripheral to and remote from the largest cities. The municipality has experienced demographic decline, and population aging as a consequence of which access to the ECEC services in rural and urban elderships is not problematic. However, the total number of ECEC establishments consistently decreased in the period from 2014 to 2018 (see Table 4.3). The total number of children enrolled in the ECEC system increased by 9.8 % in the same period mostly because the pre-school year became compulsory in 2016. There are 62 % of children aged 0–5 years attending the ECEC institutions, and 84 % of children 3–5 years (Švietimo problem analizė, 2020).

In the rural municipalities the important issue is the territorial coverage of ECEC services for all beneficiaries, especially in remote elderships.

Local policy documents define the general goal of education policy and assert a commitment to "promote high-quality education and life- long learning" and to secure "provision of the education services, which are of high quality, accessible and oriented towards the needs of the population" (Pakruojo rajono savivaldybės 2014–2022 metų srateginis plėtros planas, 2013). For the period under study, no other available local policy documents articulated and set the agenda for the ECEC in the locality. Although the Strategic Plan sets high-quality education as the priority of the local policy, it focuses on primary and secondary education. The ECEC is discussed only implicitly and indicated marginally in relation to the restructuring of the network of educational institutions. There is a need to

Table 4.3. Pakruojis district municipality ECEC institutions (public and private).

Year	Enrolment of children to ECEC, thousands	Number of ECEC establishments
2018	610	7
2017	596	7
2016	610	8
2015	593	9
2014	553	9

Source: Statistics Lithuania (2020).

establish multifunctional centers in some localities of the municipality. In addition, the Plan notes the actions related to the reconstruction and renovation of the ECEC institutions. Very sporadic attention to the ECEC in the policy discourse could be a result of a sufficient supply of the ECEC places for the residents. On the other hand, as the field study revealed, many issues related to the ECEC are solved through informal networks and in a non-bureaucratic manner.

In 2017, the municipality initiated a service provision in rural multifunctional centers to provide formal childcare, including the safe transportation of children to childcare rooms, for up to 4 hours a day. In order to attract families to use the ECEC services, the municipality provides transport to the kindergarten for children aged 4–5 years and preschoolers (Local authority actors, Pakruojis district municipality). In addition, the obligatory pre-school education for 4 hours per day (number of hours subsidized by the state), was expanded to a full day service. This required parents to cover the expenses and they enrolled after recognizing the benefits of pre-school education. As one local public policy actor explained: "*We were not sure if parents will want the service. So, in the beginning, we started to provide service only for 4 hours and this was oriented only towards the educational activities, no care services. But later parents understood that these educational activities are good for children, thus, they started to ask to extend the childcare, to provide services for the whole day. We explained to them, that this implies additional expenses, which need to be covered by the parents and there were no objections*" (Local authority actor, Pakruojis district municipality). This measure secures within the ECEC system the inclusion of children from remote areas and sometimes from disadvantaged socio-economic backgrounds while at the same time, assists in sustaining the network of the ECEC institutions by securing a sufficient number of children in the kindergartens.

As accessibility to the ECEC is not an issue in the municipality, the quality of ECEC services becomes an issue. Only one kindergarten which has been in operation for more than 20 years, implements the innovative educational methodology (different educational rooms are created, and children might choose different places and activities) and is the only one in the country to do so. The other kindergarten bases its educational methodology on the health program; there is special equipment for children with special needs (disabled), and the kindergarten implements special healthy lifestyle programs for children and parents – "from birth to the age of three". With regard to the diversity of the services, ECEC institutions in rural areas organize summer camps, secure the uninterrupted provision of childcare services during the summer, and introduce late working hour days in order that parents could have time off after work.

Funding of the innovations in ECEC in some cases flows from the local business actors. The small scale of the municipality enables inter-relatedness based on inter-personal networks. As one local actor leading the kindergarten articulated: "*I know local people, business people. Their children attended our kindergarten, their grandchildren. All of them are local and if I ask for help, they always help*" (Local authority actor, Pakruojis district municipality). For example, finance from industries, business associations or individual local businesspeople supports kindergartens in acquiring educational means, covering the traveling expenses of teachers for the conferences, and project meetings.

One of the initiatives of the municipality was linked with improvement of the quality of nutrition in the public kindergartens that were implemented under the national level regulations in 2018 (Nutarimas dėl vaikų maitinimo organizavimo, 2018). The initiative is related to higher consumption of healthy products and vegetables in the children's diet. The kitchens of the ECEC institutions adopted a new menu for daily hot meals. On the one hand, the existing childcare service infrastructure has been renovated, but it should be also adapted to the changing needs of the community by establishing new facilities.

Social investment in the ECEC is predominantly the municipality's responsibility and is not shared with the private actors. The demand for innovative childcare solutions is relatively low, thus the role of private services providers is almost absent (there is one private kindergarten run by the Catholic Church).

Summary of the findings

All three local cases have similarities and differences in relation to the ECEC policy and system. Table 4.4 provides the summary of the three localities.

The growing numbers of children enrolling in ECEC institutions. The enrollment of children in the ECEC system is constantly increasing for all age groups. However, although the participation of children aged 1–2 has also improved, enrollment is still below the EU average. There is a significant gap in the participation in the ECEC between children aged 1–2 from households at risk of poverty and social exclusion and children from a more advantaged background. The municipalities are trying to solve the problem of supply and demand by renovating old facilities and establishing multi-functional centers in rural areas.

Regional dispersion and better accessibility. There are territorial disparities regarding the supply and demand for pre-school childcare in Lithuania. The demand for childcare services is substantially higher in urban than in rural areas, however, the supply is higher in rural areas. Nonetheless, childcare attendance rates in rural areas are significantly lower and this has been recognized as the key challenge to territorial cohesion and social inclusion. Thus, there is a need to increase the demand in rural areas (through increased accessibility, raising parental awareness of the benefits of the child's participation in ECEC). On the other hand, there is a need to increase supply and accessibility in urban areas, where there is a shortage of places in public ECEC institutions.

Equalization of the financial mechanisms of the ECEC system. The ECEC funding scheme (mixed model of funding based on "student basket" and "class basket" principles), results in the low level of standardization of the ECEC policies in the territorial units as only the basic funds ("student basket") are provided from the national budget. The level of the centralized funding is too low to secure high-quality services in all territorial units, thus, the responsibility for the supply and the quality of the ECEC is transferred to the municipalities as a consequence of which, there is great spatial variation in securing the ECEC services. Some municipalities subsidize family expenses in the private ECEC institutions, but the size of the subsidy and number of families receiving it differs. Only some of the municipalities provide free transportation services.

Generally, in all localities high quality and accessibility of the childcare services are articulated and recognized as a priority. In all localities, this is the ultimate goal, however, the municipalities emphasize different aspects of this objective. For example, in urban municipalities, the three main issues related to childcare services are identified as: *accessibility, quality of the infrastructure and capacity building of ECEC providers.* In suburban municipalities, the focus is *the infrastructure ("rationally planned development of the educational institutions*

Table 4.4. Similarities and differences in ECEC policies in three localities.

	Localities	**Characteristics**
Similarities	Kaunas city municipality (urban) Kaunas district municipality (suburban) Pakruojis district municipality (rural)	1. Accessibility and availability of ECEC services in more remote areas and beneficiaries targeting problems (ensuring equal access for families with children who needed assistance or disabilities). 2. Low participation of children from aged 3 to the mandatory school age from households at risk of poverty and social exclusion. 3. Insufficient childcare provision for early-age children below 2 years old. 4. Re-organization of ECEC institutional network and costs optimization strategies. 5. Issues in balancing supply and demand of ECEC vacancies based on territorial needs. 6. Dependence on public funding mechanism defined by "student-basket" and "mixed funding method" principles. 7. The increasing number of private ECEC providers targeting ECEC services that are more accessible in urban areas for higher-income families. 8. Low participation of social stakeholders in ECEC institution boards. 9. Municipal efforts for the renovation of ECEC facilities and buildings.
Differences	Kaunas city municipality (urban)	1. Insufficient supply and demand of ECEC services in central and peripheral urban areas. 2. High costs of private ECEC providers that are available only for families with higher income. 3. Changes of fees policy since 2020 for the families that are not registered in the territory of Kaunas city municipality and prioritizing of ECEC service beneficiaries.
	Kaunas district municipality (suburban)	1. High competition for ECEC vacancies and insufficient supply of ECEC services in rural and urban elderships (territorial units). 2. Accessibility and availability of ECEC services in more remote areas. 3. Spatial distribution of ECEC services in more rural and more urban elderships (territorial units). 4. High level of municipal and public investments in the renovation of ECEC facilities and establishments. 5. Innovative models of ECEC services (family kindergartens) and an increasing number of private providers.

(*continued on next page*)

Table 4.4. Continued

	Localities	Characteristics
	Pakruojis district municipality (rural)	1. Sufficient supply for the ECEC services demand 2. Transportation problems for children in remote rural areas (where children are at a higher risk of poverty and exclusion) 3. The high negative impact of demographic decline and spatial remoteness of the ECEC institutions. 4. Accessibility and availability of ECEC services in more remote rural areas and spatial distribution of services. 5. The need for the reconstruction of multi-functional centers and childcare rooms in rural areas.

and modernization of existing educational infrastructure") and the *quality of the educational process*, but the issue of accessibility is not part of the strategic policy agenda. In rural areas, ECEC is discussed only implicitly. It is indicated marginally in relation to the restructuring of the network of educational institutions, in the establishing of the multifunctional centers in some localities, and the reconstruction and renovation of the ECEC institutions. The components of the goals and even the internal interpretation of each goal is linked to the actual situation in the locality. For example, the issue of accessibility in urban municipalities is related to the shortage of kindergartens, preschool institutions and primary schools in some elderships. In contrast, in rural municipalities, the issue of accessibility is linked to the inclusion of children from disadvantaged families in the formal childcare system.

Re-organization and re-modification of educational services network. Demographic developments in individual localities alter the supply-demand chain of educational services. Internal migration, growth of the number of young families with children or aging of the population necessitates a re-structuring of the infrastructure. For example, in the Kaunas district municipality in some localities, there is a growing number of young families and a demand for the expansion of the ECEC network. In rural municipalities, an aging population combined with a decrease in the size of the younger populace, necessitates a re-modification of the educational institutions and a transformation of the kindergartens or schools into multifunctional community centers. Voluntary organizations or citizens groups employ various strategies to pressurize the municipality to satisfy the needs of the residents.

Innovations related to the accessibility of the ECEC services. In suburban and particularly in rural municipalities, the re-structuring of the network of the ECEC institutions due to the demographic developments in specific areas raises the issue of the accessibility of the services. Thus, municipalities organize transportation for children from home to the pre-school institution or even to the kindergarten.

Innovations related to the quality and diversity of the ECEC services. In all localities, there are implemented innovations related to the health of children, educational curricula, and diversity of the services. The health of the children is one of the concerns shared by service providers and parents.

Educational quality. The responsibility for the curricula of the ECEC and the quality of the services is decentralized and thus, there is no comprehensive system of quality control. The internal and external evaluations are conducted by the specific institution and municipalities respectively, however, municipalities lack clear guidelines and instruments for quality control and in many cases also lack the competence for assessment (the exception might be the large urban municipalities). Thus, the level of quality of the ECEC services might differ between the municipalities.

Policy priorities and social investment strategy

In summarizing, we could determine the list of main priorities in the local policy agenda for developing the ECEC policy field in terms of increasing the accessibility and availability of ECEC places especially for families with different socio-economic statuses, educational quality, and participation of stakeholders in defining local needs. The priorities reflect the main goals of the social investment approach (SI).

1. **ECEC institutional network development and spatial coverage**. The criteria for urban-rural distribution of ECEC services coverage in the municipalities should be applied. When analyzing rural municipalities, the criteria for the participation rates in the ECEC should be considered (i.e., inclusion of the rural municipalities where the enrollment rates of children are relatively lower, especially in families socially and financially at risk). When referring to urban municipalities, the criteria for the public-private structure of the ECEC institution should be considered. It is important to take a differentiated approach to urban municipalities with a high as opposed to a moderate shortage of places in ECEC.
2. **Improvement of service provision for children with special needs**. The current ECEC system needs more efficient instruments to improve access for children with special needs to formal childcare services. The greater inclusiveness could be fostered by financial instruments in municipalities and better qualified ECEC teachers.

3. **Accessibility and availability of ECEC services.** Considering the urban-rural inequalities in participation in the ECEC, special attention should be given to issues linked with the role of the municipalities in raising parental awareness of the benefits of the ECEC, particularly for the children from socio-economically disadvantaged backgrounds. Therefore, issues around the organization of the transportation services provided by municipalities are very important (funding, problems in organizing transportation and keeping safety rules for transporting small children).
4. **The innovative models for formal childcare.** The manner in which all municipal stakeholders and social partners in ECEC services development are involved is important. The innovative models of providing formal child-care are only in the initial phase and implemented by few municipalities.
5. **Public-private partnership and equality of opportunities.** The involvement of private actors in the ECEC provision increased the supply of services particularly in the urban or demographically growing municipalities. The public-private partnerships were institutionalized through partial subsidies provided by the municipalities to the families. Though the partnership helped to solve the supply-demand problems, it also added to the growing inequality of the educational opportunities for the children from less socio-economically privileged families. This is an unfavorable trend in relation to the social investment approach and should be given special attention in the development of the educational policies at both national and local levels.

References

Aidukaitė, J., Bogdanova, N., & Guogis, A. (2012). *Gerovės valstybės kūrimas Lietuvoje: mitas ar realybė?* [Creation of the Welfare State in Lithuania: Myth or the Reality?]. Vilnius: Lietuvos socialinių tyrimų centras.

Aidukiene, T. (2014). Lithuanian experience: Towards accessible and inclusive early childhood education. Available at: https://www.worldbank.org/content/dam/Worldbank/Event/ECA/romania/Teresa%20Aidukiene-Lithuania-2014-04-02-.pdf (Accessed at 13 March 2020).

Baranauskienė, V. (2021). *Socioteritorinė atskirtis Lietuvos retai apgyventose teritorijose. Daktaro disertacija [Socio-spatial exclusion in sparsely populated territories of Lithuania. PhD thesis*] VDU, LSMC, KTU.

Bučaitė-Vilkė, J., Purvaneckienė, G., Vaitkevičius, R., & Tereškinas, A. (2012). *Lyčių politika ir gimstamumo ateitis: monografija*. Kaunas: Vytauto Didžiojo universitetas.

Bukelevičiūtė, D. (2016). 'Švietimo prieinamumo socialiniai aspektai, slinktys ir pokyčiai' [Social Aspects of the Accesiblity of the Education: Trends and Changes]. In D. Bukelevičiūtė, Z. Butkus, N. Černiauskas, A. Grodis, A. P. Kasperavičius, & G. Polkaitė-Petkevičienė (Eds.), *Socialiniai pokyčiai Lietuvos valstybėje 1918–1940 metais.* [Social Changes in Lithuanian State in 1918–1940] (pp. 314–365). Vinius: Vilniaus universiteto leidykla.

Čižauskaitė, A., & Gruževskis, B. (2018). Ikimokyklinių ugdymo paslaugų įtaka tėvų užimtumui Lietuvoje. *Socialinė teorija, empirija, politika ir praktika, 17*, 74–91.

Dėl ikimokyklinio ir priešmokyklinio ugdymo 2011–2013 metų plėtros programos patvirtinimo [Pre-school and Pre-Primary Education Development Programme for 2011–2013] (2011). Valstybės žinios, 2011-03-10, Nr. 30-1421. Available at: https://e-seimas.lrs.lt/portal/legalAct/lt/TAD/TAIS.393941

Dėl mokyklų aprūpinimo geltonaisiais autobusais 2018–2020 m. projektas [Regarding the school's equipment with the yeallow buses in 2018–2020]. (2017). Available at: https://e-seimas.lrs.lt/portal/legalAct/lt/TAD/d13fbaf26b2b11e7aefae747e4b63286?jfwid

Demographic Yearbook 2017. (2018). Vilnius: Lietuvos statistikos departamentas.

Education and Training Monitor. (2017). Available at: https://op.europa.eu/en/publication-detail/-/publication/38e7f778-bac1-11e7-a7f8-01aa75ed71a1

Education and Training Monitor. (2019). Available at: https://op.europa.eu/en/publication-detail/-/publication/15d70dc3-e00e-11e9-9c4e-01aa75ed71a1/language-en/format-PDF/source-171178208

Esping-Andersen, G. (2002). A new European social model for the twenty-first century. In M. J. Rodrigues (Ed.), *The new knowledge economy in Europe: A strategy for international competitiveness and social cohesion* (pp. 54–94). Cheltenham: Edward Elgar.

European Commission Country Report Lithuania. (2019). Available at: https://ec.europa.eu/info/sites/info/files/file_import/2019-european-semester-country-report-lithuania_en.pdf (Accessed at 30 October 2019).

European Commission/EACEA/Eurydice (2019). Key data on early childhood education and care in Europe – 2019 edition. Eurydice report. Luxembourg: Publications Office of the European Union. Available at: www.eacea.ec.europa.eu%2Fnational-policies%2Feurydice%2Fsites%2Fdefault%2Ffiles%2Fec0319375enn_0.pdf&clen=7925436&chunk=true (Accessed at 10 March 2020).

Ikimokyklinis ugdymas [Early child care and education]. (2021). Available at: https://www.renkuosilietuva.lt/lt/ikimokyklinis-ugdymas (Accessed at 08 August 2021).

Information of the Ministry of Science, Education and Sports. (2019). Available at: https://www.sac.smm.lt/projektai-ir-programos/projektai/vykdomi-projektai/es-projektai/ (Accessed at 12 December 2019).

Kaunas district municipality information, 2020. Available online www.krs.lt/savivaldybe Acceced online 2021 08 16.

Kauno miesto savivaldybės 2013–2015 metų strateginis veiklos palanas. (2013). Available at: http://www.kaunas.lt/administracija/veikla/planavimo-dokumentai/strateginiai-veiklos-planai/.

Kauno miesto savivaldybės 2016–2018 metų strateginis veiklos palanas. (2016). Available at: http://www.kaunas.lt/administracija/veikla/planavimo-dokumentai/strateginiai-veiklos-planai/

Kauno miesto savivaldybės 2019–2021 metų strateginis veiklos palanas. (2019). Available at: http://www.kaunas.lt/administracija/veikla/planavimo-dokumentai/strateginiai-veiklos-planai/

Kauno miesto savivaldybės strateginis plėtros planas 2015–2022 [*Strategic plan of Kaunas city municipality* 2013–2022]. (2015). Available at: http://www.kaunas.lt/wp-content/uploads/sites/8/2015/03/t157127planaspatvirtintas.pdf (Accessed at 08 March 2017).

Kauno miesto savivaldybės švietimo pažangos ataskaita (2017). Available at: http://svisold.emokykla.lt/lt/index/a_view/51.

Kauno miesto savivaldybės švietimo pažangos ataskaita [Kaunas city municipality Advancement of Education Report] (2017). Kaunas: Kauno miesto savivaldybė.

Kauno rajono savivaldybės strateginis 2013–2020 metų plėtros planas [Strategic Plan of the Kaunas district municipality development 2013–2020]. (2013). Available at: https://www.krs.lt/savivaldybe/administracine-informacija/planavimo-dokumentai/ (Accessed at 08 February 2017).

Kauno rajono savivaldybės strateginis plėtros planas 2021–2027 [Strategic Plan of the Kaunas district municipality development 2021–2027]. (2019). Available at: https://www.krs.lt/savivaldybe/administracine-informacija/planavimo-dokumentai/ (Accessed at 21 February 2020).

Kauno rajono savivaldybės švietimo pažangos ataskaita [Kaunas district municipality report on the advancement of the education] (2017). Available at: https://www.svis.smm.lt/savivaldybiu-pazanga-test/.

Leinarte, D. (2021). *Family and the state in Soviet Lithuania: Gender, law and society*. London: Bloomsbury Publishing.

Lietuvos Respublikos Švietimo įstatymas [Law on Education of the Republic of Lithuania] (2011). Nr. XI-1281, 2011-03-17, Žin., 2011. Available at: https://e-seimas.lrs.lt/portal/legalAct/lt/TAD/TAIS.1480/asr (Accessed at 05 March 2017).

Lithuania. Organization of Private Education. (2018). Available at: https://eacea.ec.europa.eu/national-policies/eurydice/content/organisation-private-education-44_en (Accessed at 03 February 2020).

Liukinevičienė, L., & Paulauskienė, V. (2019). Nauji viešųjų paslaugų teikimo būdai ir kanalai ikimokyklinio ugdymo įstaigose. *Socialiniai tyrimai*, *42*, 50–66.

Martišauskienė, D. (2010). Ikimokyklinio ugdymo paslaugų kokybės valdymo modeliavimas tiriant tėvų-vartotojų poreikius. Daktaro disertacija. Šiaulių universitetas.

Martišauskienė, D. (2011). Ikimokyklinio ugdymo įstaigos kokybės vadybos sistemai būdingų požymių dinamika, įvairiapusiškumas ir jos vertinimas: paslaugų teikėjų (vadovų, pedagogų) požiūriu. *Tiltai*, *55*(2), 163–176.

Nacionalinė švietimo strategija 2013–2020 [National Education Strategy 2013–2022] (2013). Vilnius: Lietuvos švietimo ir mokslo ministerija. Available at: www.sac.smm.lt%2Fwp-content%2Fuploads%2F2016%2F02%2FValstybine-svietimo-strategija-2013-2020_svietstrat.pdf&clen=1160725&chunk=true (Accessed at 22 April 2017).

Norgėlaitė, A. (2020). 'Vaiko priežiūros išmokų gavėjų struktūros pokyčiai lietuvoje: lyčių egalitarizmo šeimoje ženklas?' *Kultūra ir visuomenė: socialinių tyrimų žurnalas*, *11*(1), 55–78.

Nutarimas dėl vaikų maitinimo organizavimo ikimokyklinio ugdymo, bendrojo ugdymo mokyklose ir vaikų socialinės globos įstaigose tvarkos aprašo patvirtinimo. [On the Nutrition regulation in the ECEC, schools and other childcare institutions]. (2018) Available at: https://e-seimas.lrs.lt/portal/legalAct/lt/TAD/TAIS.411986/asr (Accessed at 10 December 2018).

OECD. (2016). Reviews of school resources. Paris: OECD Publishing. Available at: https://www.oecd.org/countries/lithuania/oecd-reviews-of-school-resources-lithuania-2016-9789264252547-en.htm.

OECD. (2017). Education in Lithuania, reviews of national policies for education. Paris: OECD Publishing. Available at: https://doi.org/10.1787/9789264281486-en (Accessed at 20 May 2018).

OECD. (2019). *Education at a Glance 2019: OECD Indicators*. Paris: OECD Publishing. Available at: https://doi.org/10.1787/f8d7880d-en (Accecced at 20 February 2020).

Pakruojo rajono savivaldybės 2014–2022 metų srateginis plėtros planas [Strategic Plan of Pakruojis district municipality for 2014–2020] (2014). Available at: www.pakruojis.lt%2Ffiles%2Fveikla%2F2014-2020%2520SPP.pdf&clen=37008542&chunk=true (Accessed at 06 May 2020).

Purvaneckienė, G. (2005). Švietimo politika ir ikimokyklinio bei priešmokyklinio ugdymo plėtra. *Acta Paedagogica Vilnensia*, 15, 176–187.

Sekeráková Búriková, Z. (2019). Paid home-based childcare in Slovakia: Informal markets and care loops. *European Journal of Social Policy. 29 (5): 653-665. https://doi.org/10.1177/0958928719873834.*

Siarova, H., & Buinauskas, D. (2017). Lithuania – ECEC Workforce Profile. In P. Oberhuemer, & I. Schreyer (Eds.), *Workforce profiles in systems of early childhood education and care in Europe*. Available at: www.seepro.eu/English/Country_Reports.htm.

Stankūnienė, V., Jasilionienė, A., & Jančaitytė, R. (2005). *Šeima, vaikai, šeimos politika: modernėjimo prieštaros*. Socialinių tyrimų institutas.

Stankūnienė, V., Maslauskaitė, A., & Baublytė, M. (2013). *Ar Lietuvos šeimos bus gausesnės?* [Are Families to be Larger in Lithuania?]. Vilnius: Lietuvos socialinių tyrimų centras.

Statistics Lithuania. (2021a). Fertility statistics. Available at: https://osp.stat.gov.lt/statistiniu-rodikliu-analize?indicator=S3R692#/ (Accessed at 30 August 2021).

Statistics Lithuania. (2021b). Children's participation in the ECEC institutions. https://osp.stat.gov.lt/statistiniu-rodikliu-analize?hash=d909e7c3-6c3c-40ea-8739-9af95163d203#/ (Accessed at 30 August 2021).

Šveitimo būklės apžvalga [Overview of the state of the Education]. (2019). Available at: www.smm.lt%2Fwp-content%2Fuploads%2F2019%2F10%2FSvietimo-bukles-apzvalga-2019-web.pdf&clen=14088051&chunk=true (Accessed at 12 August 2021).

Švietimo problemų analizė (2020). Available online: https://www.nsa.smm.lt/wp-content/uploads/2020/12/Ikimokyklinio-ugdymo-apreptis.pdf Acceced on 2021-03-14.

Artūras Tereškinas

Chapter 5 Active labor market policies as a part of social investment approach

Abstract: Focusing on active labor market policies in Lithuania, this chapter examines principal institutions and actors, division of responsibility between central administrative and municipal levels, policy goals, planning, beneficiaries, and expenditures. In Lithuania, the primary responsibility for implementing an active labor market policy is allocated to the central authorities, primarily the Ministry of Social Security and Labor. The analysis of urban (Kaunas city), suburban (Kaunas district), and rural (Pakruojis district) municipalities demonstrates that they have no discretion with regard to implementing, managing, and supervising active labor market policy measures. The findings indicate a need for early labor market interventions, a reconsideration of the financing system, and a fostering of regional and municipal initiatives and social dialogue as a part of the Social Investment approach.

Keywords: active labor market policy, Lithuania, municipalities, Social Investment approach, policy design and implementation

Introduction

Social Investment (hereafter SI) emerged as a policy approach at the end of the 1990s, supporting the notion of welfare state expenditure as a productive element which combines social inclusion with economic competitiveness (Morel et al., 2012). From this perspective, the welfare state should not be viewed as a barrier to economic development but rather as a coordinator, promoter, and stimulator. The development of human capital through education and training is one of the central goals of social investment policy that attempts to prepare people for societal hazards rather than compensate them after they arise (Morel et al., 2012). In the sphere of social policies, SI might be considered a paradigm shift. According to this viewpoint, policy interventions should shift from protection to prevention, training people to deal with the less predictable and dynamic nature of social risks that plague today's communities (Esping-Andersen et al., 2002; Magnusson & Pascual, 2007). The primary purpose of SI is to boost labor market productivity and inclusive growth by enacting policies that train and equip people to meet new social risks and participate meaningfully in a globalized knowledge economy.

SI is particularly relevant to labor market issues as Lithuania's labor market is characterized by considerable flexibility but persistent structural issues. Contrary to other European economies, wages in Lithuania are very sensitive to unemployment and, therefore, an increase in unemployment rapidly results in a reduction in wage growth. Wage flexibility is underpinned by one of the lowest densities of trade union and employer organization and the rare occurrence of collective bargaining. Thus, wage-setting essentially happens at the firm level. Real wages and productivity have been traditionally closely linked, and temporary deviations have been self-correcting. However, deviations at the sectoral level can be persistent, although, in the all-important manufacturing sector, wage growth has remained well below productivity growth (IMF Country Report No. 5/139, 2021). In contrast, structural unemployment has traditionally been high, although it appears to be gradually falling. Large-scale structural unemployment can have a significant long-term impact on potential growth and, therefore, employment (IMF Country Report No. 18/185, 2018).

Despite Lithuania's convergence with the EU, which surged during the economic boom of 2004–2007, fell during the crisis due to the downturn in Vilnius, and has been stable since 2013, regional disparities remain high. In terms of per capita income, the country is divided into three main regions. To begin with, the Vilnius region, which accounts for 40 % of Lithuania's GDP, has the highest level of income and has seen the most significant rises since 2010. The regions of Kaunas and Klaipėda follow Vilnius as important business and industrial centers, with the latter having the country's largest seaport. Kaunas generates 19 % of the country's GDP and has expanded faster than Klaipėda; both regions had the same GDP per capita in 2017. The remaining areas of Lithuania all have GDP per capita below 60 % of the EU average (Country Report Lithuania, 2020).

This chapter analyzes active labor market policy (hereafter ALMP) as a part of SI. The discussion will encompass employment services and active labor market policies directed at employment growth and avoiding depletion of human capital, availability and accessibility of training programs and the provision of unemployment benefits in Lithuania. The first section describes the division of responsibilities between central and municipal levels, policy goals, planning, beneficiaries, expenditures, the role of private actors, monitoring and evaluation activities. The second section examines three localities: urban, suburban, and rural, focusing on labor market policy goals and priorities at the municipal level, target groups and beneficiaries, financial mechanism, service coverage, the division of institutional responsibilities, territorial coverage and personnel issues. The chapter concludes with a discussion of the priorities for developing SI policies in the field of labor market policy. In the chapter, we employ a significant number of policy documents and statistical data.

National framework for active labor market: Shift between state priorities and centralized policy design

ALMP measures are highly centralized in the country. The Ministry of Social Security and Labor is the leading actor responsible for policy implementation at all levels; national, regional, and local. In ALMP, Lithuania is progressing with regulatory enforcement initiatives for the greater involvement of local municipalities. However, regulatory quality has not improved enough, and frequent legislation changes do not provide a stable legal environment for ALMP actions. The capacity of municipalities to execute ALMPs is lacking. Due to its limited ability to provide the required resources for ALMP implementation, local government continues to perform poorly (Country Report Lithuania, 2020).

In general, ALMPs encompass government programs to increase the efficiency of the labor market. Lithuania's ALMP measures consist of support for learning, mobility, assisted recruitment, and job creation. There are different categories of ALMPs:

- Job search assistance (JSA) includes municipally located employment service centers and labor exchanges that attempt to improve labor market matching by disseminating information on job vacancies, equipping the unemployed with interview skills, or assisting in writing a curriculum vitae.
- Vocational training schemes that encompass classroom training, on-the-job training, vocational education and apprenticeships, aim to help the unemployed improve their vocational skills and productivity and increase their employability. They are partly compatible with the existing VET system in the country in terms of organizing adult learning and requalification courses.
- Employment state subsidies comprise wage subsidies, hiring subsidies, business start-up subsidies, and in-work benefits to encourage worker labor market attachment and job creation by firms. It includes Public works programs (PWP), which provide the temporarily unemployed with short-term employment. The employment state subsidies are organized and managed centrally. The local employment service centers take the role of implementing the programs at the local level.

The new Labor Code of 2017 brought about changes in ALMP measures, including promoting self-employment and internship, encouraging self-education and non-formal adult education, and providing mobility support. Vocational training schemes that incorporate classroom training, on-the-job training, vocational education and apprenticeships, aim to assist the unemployed to improve their vocational skills and productivity and increase their employability. Employment subsidies have become the primary ALMP measure. Unlike other programs, which have maintained almost the same level of spending relative to GDP, expenditure on training has fluctuated over time and increased recently subsequent to very low levels between 2011 and 2014. In addition, despite the introduction of the training voucher scheme in 2012, training programs are predicated on curricula for low-skilled tasks, such as logistics (truck drivers), construction, cooking and beauty services, which already exceed the demand for labor. The cost-effectiveness of ALMPs could be enhanced by improving program design based on a more systematic program evaluation (Labor Code, 2017).

The ALMP policy is designed around a few primary target groups of beneficiaries. According to the Description of the Conditions and Procedure for the Implementation of the Employment Support Measures, approved by the Minister of Social Security and Labor (2017, June 30 No. A1-348), the ALMP measures are targeting the following groups: (1) unskilled unemployed (providing support for the acquisition of work skills and support for mobility, subsidized employment and mobility support, apprenticeship employment); (2) unemployed persons under the age of 29 and the long-term unemployed (providing support for the acquisition of work skills and support for mobility, vocational training, subsidized employment and support for mobility, internship, recruitment through apprenticeship, support for learning measures and support for self-employment), (3) unemployed over the age of 50 and (4) individuals with refugee status, or persons granted subsidiary or temporary protection for immigration purposes (Report, 2016, Government of the Republic of Lithuania).

The purpose of ALMP monitoring and evaluation is to enable employment policymakers to make informed decisions. Employment monitoring is carried out by the Government Strategic Analysis Centre (STRATA) according to the procedure established by the government or its authorized institution. STRATA agency monitors two indicators: employment and labor market tendencies. Assessment of employment status, changes, and trends in the Lithuanian population, taking into account the needs of the state, municipalities, society, and economy, employment forecasts for the Lithuanian population and the collection, processing, and publication of employment statistics are all part of employment monitoring (Report, 2016, Government of the Republic of Lithuania). Monitoring the labor market entails (1) keeping track of job searchers and vacancies, assessing the labor market's position, and anticipating changes; and (2) evaluating the implementation and efficacy of labor market services and active labor market policies (Ministry of Social Security and Labor information, 2020). The Employment Service Office also develops and publishes labor market reports (annual, half-year, and quarterly) as well as market projections.

In the regulation of the employment relationship, working conditions, and industrial relations structures, trade unions, employer groups, and state institutions play a critical role. They are interconnected components of a multilevel governance system that covers the European, national, sectoral, regional (provincial or local), and company levels (Living and Working in Lithuania, 2021).

Although social dialogue is improving, there are still some weaknesses. In 2019, new collective agreements were signed at the national, sectoral, and company levels. The percentage of employees covered by collective agreements climbed to 15 % in the same year. The public sector is where the majority of collective agreements are signed. However, a lack of capacity and resources is a barrier to social partners engaging in effective social dialogue at the sectoral or company level (Müller et al., 2019). Some relevant public institutions continue to undervalue the role of social partners. However, there is also a trend toward increased constructive participation of social partners in the European Semester process (Country Report Lithuania, 2020).

The Labor Code, which has been in effect since July 1, 2017, establishes representation rules for social partners in the Republic of Lithuania's Tripartite Council (hereafter LRTT). Three trade unions and six employer organizations were represented at the LRTT at the start of 2019 (Living and Working in Lithuania, 2021). Trade unions include the Lithuanian Trade Union Confederation, Lithuanian Trade Union 'Solidarumas' [Solidarity] and the Federation of Lithuanian Trade Unions 'Sandrauga' [Community] (the latter joined the Council in 2017). The Lithuanian Confederation of Industrialists, the Confederation of Lithuanian Employers, the Association of Lithuanian Chambers of Commerce, Industry and Crafts, the Chamber of Agriculture of the Republic of Lithuania, the Investors' Forum and the Lithuanian Business Confederation (the latter two joined the Council in 2017) are all employer organizations. These organizations regularly participate in national-level social dialogue. Collective bargaining is most common at the company level in Lithuania. Despite the fact that sectoral collective bargaining is still in its infancy, numerous sectoral collective agreements covering wage-related problems were signed for the first time in 2017–2018 in the education, health care, and social care sectors. Collective bargaining in Lithuania takes place most prevalently at a company level levels (Living and Working in Lithuania, 2021). The Republic of Lithuania's Tripartite Council's primary role in ALMPs is to develop sectoral agreements for more active participation of unemployed persons.

In 2019, social partners at the Tripartite Council of the Republic of Lithuania (hereinafter TCRL) and members of the Parliament looked at ways to encourage social dialogue by adapting and enacting new social dialogue legislation. A number of sectoral collective bargaining agreements have been signed. In addition, a national (public sector) collective agreement for 2020 was reached, and long-term public sector finance negotiations were started. Furthermore, at the TCRL, social partners agreed to form a Bipartite Social-Partner Commission for Competence Building at the end of 2019.

To promote social dialogue, the Law on the Promotion of Social Dialogue was prepared and debated in 2019. The proposed legislation includes a mediation system that would be used to help with problem-solving in collective bargaining or when professional assistance is needed. Relief from taxes and charges, promotional scores in public tendering and support projects, financial support, administrative services and consultations, training organization, and additional guarantees for employee and employer representatives are all examples of state aid that could be applied to social partners in the draft law.

The TCRL created a Bipartite Social-Partner Commission for Competence Building towards the end of 2019. The commission's goal is to identify the skills that social partners will need to participate in various types of social dialogue more effectively and efficiently. It will also review proposals from the parties and offer recommendations to the TCRL on how to strengthen social partners' ability and empower them. It will also assess and evaluate party performance in the area of social partner competence development, and report its results to the TCRL (Living and Working in Lithuania, 2021).

Expenditures and policy funding mechanism

Labor market services and measures for employment support are financed by the Employment Fund, state and municipality budgets, and EU structural funds amongst other sources. Disbursement of funds and coverage for active labor market policies decreased in 2019. This further pressurized integration into the labor market of the long term unemployed and of vulnerable groups. Coverage of labor market policy measures fell from 17 % in 2018 to less than 10 % in 2019, while the cost per participant increased significantly in 2019 compared to 2018, and the total budget for the measures fell.

It should be emphasized that ALMP expenditure in Lithuania is low in terms of investment and participation. Spending on ALMPs was only 0.3 % of GDP in 2016 relative to OECD countries. Participation is also limited, with only 3.7 % of the unemployed involved in training programs in 2016. The 2014–2015

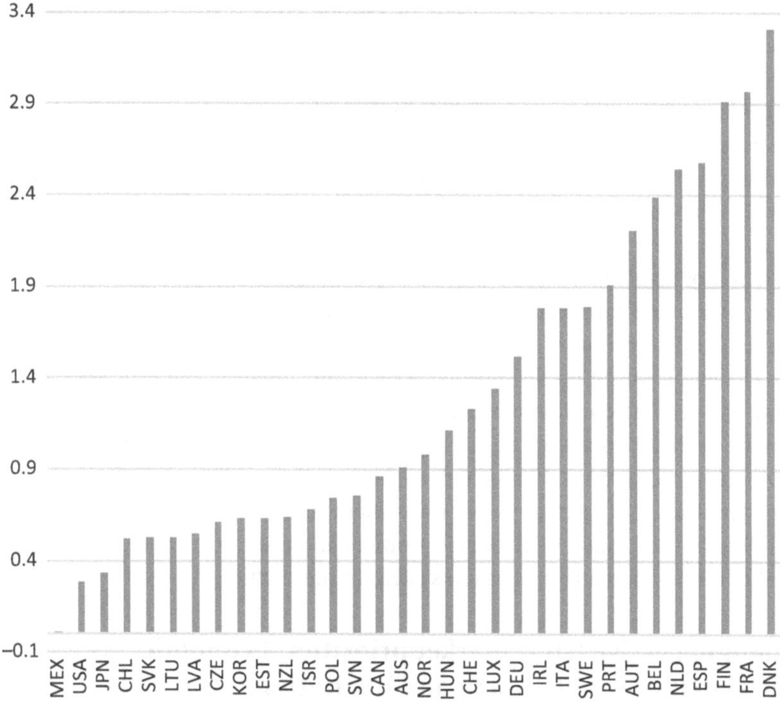

Figure 5.1. Public expenditure on ALMP measures for 2015 in OECD countries. Source: OECD report 2017. OECD Employment and labor market statistics.

budget allocation indicates that the national financing of ALMP policy remains significantly lower compared to the other OECD countries (Figure 5.1).

Referring to the data on the allocation of ALMP expenditures for national programs, the largest share of the total budget is allocated to employment incentives and administrative expenses for Employment Services Offices. Since 2003 the proportion of total expenditure for different programs has been steadily increasing.

ALMPs in Lithuania do not sufficiently reflect labor market needs or cyclical conditions and rely mainly on European funds. Since 2009, most employment policy measures have been financed almost exclusively from the EU funds. Spending is low in downturns and does not reflect increasing needs. ALMP spending relative to GDP has been commensurately constant in Lithuania even following the global financial crisis when unemployment increased sharply and participation was one of the lowest in Europe. This is partly explained by the heavy reliance on an external funding source such as the European Social Fund (ESF) – almost two-thirds in 2015. The heavy dependence on EU funding, which targeted specific groups, has resulted in the unique situation of specifying beneficiary groups in the Labor Code: older workers, long-term unemployed, youth and the disabled. The new Labor Code adopted in 2017 now lists unqualified persons as potential beneficiaries. Furthermore, training programs tend to focus on oversupplied skills.

It is possible to conclude that the role of the EU funds in implementing labor policy and supporting active labor market measures is crucial. Lithuanian municipalities encounter insufficient accessibility of employment services. Thus, the challenge would be to improve accessibility, quality, and efficiency to promote the region's employment and labor mobility. The EU funds should apply a more individualized approach to employment services, create services for clear-cut target groups (for instance, the long-term unemployed), and secure their territorial accessibility. More investment should be allocated to the capacity building of the Employment Services offices and their employers and creating a quality monitoring and evaluation system in these offices.

Changing active labor market priorities: Economic performance, employment and institutions

The past decade marks vigorous developments in the field of ALMPs. As the labor market has recovered from the recession of 2009, total employment has continued to rise in absolute terms, but it has not yet reached its pre-crisis level. Both employment and unemployment rates have steadily improved since 2010, with unemployment at 6.4 % in 2019 and activity rate at 82.9 % in the third quarter. In the third quarter of 2019, long-term unemployment stayed below 2 % (2.4 % in the EU).

In this quarter, youth unemployment (at 11.7 %) and the rate of young people not in employment, education, or training were also below the EU average (at 7.8 %). The decreasing number of long-term unemployed persons and the improved labor market condition for young people not in education, employment, or training (NEET) mirrored the continuing drop in unemployment (Country Report Lithuania, 2020). However, although on a downward trend, the unemployment of older people (50–59) was higher than in the EU (6.7 % vs 5.2 % in 2018). During the later years, the stabilization of unemployment and a drop in the vacancy rate indicate a suppression in the labor market (Statistics Lithuania, 2021).

Despite significant economic growth and ambitious changes during the last 25 years, Lithuania faces a number of problems in the future. Labor productivity remains at two-thirds of the OECD average, owing in part to informality and skill mismatch. Wage disparities are widespread, and work quality is frequently subpar. Significant social security contributions, as well as, until recently, strict labor market regulation, have a negative impact on labor market opportunities, worsening inequality and reducing tax revenues, while also contributing to informality. Despite the low obstacles to entry, international investment is still limited. Demography is of particular concern. Demography is a major source of concern. Lithuania's population has been quickly aging and declining, owing primarily to youth emigration. Every year, the labor force continues to drop by about 1 %. Stringent regulations and a dearth of attractive job opportunities are preventing talent from entering the country (OECD Labor Force Statistics, 2020).

In 2019, employment opportunities rose in Lithuania, while the labor force shrank, primarily due to emigration. In recent years, the labor shortage has worsened, while labor expenses have risen dramatically. Nonetheless, competitiveness threats are now limited: there are indicators that the labor shortage is reducing, with unemployment marginally increasing and the job vacancy rate somewhat decreasing. Immigration from non-EU countries increased in 2019: migrant workers from non-EU countries, primarily from Ukraine and Belarus, filled low- and medium-skilled openings in construction, industry, transportation, and services. In the longer term, Lithuania's biggest issues include a shrinking population and ongoing weaknesses in its education and health systems (Statistics Lithuania, 2020).

The Bank of Lithuania argues that the economic climate, demographic changes, and migration also affected the labor market situation, which was marked by the dearth of highly skilled workers outside the capital area of Vilnius county, and a growing labor demand in rural areas. For example, the proportion of young persons aged 25–39 has been increasing solely in the capital Vilnius region, where the number of working-age persons remains essentially stable. In Kaunas and Klaipėda regions, the number has declined, whereas, in other peripheral Lithuanian regions, the downturn halved (see Figure 5.2).

Due to the stable economic situation in Lithuania, the general unemployment rate was declining, and labor shortages were rising. The wages in the private sector saw the greatest increases since the onset of the economic recovery in 2014, rising by more than 9 % annually (Central Bank of Lithuania, Report on Lithuanian Economy, 2019). Since 2014, governmental efforts to increase tax-exempt income, pensions, and other social benefits have positively boosted household income and general consumption levels. Nevertheless, the problem

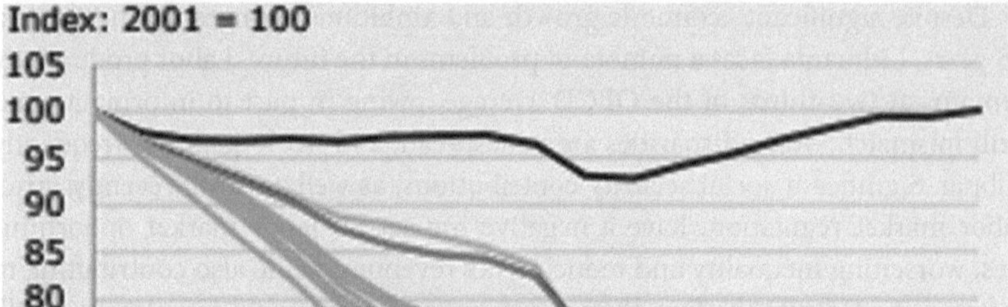

Figure 5.2. The drop of the population aged 25–39 in Lithuanian regions, in 2001–2019. Source: Statistics Lithuania (2018) and Central Bank of Lithuania (2019).

of the working-age population shortage was significant. The continuous adverse demographic trends (older cohorts leave the workforce in higher numbers than younger cohorts enter it) altered the overall picture of sustainable employment other than in the Vilnius region which has experienced a stable population growth over the last decade. For example, according to the Central Bank of Lithuania survey, approximately 17 % of Lithuanian companies declared a shortage in the labor force that also constituted the main driver of rapid wage growth. Moreover, the decrease in the unemployment rate was about 4 % in the large cities of Kaunas, Vilnius and Klaipeda. In the rest of the country, the rate exceeded about 9 %. Another important aspect is that the changing migration flows exert only a limited impact on labor market conditions. 2019 was the first year since 1990 that showed the lowest net emigration (Central Bank of Lithuania, Report on Lithuanian Economy, 2019).

Labor productivity gaps between the capital region of Vilnius and the western-middle Lithuania region create GDP disparities among regions. While labor productivity in Lithuania's western-middle region is increasing, it is still below the EU average (78 % of the EU rate after adjusting for purchasing power). Vilnius has a much greater per capita income than the rest of Lithuania (€37 700 in 2017 vs €25 600 in 2017). The gap has been slowly decreasing over the last few years, mainly because of rapidly growing productivity in specific manufacturing sectors (e.g. wood processing) located outside the capital region (Statistics Lithuania, 2020).

Rural regions have been lagging. Despite persistently high unemployment (9.3 % in rural areas in 2018, compared to 4.3 % in cities and 5.9 % in towns and suburbs), rural areas face a shortage of skilled labor. While the proportion of the population with a tertiary education is far above the EU norm in Lithuanian cities, reaching up to 49.2 %, it drops to 32.6 % in towns and suburbs and 22.2 % in rural areas (Statistics Lithuania, 2020).

Productivity has been rising, albeit at a slower pace than before the crisis, and it remains significantly below the EU average. Since the financial crisis, investment and productivity have been gradually increasing (apart from 2014 to 2016, when Russian sanctions generated uncertainty). As a result, productivity continues to catch up with the EU average, owing mostly to capital accumulation rather than technological advancements. In the short term, there has been considerable pressure on labor costs, but no discernible influence on cost competitiveness: despite the worse environment of its main trading partners, Lithuania's exports have performed well (save for 2014–2016). The low level of foreign direct investment reflects the international context. Despite the temporary rebound, investment remains below historical levels (Ministry of Economy of the Republic of Lithuania, 2019).

Furthermore, wages in Lithuania have increased significantly but are projected to normalize in the near future. Wage growth slowed in 2019, dropping from 7.7 % to a constant high of 7 %. This rate was higher than domestic labor productivity prices and unemployment would have justified, and it was also higher than the rate that would have kept the real effective exchange rate constant. However, over the next two years, a further slowdown to 4 % is expected. In 2019, real wage growth (adjusted for inflation) was 4.95.8 %, down from 5.8 % in 2017. Inflationary pressures on unit labor costs were lessened in 2019 as wages and productivity growth slowed. These advances, together with evidence of a loosening labor market, will dramatically reduce labor costs in the coming years (Statistics Lithuania, 2020).

It should be noted that several reforms affected the state of the ALMP at the national level. The Lithuanian Labor Exchange was restructured as an Employment Office from October 2018. Regional customer service offices remained in the largest cities of Vilnius, Kaunas, Klaipėda and Panevėžys, with some, but less customer service availability in all 60 municipalities. The main reasons for the reorganization were cost optimizations, more efficient management, reduction of regional autonomy, and standardization of management in finances and IT solutions. A further strategic goal was to reduce the average monthly workload with the proportion of clients per employee up to 30 % (405–275 clients). Focus on customer service and labor market analysis was also important.

More recently, the Bank of Lithuania (2016) simulated the effect of social policy proposals in Lithuania's New Social Model in 2015 on unemployment using an open economy vector autoregressive (VAR) model. They assumed an increase in ALMP expenditure financed by imposing a 15 % income tax on unemployment benefits and found a resultant reduction in the unemployment rate (Lietuvos investuotojų pasitikėjimo indeksas, 2019). The New Social Model encompassed reform of labor relations, unemployment insurance and pensions based on flexicurity. The reform entered into force in three stages in 2017 and 2018. The reform relaxed labor market regulations, increased unemployment benefits, strengthened active labor market policies and made the pension system more sustainable.

Despite these reforms, tt should be noted that progress toward enhancing the quality and efficiency of education and training at all levels, including adult learning, has been slow. More needs to be done to enhance the education and training system's low efficiency in terms of job results, as well as the allocation of resources between education levels and between urban and rural areas. Reforms in the educational system are being implemented slowly. Participation in adult learning is still significantly below the EU average (Country Report Lithuania, 2020).

It's also worth noting that, while Lithuania increased the quantity of training in the total percentage of activation measures, the number of apprenticeships remained low. The number of trilateral training and employment agreements with local businesses, as well as bottlenecks in the supply of job-relevant training, reduce the effectiveness of the measures, resulting in low levels of sustainability. The business companies (mostly in industries) are invited to participate in the apprenticeships programs organized by local Employment Service Offices; however, the first steps towards program activation have yielded limited results. More positively, Lithuania's public employment service now offers more tailored services to help long-term unemployed people get back to work, and a national pilot project involving an integrated service model aimed at the most vulnerable long-term unemployed people is currently underway, with promising results in participating municipalities (Country Report Lithuania, 2020).

Is it possible to implement active labor market policy on municipal level?

The ALMP is an example of consolidated policy in Lithuania supervised and controlled by central authorities. Concerning the assignment of responsibilities and bodies within the ALMP policy area, the Employment Services Office (since 2019 the former Labor Exchange Office) controlled by the Ministry of Social Security and Labor is responsible for the country's labor market policies. Besides this Ministry, territorial offices of the Employment Services Office, other state institutions, municipalities and other agencies are responsible for this policy area. Currently, the main measures in the labor policies include support for learning, mobility, employment subsidies, support for new workplace positions and support for new working skills. Thus, the ALMPs are centralized through the Employment Services Office; however, the Law on Employment Support of the Republic of Lithuania provides for the involvement of different-level institutions in these policies, i.e. various functions and responsibilities along with some of the implementations are divided between different national and local institutions, for example, Tripartite councils on national and municipal level negotiate on sectoral agreements.

There are five regional customer service departments in the Employment Service, covering 52 units providing customer services in municipalities and working full-time in all areas (Figure 5.2). All customer centers are administered by the Central Office in Vilnius but enjoy minimal regional or municipal program autonomy. Concerning local autonomy and territorialization, it should be pointed out that territorial Labor Exchange offices are subordinate to the Employment Services Office that is, in turn, subordinate to the Ministry of Social Security and Labor. This type of governance secures some common standards, but is less flexible regarding regional specificity and context that could be ensured by implementing local employment projects and other activities within different municipalities.

However, keeping in mind territorial disparities among different regions, it is possible to argue that territorial equalization is not ensured: on the one hand, regional specificity (demographic differences, infrastructural differences and the

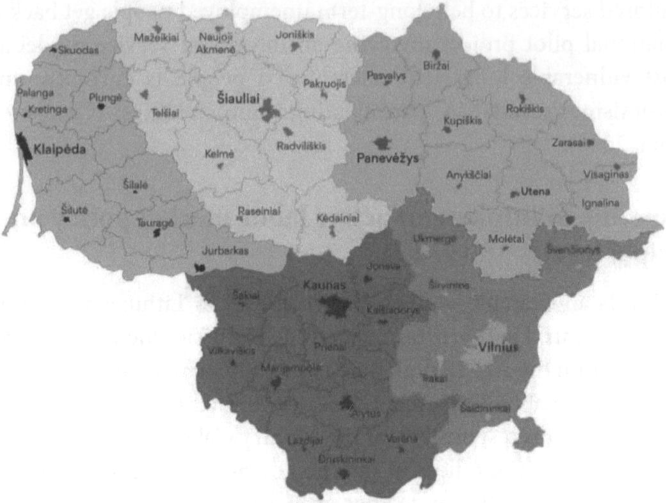

Figure 5.3. Structure of regional Employment Services Offices coverage.
Source: Employment Services Under the Ministry of Social Security and Labor of the Republic of Lithuania, 2020.

differences in labor supply and demand) determine territorial disparities; on the other hand, initiatives at the municipality level are also a factor in reducing territorial inequalities, for example, the fostering of seasonal employment programs.

Following the reorganization of the Employment Services Office, the number of professional positions has declined by 10 %, which is 143 positions less than previous numbers (in total 1290 positions in the overall system). There are 1290 employees on the overall Employment Services Office system of which 93 % were women, and only 7 % men. The average age of the employers is 47 years, 97 % of them had higher education, and 76 % were civil servants. In 2018, 89 requalification programs were organized for the employees in which 36 % of employees have participated. Greater attention is paid to skills such as customers service specialists and unit managers (Annual Report of Employment Services Office, 2019).

Regarding the relation between territorial policy goals and the ALMP system, the main body of ALMP policy implementation is the Employment Services Office under the Ministry of Social Security and Labor which is responsible for all ALMP measures and programs. These include registration of the unemployed, job vacancies, employment policy development, analysis and forecasting

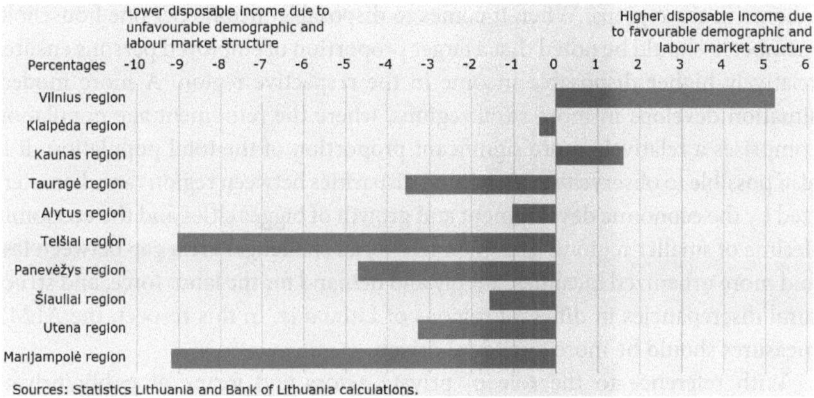

Figure 5.4. Impact of regional demographic and labor market structure on the deviation of disposable income per one household member from the country's average in 2017. Central Bank of Lithuania (2019).

of labor market data, subsidized employment, varying programs for employment and SME, and entrepreneurships for different groups of beneficiaries. The Office provides labor market services defined in the Law on Employment of Lithuania and provides ALMP measures and employment promotion programs established by this law. It also grants the status of social enterprise and provides state aid in accordance with the procedures established by the Law on Social Enterprises of the Republic of Lithuania. Another aspect of their functions involves the cooperative initiatives and implementation of different employment programs or projects. For example, it is noted that the Office works together with municipal institutions, regional development councils, and social partners in submitting proposals to the Ministry of Social Security and Labor on ALMP measures to address employment challenges in the regions. However, our previous empirical work (interviews with the stakeholders in the localities) indicates that cooperation with the Employment Services Office is inadequate. The municipal authorities have limited access to both regulation of ALMP measures and programs needed for the territories.

Nevertheless, regarding ALMPs in regions and municipalities, data from the first quarter of 2020 demonstrates that territorial inequalities are significant in terms of employment and disposable income (Figure 5.3).

According to the Central Bank of Lithuania (Lietuvos Bankas, 2021), labor market indicators significantly impact the structure of household disposable income in the regions. When it comes to disposable income per one household member, it should be noted that a larger proportion of employed persons ensures relatively higher disposable income in the respective region. A more modest situation develops in more rural regions, where the retirement age population comprises a relatively more significant proportion of the total population. It is also possible to observe that increasing disparities between regions are characterized by the economic development and growth of bigger cities and the economic decline of smaller regions. The main territorial challenges are a gap between less and more urbanized localities, supply and demand for the labor force, and structural discrepancies in different regions of Lithuania. In this respect, the ALMP measures should be more territorial driven.

With reference to the role of private actors and forms of public/private partnership, the Law on Employment Support of the Republic of Lithuania encourages cooperation between social partners via social partnership, tripartite contracts, an active role for employers in employment policies, employment projects, subsidies for new work positions, etc. Employers, NGOs, trade unions, and professional/formal/informal learning providers are essential partners in implementing ALMP measures.

The choices between municipal needs and territorial provision of activities: Active labor market in urban, suburban and rural cases

In this section, the territorial level policies related to ALMP in three municipalities of Kaunas city municipality (urban), Kaunas district municipality (suburban) and Pakruojis district municipality (rural) are presented. However, since the ALMP in Lithuania is highly consolidated, we do not consider all three localities separately.

As policy analysis and qualitative interviews with stakeholders from three localities demonstrate, the ALMP goes beyond the municipal level planning, and intervention policy as this area is centrally planned, controlled, and monitored. Therefore, innovative community practices, collaborations and local dilemmas in community and stakeholder involvement in the active labor market are rather limited.

The necessity to preserve a competitive edge within constrained labor supply conditions, according to the Ministry of Finances, urges Lithuanian industrial businesses to seek ways to boost labor productivity through modernization, automation, and more effective work processes (Lithuania's Economic Development Scenario 2018–2021, Ministry of Finances, 2018).

The Employment Services Office, controlled by the Ministry of Social Security and Labor, is responsible for ALMPs in the country, including Kaunas city, Kaunas district and Pakruojis district municipalities. Besides this Ministry, territorial offices of the Employment Services Office are responsible for this policy area. The definition of the Lithuanian Labor Exchange's functions evidences that territorial labor exchange offices function as non-autonomous units controlled by the Lithuanian Labor Exchange and are dependent on the decisions of the Ministry. Thus, ALMPs are centralized through the Employment Services Office; however, the Law on Employment Support of the Republic of Lithuania provides for the involvement of different-level institutions in these policies, i.e., various functions and responsibilities are divided among different national and local institutions. For example, municipal representatives are members of Tripartite Councils in the localities. In the case of rural Pakruojis, there is also a lesser availability of customer service in Pakruojis town. The regional Employment Services Office is based in Šiauliai, and is subordinate to headquarters in Vilnius. The public bodies of ALMP use standardized procedures and follow central office recommendations on implementing municipal ALMP measures and programs.

Nevertheless, the case of suburban Kaunas district municipality demonstrates that local authorities could indirectly foster employment in the locality. Kaunas district municipality is partially accountable for designing and implementing labor policies because the decisions of its Council and flexible tax policies are responsible for a large number of businesses and the low unemployment level. Included in these policies is the directive that newly established businesses do not have to pay land, land lease, and real estate taxes for three years.

With regard to the role of private actors and forms of public/private partnerships in localities, partnerships between local governance and social partners such as business owners and NGOs and academic experts are essential in implementing ALMP measures. Greater involvement of social partners, including businesses and NGOs and the stimulation of responsibility among potential employees and employers, should be encouraged. For example, according to the *Kaunas City Strategic Development Plan 2019–2021* (2015), '... in implementing the action programme of the development of human resources, it is sought to attract and keep people in the labor market, to encourage a more active life-long learning, to develop the labor force of the highest qualification and to perfect public administration.' However, it is difficult to trace the role of Tripartite councils in the localities. Business entities declare their demand for a labor force but often complain about the lack of professional qualifications of jobseekers and inefficient Employment Services Office programs for different groups of beneficiaries, for example, youngsters or long-term unemployed persons.

It has not been possible to retrieve the available data on funding ALMP programs for regional offices in analyzed localities. According to the Annual Report of Employment Service Office (2018), 130.1m. EUR was used for different employment services and programs in 2018, including 46.8m. EUR from the European Social Fund. The active labor market policies are financed by approximately 67.5m. EUR, which comprises 0.15 % of national GDP in 2018, more specifically the expenses for labor market services comprise 28.1m. EUR, for social companies – 31.3m. EUR (Annual Report of Employment Service Office, 2018).

The main ALMP changes at a municipal level are related to the reorganization of Employment Service Offices and the curtailing of local autonomy to regulate ALMP programs and measures. The variety of ALMP programs is standardized in all three localities; consequently, the municipal authorities only indirectly impact regulation of employment services, for example, the hosting of various public work programs.

Activities and services. As was noted in previous subchapters, there are no significant differences among ALMP institutions in terms of the beneficiaries, main goals and priorities, expenditures, and personnel requirements at a regional or municipal level. Therefore, the localities (rural, urban, and suburban municipalities) are involved in the ALMPs to a very limited degree. The low engagement of municipalities is related to the specificity of national legislation on implementing ALMPs coordinated by the National Employment Services Office. The Ministry of Social Security and Labor is responsible for all ALMPs and services provided in regional Employment Services Offices. The local municipalities enjoy very little autonomy in implementing the ALMP, other than suggesting the unemployment actions and measures needed for the local labor market; for example, the municipal administration can initiate the seasonal employment program for the municipal Employment service office. The Tripartite councils operate in many municipalities involving local authorities, business stakeholders, and municipal Employment Services Office representatives. The main activities, goals, and beneficiaries of ALMP institutions are defined in national legislation and applied in all national Employment Services Office networks.

The ALMP services supplied by local Employment Service offices include: (1) job postings and job seekers registration; (2) information; (3) counseling; (4) employability assessment; (5) recruitment mediation; and (6) personalized employment planning. According to the Employment Law, ALMP services must be offered to people who do not work, people who work under any sort of employment contract or on the basis of other legal contacts that are comparable to labor relations, self-employed people, people who are unable to work, and employers (Report, 2016, Government of the Republic of Lithuania).

The new Labor Code that entered into force on 1 July 2017 extended the area of application of the Law on Employment Support and service delivery by the Employment Office. The legislation has defined the organization and financing of the labor market services and employment support measures. For example, additional target groups of persons receiving added support in the labor market have been introduced: disabled persons of working age, unemployed persons who have not acquired any professional qualifications, the long-term unemployed under 25, and unemployed persons over 50 but within working age, amongst others. Such a novel method of classifying target groups is based on criteria that hinder their employment opportunities rather than on the relevant social status (Labor Code, 2017). In February 2018, the Labor Code was amended, allowing for the financing of vocational training for employees seeking to change both their profession and their employer. Individuals who seek to establish new job opportunities will profit from this expansion of the vocational training target group. However, due to widespread questionable practices by people avoiding payment for compulsory health insurance contributions, the measure of self-employment support - subsidies for registered individual activities under a business license – has been abandoned.

Given the ALMP structure, goals, targets, services, their territorial distribution and personnel (requirements and working conditions) are applied similarly in all territories. Indeed, the main goals and targets of ALMPs in localities are described in the overall strategy by the Employment Services Office. The main activities and targets are also defined by legislation and recommendations of the Ministry of Social Security and Labor. Kaunas region and Pakruojis district Employment Services Office provide centralized services comparable to the other regional offices. The offices are using the same centralized protocols for the activities and ALMP programs and the services are available to all beneficiaries.

In terms of personnel (requirements, working conditions), the staff in municipal Employment service offices are working under public employee condition. The national regulation defines the working conditions, the length of the contract, working hours, and remuneration system amongst other aspects. The central Office in Vilnius hires the personnel for the municipal Employment Service offices. The main differences between localities relate to ALMP users and service coverage.

Kaunas region and Pakruojis district Employment Services Office provide centralized services commensurate with the other regional offices and employ the same centralized protocols for the activities and ALMP programs. Concerning territorial distribution, the services are available to all beneficiaries. However, the rural municipality of Pakruojis district provides additional benefits for the unemployed in terms of transportation from the remote areas to the Office.

The staff in municipal Employment Service offices work under the same conditions as public employees. The national regulations define the working conditions, the length of the contract, working hours, and remuneration system amongst other aspects. The personnel for the municipal Employment Service Offices are hired by the Central Office in Vilnius (Užimtumo tarnyba, 2021).

Looking more specifically at analyzed urban case (Kaunas city municipality), the active labor market strategies formulated in the policy documents of Kaunas city municipality documents are described in terms similar to EU strategic documents and the dominant discourse on the highly educated and flexible workforce. It is possible to identify two distinct ways in which these problems are discussed in the policy documents. Firstly, the intention is to reduce unemployment and, secondly, to address structural problems in the labor market such as inadequate workforce education, professional training or, in other words, the lack of employability. Inadequate social services for the unemployed are also mentioned in the documents.

Furthermore, the documents identify the chief strategies to improve the labor market: increased investment in education and professional development; the creation of special training programs; investment in new enterprises; and improvement in social services so as to assist the workforce adjust to the labor market requirements. The changes in labor market participation could be achieved by investing in human resources development through continuous education and by strengthening the social service system for people at risk of social exclusion (Kaunas City Strategic Development Plan, 2019–2021).

Regarding labor market processes, the trends in Kaunas city development reflect the main trends and problems in Lithuania including slowly decreasing unemployment, and low income with concomitant economic migration. A significant level of unemployment reflects the general unemployment level in the country. Regarding low salaries, in 2014, gross salary remained significantly lower in Kaunas city compared to Vilnius and Klaipėda (by 17 % and 6 % respectively) (Statistics Lithuania, 2020). For this reason, Kaunas city lacks a competitive advantage in attracting a labor force from less economically developed territories in western or eastern Lithuania.

All regional Employment Services offices provide the same standard for ALMP programs and services for the same beneficiaries: unemployed persons in different age groups, long-term unemployed, qualification programs for the unemployed, entrepreneurship initiatives for youngsters and social enterprises, disabled people, etc. There are no particular access limitations to the ALMP services in the territories for disparate beneficiary groups.

Table 5.1. Registered unemployed, percentage from the working-age population in Kaunas city municipality (2012–2019).

Annual average of the registered unemployed, percentage from working age population									
Year	**2012**	**2013**	**2014**	**2015**	**2016**	**2017**	**2018**	**2019**	**2020**
Kaunas city municipality	10,6	9,6	8,2	7,3	6,7	7,2	8,6	8,8	9,6

Source: https://uzt.lt/en/market/statistical-indicators/.

Table 5.2. Coverage of users and services in Kaunas city municipality, 2020.

Local labor exchange and munici-palities	**Unemployed registered**		**Placed into job by the end of month (2020 03 30)**	**Referred to active labor market programs**	**Unemployment, percentage from working age population**		
	per month	**In total by the end of month (2020 03 30)**			**2020 02 01**	**2020 03 01**	**change +/–**
TOTAL of Lithuania	**21304**	**161594**	**28126**	**2212**	**9,2**	**9,4**	**0,2**
Kaunas county	***4324***	***33266***	***5581***	***366***	***9,4***	***9,7***	***0,3***
Kaunas city munici-pality	2168	16826	3135	141	9,4	9,7	0,3

Source: Employment Services Office (2020). https://uzt.lt/en/market/situation/.

In terms of the quantifiable reportage of users of ALMP programs and measures; from 2012 to 2020, the number of registered unemployed as a percentage of the working-age population in Kaunas city remained almost stable (approximately 9 % annually) (see Table 5.1).

The recent data from the Employment Services Office (2020) provides user profiles in terms of registered unemployed persons placed in job vacancies and participating in different ALMP programs. The data demonstrates that the total number of persons in ALMP programs is relatively low compared to the total registered unemployed (Table 5.2).

In implementing the ALMP policy at the municipal level, one of the main goals is to create more workplaces by creating new business centers while strengthening the old ones in the target territories of the Kaunas city municipality. An additional challenge related to the ALMPs in Kaunas city municipality is the underemployment of socially excluded groups such as formerly incarcerated persons, persons with various addictions and persons who have been subject to violence. Various Kaunas city strategic planning documents describe the labor market problems in terms of the need for a highly educated and flexible workforce. The municipality underlines that it is obligated to address structural problems of the labor market such as inadequate workforce education, professional training or, in other words, the scarcity of persons who are employable. Thus, the main policy strategies to improve the labor market include increased investment in education and professional development; the creation of special training programs; investment in new enterprises; and the improvement of social services that help the workforce to adjust to the labor market requirements (Kaunas City Strategic Development Plan 2019–2021; also see Integrated Territorial Development Program of Kaunas City, 2016).

The development of workforce capacities, greater involvement of social partners including business and NGOs and the stimulation of responsibility both among potential employees and employers, are mentioned in policy documents. Thus, the principle of partnership is emphasized in the policy documents: local governance, the Labor Exchange, NGOs and entrepreneurs should be involved in setting up plans for the employability of Kaunas inhabitants. Two additional discourses are manifest in the policy documents: the discourse on local governance as a partner in solving the labor market problems and the discourse on human capital, which requires investment (in education and life-long learning processes). To increase the employment capacity of the workforce, it is necessary to deal with the problems of the labor market, such as limited educational possibilities for the workforce and the absence of a comprehensive professional development system that would respond to the changing needs of the labor market. According to the *Kaunas City Strategic Development Plan 2019–2021* (2015), '… by implementing the action programme of the development of human resources, we seek to attract and keep people in the labor market, encourage a more active life-long learning approach, develop a highly qualified labor force and improve public administration.'

The relationship between central government, local governance, and socio-economic change in the city could either impede or encourage improvement of the labor market. In describing the labor market through a particular set of relations – between economic issues and local governance – the documents also point to the issue of regulation and the involvement of stakeholders. They emphasize the mechanisms of partnerships between local governance and social partners such as business owners and NGOs, and academic experts. As the *Program of Sustainable City Development* (2013) states, it is essential to 'to encourage the cooperation of business, the science community and local governance to develop scientific research, technologies and innovations.' The participation of citizens through surveys and other mechanisms is also envisioned in these policy documents. The active participation of citizens for their own good is considered desirable.

As the official website of **Kaunas district municipality** states, Kaunas district is a locality with favorable conditions for labor participation and business development (Kaunas district municipality 2021). The statistics demonstrate that unemployment was at its lowest during the past several years, and the number of small and middle-range businesses was the highest among most small municipalities. As of February of 2018, according to the data of the Lithuanian Labor Exchange, there were 7.4 % registered unemployed in Kaunas district municipality. From 2012 to 2020, the total number of registered unemployed consistently decreased by 16 % (Table 5.3). In 2018, there were 2073 small and middle-range businesses registered.

As the data in Table 5.4 demonstrates, the proportion of users in ALMP programs is very small compared to the overall number of registered unemployed persons. One of the reasons is the high level of employment and the number of SME businesses in the territory.

In Kaunas district municipality, high economic productivity and industrial investments in a suburban area are often emphasized because they influence and foster lower unemployment rates. The largest proportion of labor force supply is directly generated through inter-institutional agreements with universities in Kaunas and Vilnius. In this sense, the role of the National Labor Exchange Office and VET (only one vocational school in the suburban locality) is very fragmented and insignificant.

Table 5.3. Registered unemployed, percentage from the working-age population in Kaunas district municipality (2012–2019).

Annual average of the registered unemployed, percentage from working age population									
Year	**2012**	**2013**	**2014**	**2015**	**2016**	**2017**	**2018**	**2019**	**2020**
Kaunas district municipality	10,3	9,5	7,7	6,6	6,3	6,6	7,4	7,7,	8,2

Source: https://uzt.lt/en/market/statistical-indicators/.

Table 5.4. Coverage of users and services in Kaunas district municipality, 2020.

Local labor exchange and munici-palities	Unemployed registered		Placed into job by the end of month (2020 03 30)	Referred to active labor market programs	Unemployment, percentage from working age population		
	per month	In total by the end of month (2020 03 30)			2020 02 01	2020 03 01	change +/–
TOTAL of Lithuania	21304	161594	28126	2212	9,2	9,4	0,2
Kaunas county	*4324*	*33266*	*5581*	*366*	*9,4*	*9,7*	*0,3*
Kaunas district munici-pality	686	5083	885	63	8,1	8,3	0,2

Source: Employment Services Office (2020). https://uzt.lt/en/market/situation/.

Kaunas district municipality seeks to promote economic growth in the area, developing business support and informational systems. A further strategic goal is to promote cooperation between business, municipality and state institutions, and foster entrepreneurship and economic mobility. These priorities are indirectly related to the ALMP through fostering business initiatives and creating job placements.

However, the ALMPs are almost absent in suburban locality strategic documents. These policy areas are centrally planned and implemented, leaving very little functional discretion to the municipality. Economic competitiveness, entrepreneurship, and labor market problems overcome the boundaries of single elderships and are perceived as integral to district infrastructure development and resource mobilization. Moreover, the labor market resources are not considered an economic development priority which comes with municipal responsibility (Kaunas District Municipality Strategic Development Plan for 2013–2020, 2013).

Pakruojis district municipality encounters a similar challenge of depopulation and unemployment. Here the working-age population loses employment due to the centralization and optimization of the public sector (Labor Exchange Office, National Foresting Agency). However, the programs implemented by

Table 5.5. Registered unemployed, percentage from the working-age population in Pakruojis district municipality (2012–2019).

Annual average of the registered unemployed, percentage from working age population									
Year	**2012**	**2013**	**2014**	**2015**	**2016**	**2017**	**2018**	**2019**	**2020**
Pakruojis district municipality	11,2	11,5	9,9	9,5	8,9	8,8	8,6	8,0	10,0

Source: https://uzt.lt/en/market/statistical-indicators/.

Table 5.6. Coverage of users and services in Pakruojis district municipality, 2020.

Local labor exchange and munici-palities	**Unemployed registered**		**Placed into job by the end of month (2020 03 30)**	**Referred to active labor market programs**	**Unemployment, percentage from working age population**		
	per month	**In total by the end of month (2020 03 30)**			**2020 02 01**	**2020 03 01**	**change +/–**
TOTAL of Lithuania	**21304**	**161594**	**28126**	**2212**	**9,2**	**9,4**	**0,2**
Šiauliai county	***2061***	***15904***	***2422***	***224***	***9,6***	***9,9***	***0,3***
Pakruojis	140	1166	157	11	9,7	10,2	0,5

Source: Employment Services Office (2020). https://uzt.lt/en/market/situation/.

the regional Office of National Labor Exchange differ from the local needs and cannot respond to the socio-demographic changes.

The Employment Services Office data demonstrates that the average percentage of registered unemployed in Pakruojis district municipality was stable between 2012 and 2020 (9,5 %) (Table 5.5). Further data on ALMP beneficiaries indicates that the number of persons involved in ALMP programs is even smaller than the overall number of registered unemployed (Table 5.6).

Although the ALMPs are marginal in the strategic planning documents of Pakruojis district municipality, the dearth of working-age population and skilled workers is recognized as one of the principal territorial disadvantages. The *Pakruojis Strategic Development Plan for 2014–2020* acknowledges that the main territorial problems are demographic decline, limited working-age population, dependency on social benefits, insufficient public infrastructure and roads: 'the unsatisfactory condition of the roads and streets limits business development and increases social exclusion,' therefore, 'the geographical location is a disadvantageous factor that affects the attractiveness of investments in the [Pakruoiis] territory.'

The 2014–2020 Pakruojis Region Strategic Development Plan (2014) includes stimulating the development and support of business and agriculture. Among the strategic measures, the implementation of a campaign supporting businesses and entrepreneurship and creating a business-friendly environment in Lithuania and Latvia's border region are mentioned. The encouragement of entrepreneurship and small and middle-size businesses is also essential in order to lower unemployment and foster efficient labor policies in rural localities (also see Pakruojis Local Action Strategy for 2014–2020, 2015; and Pakruojis Strategic Action Plan 2019–2021, 2018).

However, in the case of Pakruojis district municipality, it is also essential to bear in mind that programs that require the intervention of the ALMP go beyond the municipal level. Following the reorganization and optimization of the national Labor Exchange Agency in 2018, the Pakruojis municipal labor exchange agency became a branch of Šiauliai regional agency with limited autonomous functions. Consequently, little attention has been paid to ALMP.

Moreover, the central government control authority of the ALMPs cannot guarantee that the municipality would be able to access decisions about interventions in territorial development problems. The local capital mobilization and economic growth approach interferes with the diverse interests of local stakeholders, primarily via formal institutionalized forms of intervention (associations, boards or municipal councils). Therefore, the well-balanced local mechanism involving agreements, considerations and cooperation should be maintained as a substitute for the 'traditional' top-down governance model. However, this mechanism is more intentional than actually practiced.

Similarities and differences among the three case studies

Looking at the ALMP policy in three different municipalities, it is possible to summarize their similarities and differences. The ALMP policy is highly consolidated in the country. In most cases, the differences are not very significant.

As previously specified, the ALMPs go beyond municipal level planning and intervention policy since these areas are centrally planned, controlled, and monitored. Usually, ALMP measures are indirectly incorporated into the

Table 5.7. Similarities and differences in ALMP policies in three localities.

	Localities	Characteristics
Similarities	Kaunas city municipality (urban) Kaunas district municipality (suburban) Pakruojis district municipality (rural)	1. Centralized and consolidated approach to ALMP measures and programs and no clear traces of responding to local labor market needs. 2. Dependence on the EU funding mechanism for different ALMP measures. 3. Low support for entrepreneurship and self-employment programs for different beneficiaries. 4. No clear traces of relationships between local labor market needs and the implementation of specific ALMP measures, for example, entrepreneurships programs are provided only for youngsters. 5. Low participation of social and business stakeholders in Employment Services Office boards and municipal Tripartite councils. 6. Modification of training and qualification programs adopted to local labor market needs.
Differences	Kaunas city municipality (urban)	1. More active role of the Kaunas city Tripartite council. 2. Low level of inter-institutional cooperation and engagement in local policy agenda on labor market needs, professional skills and re-shaping qualifications. 3. Different measures and programs for entrepreneurships and SME provided by local authorities, for example, the establishment of working co-spaces and hubs.
	Kaunas district municipality (suburban)	6. Low participation of the beneficiaries in ALMP programs. 7. Low engagement in recognizing local needs and advantages. 8. Favorable economic climate and active labor market for different professional groups. 9. Different measures and programs for entrepreneurships and SME provided by local authorities.
	Pakruojis district municipality (rural)	6. Low participation of the beneficiaries in ALMP programs. 7. Negative impact of demographic decline and spatial remoteness that shape the profile of ALMP policy beneficiaries (long-term unemployed, unskilled unemployed, pre-retirement persons, lower participation of youngsters in entrepreneurship programs by Pakruojis Employment Services Office).

overall strategic planning documents on the economic development of three municipalities.

With regards to vertical and horizontal coordination of implementing ALMPs, the Ministry of Finances underlines the need to maintain a competitive advantage under limited labor supply conditions in order to encourage the Lithuanian industrial enterprises to search for ways to increase labor productivity through modernization, automation and more effective work processes (Lithuania's Economic Development Scenario 2018–2021, 2018). The document draws attention to the risks of a limited labor supply, particularly relevant to Kaunas city and Pakruojis district municipality.

Although the ALMPs are not considered as a priority in the list of municipal responsibilities, a variety of policy documents related to all three cases identify the main strategies to improve the labor market: increased investment in education and professional development; the creation of special training programs; investment in new enterprises; and the improvement of social services that help the workforce to adjust to the labor market requirements. At the national level, the regional economic policy mainly focuses on supporting entrepreneurship, SME's development and investment policy, which directly affects labor market intensity and economic productivity at the regional level. It could be argued that as a consequence of central control and monitoring, the dimension of vertical coordination dominates in the coordination of ALMPs.

Despite centrally controlled labor market policies, some policy documents related to all three municipalities declaratively indicate the importance of a variety of stakeholders in implementing active labor market strategies. The example of Kaunas city municipality is illustrative in this regard. The policy documents related to Kaunas city municipality consistently mention the development of workforce capacities, greater involvement of social partners including business and NGOs and the stimulation of responsibility both among potential employees and employers. Thus, the principle of partnership is emphasized in the policy documents: local governance, the Labor Exchange, NGOs and entrepreneurs should be involved in the process of setting up plans for employability of Kaunas inhabitants.

To increase the employment capacity of the workforce it is necessary to deal with the problems of the labor market, such as limited educational possibilities and the lack of a comprehensive professional development system that would respond to the changing needs of the labor market. The same policy discourses on the involvement of social stakeholders in labor market policies apply to Kaunas district and Pakruojis district municipalities. Here the joint actions of different stakeholders, particularly local businesses, are considered a significant stimulus to mobilizing labor force capital and improving labor market efficiency.

In all three cases; Kaunas city, Kaunas district and Pakruojis district municipalities, territorialized collective actions are implied in policy documents by pointing to the process of forging partnerships between local governance and social partners such as business owners and NGOs and academic experts. For instance, policy documents related to Kaunas city municipality state that it is important to encourage the cooperation of business, the science community and local governance in the development of scientific research, technologies and innovations. The participation of citizens in contributing to the formation of ALMPs through surveys and other mechanisms is also envisioned in these policy documents. The active participation of citizens for their own good is considered desirable.

However, because of the dependence of ALMPs on EU and central government funding, strategies related to the labor market are somewhat uniform and lack diversity. It could also be argued that collective actions in the field of both labor market policies and strategies are not sufficiently territorialized in the Lithuanian policy documents related to all three analyzed cases. The central government control authority of ALMPs cannot guarantee the access of three municipalities to effect interventions with regard to territorial development problems. Moreover, ALMPs reflect the increasing centralization and cost optimization tendencies.

National active labor market priorities and options for social investment strategy

The ALMP is typically divided into training, employment subsidies, public work programs, and activation, i.e., increasing incentives for participation in the labor market. The positive aspects of ALMP include improvement and acquisition of skills demanded by the labor market and less uncertainty regarding employee suitability. The negative impact might be related to the fact that job search intensity may decrease when individuals participate in a public employment program and receive benefits, as in the Lithuanian case.

In general, the ALMP system in Lithuania encounters various problems related to the effectiveness of ALMP measures and programs; targeting the beneficiaries, responding to labor market needs and consolidating policy pressures. At a municipal level, improvement of the labor market is often discussed in terms of supporting business, creating new jobs, and life-long learning. The analysis of the ALMP field also points to an increase in the system's capacity and a necessity for a more precise definition of the priorities for SI strategy.

Greater attention should be paid to the upgrading of professional skills and adult learning. Given the degree of skills upgrade needed in Lithuania, the recent increase in training disbursement is welcome and should continue. With 40 % of the unemployed in 2018 without professional qualification, the 3 % of the participation rate in training is inadequate. Training and retraining programs will directly address the issue of the over-supply of low-skilled workers for which there is no additional demand. Participation rules could be adapted to allow for extended programs and those that require expensive equipment to increase the participation of low-skilled, older workers and workers in rural areas (Ministry of Social Security and Labor, 2020).

Beneficiaries should participate to a greater extent in SI strategy. Currently, almost 60 % of the unemployed persons registered annually received additional support in the labor market; one in four was older than 50 years of age (25.5 %). One in three unemployed persons lived in a rural area (31.4 %). Women accounted for 44.5 % and men for 55.5 % of all registered unemployed persons in 2018. In 2019, 8.6 % of all women of working age were without employment (Ministry of Social Security and Labor, 2020). The ALMP measures and programs should cover a wide range of unemployed groups and clients. For example, employees who lose their jobs are often more likely to be working in declining industries or services in crisis, may take longer to obtain a new job, and can experience professional skill challenges and wage reductions once re-employed. The ALMP must be a key element in improving the employability of different age groups such as older workers or pre-retirement age groups, and particularly those who are vulnerable due to job displacement. The ALMP should encourage employees to remain in the labor market, foster hiring, support job-search assistance and improve matching by using the assistance of regional Employment Services Offices.

Lithuania's economic and labor market performance has been strong in recent years. Strong economic development resulted in lower overall and long-term unemployment rates, while the proportion of the economically active population and employment levels hit new highs. Despite this, disparities in employment continue across regions and skill levels. The data demonstrates that in 2019 the largest number of working-age persons registered as unemployed lived in the rural municipalities of Lazdijai (15.7 %), Kelmė (15.3 %) and Zarasai (14.8 %) (Ministry of Social Security and Labor, 2020). Due to the unfavorable ratio between supply and demand of the labor force in different urban and rural regions, the small number of active economic entities and a slow development of local economies, territorial inequalities have been increasing. These inequalities point to the economic development and growth of bigger cities, the economic decline of smaller regions, and the lack of territorial cohesion in the latter. A regional diversity and adaptability of ALMP measures and programs is necessary. Also, despite its increase in 2018, the gender employment gap remains one of the lowest in the EU. The Employment Service Office implemented the pilot project to respond to the disparities in different regions and individual needs of the job seekers (introduced in 2018) in six different municipalities. This pilot project aimed to facilitate the transition of the long-term unemployed from unemployment to employment and harmonize employment promotion and motivation services through active social assistance services.

It should also be noted that a sound national strategy for territorial development that would include the use of ALMP instruments is still absent in Lithuania. The ineffectiveness of national and cohesion policy investments is hampered by the lack of a cohesive regional development vision and 'space aware' planning documents, as these are often driven by national sectoral priorities and do not necessarily provide for regional and local development needs (Country Report Lithuania, 2020). The significant emphasis on regional development in the draft national development programme for 2021–2030, which incorporates regional and territorial aspects as vertical and horizontal priorities across all policy areas, is a positive step forward (2021–2030 Draft National Development Programme, 2021).

As regards changes in consolidating the networks of public services, the ALMPs are implemented in a somewhat centralized manner in Lithuania, and this means of governance does not provide for regional specificity and sensitivity to regional issues. The restructuring of the Lithuanian Labor Exchange as an Employment Office came into being in 2018 and affected ALMP. The regional and municipal Employment Services offices are the most active bodies in this area. Although territorial Labor Exchange offices exist in municipalities, they are controlled by the headquarters of the Employment Services Office in Vilnius that monitors the standardized ALMP measures and projects. Thus, although the cooperation between different stakeholders such as employers, NGOs, trade unions, and professional/formal/informal learning providers is encouraged by the Lithuanian laws, it remains deficient in implementing employment policies.

Lithuania lacks sustainable financial measures for low-skill employment. The situation indicates that about 34.3 % of unemployed persons applying to employment services have no vocational training, and in 2018 15.6 % had not worked for more than two years (Ministry of Social Security and Labor, 2020). The financing mechanisms of most ALMP measures since 2008 have been dependent on EU funds, which remain crucial. As our previous analysis demonstrates, the total proportion of public funding for different ALMP programs is one of the lowest in the OECD countries. Spending on ALMPs could be increased with funding stabilized and secured by predictable and reliable public resources. In this regard, the scope and dimension of the ALMP programs should not be linked to European funds and the funding level should be responsive to cyclical developments in the labor market.

Conclusion

In summary, it is possible to argue that the fact that the ALMPs are dependent mainly on central government and EU funding does not allow for significant diversity in choosing these strategies or for the active involvement of different stakeholders in these strategies. The improvement of the labor market is discussed largely in terms of supporting business, creating new jobs, and life-long learning, but does not indicate any innovative practices or specific collaborations that could be beneficial in overcoming the labor market problems, combating unemployment and creating new jobs.

ALMP goes beyond the municipal level planning and intervention policy since this area is centrally planned, controlled, and monitored. Municipal capacity for ALMP implementation is fragmented and limited. Therefore, innovative community practices, collaborations and the involvement of local communities and stakeholders in the ALMPs are rather episodically implemented than systematically organized. The performance of local municipalities remains weaker due to its limited ability to ensure the necessary resources for ALMP implementation and ensure a sustainable relationship with territorial cohesion policies. In this respect, the recent ALMP changes demonstrate a decreasing input of municipalities in the regulation of labor market needs, for example, the reorganization of Employment Service Offices into one central office and reduction of local autonomy to regulate the need for programs and measures in the ALMP field. The variety of ALMP programs are standardized in all three localities in which the municipal authorities exert only a low-level indirect impact in regulating employment services, for example, the hosting of various public work programs. The ALMP standardization trend is mainly related to national cost efficiency and resource optimization rather than other factors, e.g., conflicts between municipalities and national authorities.

Thus, in Lithuania, the system of ALMP measures consists of support for learning, work mobility, employment and job creation. The policy goals on supporting learning include vocational training (in cooperation with VET schools in organizing formal learning for adults), employment under an apprenticeship contract, internship, and recognition of non-formal and informal learning competencies. At the national level, the ALMP measures are combined and applied in an integrated manner.

In summarizing the analysis, it is possible to list the main priorities in the local policy agenda for developing the ALMP field in terms of targeting users, increasing accessibility and quality and participation of stakeholders in defining local needs. The priorities reflect the main goals of SI approach.

(1) **A need for ALMP measures for early interventions**. Early interventions can increase the likelihood of re-employment, for instance, through job search assistance which is often relatively cost-effective. Either way, this requires a balance of active and passive support for the unemployed which could facilitate re-employment with better outcomes and skill upgrading. It calls for targeted policy actions to gradually shift the economy towards higher value-added activities, especially in the service sector. Meanwhile, it is crucial that this transformation process is accompanied by policy measures to improve employment quality and skill profiles, which is one of the main drivers of sustainable long-term productivity growth.
(2) **Financing system for low-skilled employment**. Currently, Lithuania expends very little on ALMP programs and projects in comparison to other EU countries. Recent ALMP spending in Lithuania is at just over 0.2 % of GDP (2018) and is significantly less than the EU-28 average (0,7 % on average) (OECD, 2019). To meet the growing demand for better ALMP services, the Employment Services Office needs to be adequately resourced. Further, the importance of employment subsidies in ALMPs should decrease. Given the challenges regarding the large number of low-skilled unemployed and the lower effectiveness of employment subsidies discussed above, these should be directed towards the most disadvantaged groups (i.e., those unlikely to find a job in their absence), and additional resources should be channeled towards training programs.
(3) **Adult learning and recognition of competencies** is one of the ALMP aims, which helps sustain and increase the employability of different beneficiary groups. Adult learning measures play a fundamental role in addressing any initial inequalities in formal education qualifications and can address skill deficiencies; however, individuals need to be upgraded throughout their lives. While training should be tailored as much as possible to correspond to different professional skills and regional needs for the local labor market, special attention is necessary to target older cohorts in regions with

demographic decline. The recognition of competencies acquired through non-formal and informal learning is intended to test the knowledge, skills and abilities of individuals seeking to obtain a diploma or certificate of competence for the relevant professional qualification and be re-employed within the field of a new recognized professional qualification or competence.

(4) **Fostering regional and municipal initiatives**. Initiatives in implementing the ALMPs at the municipal level are likely to reduce territorial inequalities and promote social cohesion. The ALMP programs and measures should also address an increasing centralization of national labor policy, reduction of regional autonomy and standardization of management and consequent effects on the ALMPs.

(5) **Social dialogue**. Active collaboration with the social partners, further education in the workplace and the sharing of best practice among employers could also be helpful. In Lithuania, social dialogue occurs within the National Tripartite Council and municipal Tripartite Councils which, however, do not necessarily operate in each municipality. Therefore, it is necessary to more comprehensively discuss the ALMP measures that support learning, mobility, employment subsidies and support for new workplace positions. Local initiatives and partnerships with different stakeholders to assist people in acquiring employment and strengthen the service sector in the regions with the highest unemployment level, should also be encouraged.

(6) **More active implementation of apprenticeship programs**. This measure could be attractive because practical training takes place in the actual workplace (in the production plant or organization), while the initial theoretical knowledge underpinning the practical skills are acquired at an educational institution. This program was introduced in 2018 but has not been actively implemented. However, it could strengthen the cooperation between labor supply, training, educational institutions and local business needs.

(7) **Development of the Youth Employment Centers** for targeted young unemployed groups. The measure would link the vocational guidance of youth (young women and men) with occupations in demand in the labor market with their career opportunities to reduce the occupational and labor market segregation by gender and age.

These strategic goals should not only be incorporated into the municipal documents on economic growth, but also be considered as immediate goals for territorially driven ALMP. National sectoral priorities that do not necessarily satisfy regional and territorial development needs are often to blame for a lack of a coherent regional development strategy and a deficiency in the effectiveness of national and cohesion policy initiatives. A positive step forward would be a strong emphasis on regional development in the recently approved *2021–2030 National Development Programme*, which integrates regional and territorial aspects both as vertical and horizontal priorities across all policy sectors (White Papers on Lithuania Regional Development for 2017–2030, 2017) and the new *Government Program for 2020–2024* (2020). This would likely open political discussion on expanding the responsibilities of municipalities and regional Councils to contribute more actively to ALMP issues and could potentially lead to a reconsideration of the principles of subsidiarity, proportionality and financial compensation for new obligations imposed on local municipalities in implementing ALMP measures.

References

2021–2030 Draft National Development Programme. (2021). Government of the Republic of Lithuania. Available at https://www.esinvesticijos.lt/uploads/main/documents/files/Post%202020/2_%20LRVK_NPP.pdf (Accessed 15 September 2021).

Annual Report of Employment Services Office. (2019). Vilnius. Available: https://uzt.lt/wp-content/uploads/2019/07/2018-m.-veiklos-ataskaita.pdf.pdf (Accessed 14 June 2021).

Country Report Lithuania 2020. (2020). European Commission. Commission Staff Working Document. Accompanying the document Communication from the Commission to the European Parliament, the European Council, the Council, the European Central Bank and the Eurogroup. 2020 European Semester: Assessment of progress on structural reforms, prevention and correction of macroeconomic imbalances, and results of in-depth reviews under Regulation (EU) No 1176/2011. Brussels, Belgium. Available at https://eur-lex.europa.eu/legal-content/EN/TXT/?qid=1584543810241&uri=CELEX%3A52020SC0514 (Accessed 12 December 2021).

Description of the Conditions and Procedure for the Implementation of the Employment Support Measures. (2017). Available at. https://e-seimas.lrs.lt/portal/legalActEditions/lt/TAD/7a621d00602b11e7a53b83ca0142260e (Accessed 15 July 2021).

Esping-Andersen, G., Gallie, D., Hemerijck, A., and J. Myles (2002). *Why we need a new welfare state*. Oxford: Oxford University Press Government Program for 2020–2024. (2020). Available at https://lrv.lt/uploads/main/documents/files/PROGRAMME%20OF%20THE%20EIGHTEENTH%20GOVERNMENT%20OF%20THE%20REPUBLIC%20OF%20LITHUANIA.pdf (Accessed 15 September 2021).

IMF Country Report No. 5/139. (2021). Available at https://www.elibrary.imf.org/view/journals/002/2021/139/article-A000-en.xml (Accessed 10 August 2021).

IMF Country Report No. 18/185. (2018). Available at https://www.elibrary.imf.org/view/journals/002/2018/185/article-A000-en.xml (Accessed 10 August 2021).

Integrated Territorial Development Program of Kaunas City. (2016). Approved in 2016 January 15, No.1V-32, last amendment 2019 February 21, Ministry of Interior of Republic of Lithuania.

Kaunas City Strategic Development Plan 2019–2021. (2015). (previous versions from 2012), approved in 2015 April 2, No. T-127, Kaunas city municipality. Available at: http://www.kaunas.lt/wp-content/uploads/sites/8/2015/03/t157127planaspatvirtintas.pdf (Accessed 30 June 2021).

Kaunas District Municipality Strategic Development Plan for 2013–2020. (2013). Kaunas district municipality. Available at: https://www.krs.lt/media/2553/2013-06-27plus01-1mplusts-256-1.pdf (Accessed 30 June 2021).

Labour Code of the Republic of Lithuania. (2017). Available at https://e-seimas.lrs.lt/portal/legalAct/lt/TAD/da9eea30a61211e8aa33fe8f0fea665f?positionInSearchResults=0&searchModelUUID=6a53d828-eda2-4945-a9fb-6ce37316f0cf%20f (Accessed 10 August 2021).

Lietuvos Bankas. (2021). Darbo rinka. Available at https://www.lb.lt/lt/darbo-rinka#ex-1-1 (Accessed 14 June 2021).

Lietuvos investuotojų pasitikėjimo indeksas. (2019). Available at https://investorsforum.lt/wp-content/uploads/2019/12/Q4_2019_LIPI.pdf (Accessed 14 June 2021).

Lithuania's Economic Development Scenario 2018–2021. (2018). Ministry of Finances. Available at https://finmin.lrv.lt/uploads/finmin/documents/files/ERS%20aprasymas%202018-03-21_EN.pdf (Accessed 30 June 2021).

Lithuanian Central bank. Lithuanian Economic Review. (March 2019). Report on Lithuanian Economy. Available at https://www.lb.lt/en/publications/lithuanian-economic-review-march-2019 (Accessed 14 June 2021).

Living and Working in Lithuania 2021. (2021). *Living and working in Lithuania*. Eurofound. European Foundation for the Improvement of Living and Working Conditions. Available at https://www.eurofound.europa.eu/country/lithuania#background (Accessed 12 December 2021).

Magnusson, L., & Pascual, A. (2007). *Reshaping welfare states and activation regimes in Europe*. Bruxelles: P.I.E-Peter Lang S.A.

Ministry of Economy of the Republic of Lithuania. (2020). Lithuania's labour productivity assessment. Available at: https://eimin.lrv.lt/uploads/eimin/documents/files/LPA%202019_EN.pdf (Accessed 30 August 2021).

Ministry of Social Security and Labour information (2020). 2019 metų veiklos ataskaita (Annual Report for 2019). https://socmin.lrv.lt/uploads/socmin/documents/files/ataskaitos/sadm/SADM%202019%20metu%20veiklos%20ataskaita%20-02_25.pdf (Accessed 24 June 2021).

Morel, N., Palier, B., & Palme, J. (2012). *Towards a social investment state? Ideas, policies and challenges*. Bristol: Policy Press.

Müller, T., Vandaele, K., & Waddington, J. (Eds.). (2019). *Collective bargaining in Europe: Towards an endgame*. Brussels: European Trade Union Institute.

OECD Economic Surveys, Lithuania. (2019). Available at http://www.oecd.org/economy/lithuania-economic-snapshot/ (Accessed 15 September 2021).

OECD Labour Force Statistics. (2020). Available at https://www.oecd-ilibrary.org/employment/oecd-labour-force-statistics_23083387 (Accessed 14 June 2021).

Pakruojis Local Action Strategy for 2014–2020. (2015). Approved in 2015, Pakruojis Local Action Board. Available at http://www.pakruojovvg.lt/upload/Pakruojo_rajono_2014-2020_m._vietos_pltros_strategija_pakeitimas_2018_10_18.pdf (Accessed 14 August 2021).

Pakruojis Strategic Action Plan 2019–2021. (2018). Approved in 2018 December 20, No.T-300, Pakruojis district council. Available at http://www.pakruojis.lt/go.php/Strateginis%20veiklos%20planas743 (Accessed 14 August 2021).

Pakruojis Strategic Development Plan for 2014–2020. (2014). Approved in 2014 April 24, No.T-166, Pakruojis district council. Available at http://www.pakruojis.lt/go.php/Strateginis%20veiklos%20planas743 (Accessed 14 August 2021).

Report 2016, Government of the Republic of Lithuania. (2016). *Report for the period ending June 2016 by the Government of the Republic of Lithuania on the Employment Policy Convention*, 1964 (No. 122) (ratification registered on 03 March 2004). Available at https://socmin.lrv.lt/uploads/socmin/documents/files/ataskaitos/ratifikuotu%20konvenciju%20taikymas/2019/C122.pdf (Accessed 12 December 2021).

Statistics Lithuania. (2020). Employment statistics. Available at https://osp.stat.gov.lt/darbo-rinka-lietuvoje-2020/tyrimai (Accessed at 30 August 2021).

Statistics Lithuania. (2021). Unemployment statistics. Available at https://osp.stat.gov.lt/en/gyventoju-uzimtumo-tyrimo-duomenys (Accessed 30 August 2021).

Užimtumo tarnyba. (2021). Available at https://www.ldb.lt/LDBPortal/Pages/ServicesForEmployees.aspx?pageId=0aa389b9-32d6-4622-935e-8c2da48cbbd8 (Accessed 30 June 2021).

White Papers on Lithuania Regional Development for 2017–2030. (2017). Approved at the 15 December 2017 meeting of the National Regional Development Council. Available at https://vrm.lrv.lt/uploads/vrm/documents/files/ENG_versija/Lithuanian%20Regional%20Policy%20(White%20Paper).pdf (Accessed 15 September 2021).

Jurga Bučaitė-Vilkė

Chapter 6 Social investment and vocational education and training policy: The architecture of combining national standardization and territorial needs

Abstract: Lithuanian vocational education and training (VET) policy exemplifies highly consolidated policy elements that reveal the specific relationship between state authorities and municipalities in connecting professional education with labor market needs. This chapter offers a summary of the main challenges facing the implementation of a national VET system at municipal level. We argue whether the institutional architecture of top-down policy design could be responsive to social, demographic, and economic inequalities at a local level. We take a close look at state subsidy expenditure, vertical and horizontal governance, stakeholder participation, and policy realization (through infrastructure and services) that provides a comprehensive perspective on national VET policy in relation to social investment policy paradigms. Particular attention is given to urban, suburban and rural municipal cases and their approach to vocational education which is explored together with the national policy regulations.

Keywords: vocational education and training policy (VET), professional qualifications, municipality, territorial differences, policy design.

Introduction

Academic and political interest in vocational education and training (VET) has increased in recent years as a response to unpredictable shifts in labor market and economic development. While there have been are some efforts to develop private VET services provision, e.g., training vouchers or levy-grant schemes, the dominant perspective underlines the central authority's jurisdiction and responsibility for developing formal and informal qualifications in vocational training. Together with the VET policy discourse stipulated in many internationally acclaimed reports by supra-national organizations (e.g., World Bank, OECD, the WTO, European Training Foundation (ETF)), two main arguments explain VET policy importance. Firstly, training leads to productivity and economic growth (training for growth). Secondly, development of necessary/required skills leads to employability (skills for work) (Anderson, 2009). Over the past twenty years, several major policy tools were implemented to sustain the direction of economic growth and employability: (1) systematic and sectoral governance reforms to further empower employers and foster more responsive education, (2) vertical and horizontal qualification frameworks including the accreditation of informal and non-formal learning, (3) a quality assurance system, (4) new funding mechanisms that are more outcomes-oriented and (5) increased autonomy for public providers so as to allow the voice of other stakeholders to be heard and further empower decision-making (McGrath, 2012, 625). Much educational research is conducted which attempts to conceptualize vocational qualification frameworks across countries that are needed to develop systematic VET policy tools (Young, 2005; Valk, 2009; Chakroun, 2010). A number of the academic debates underline the relevance of vocational competences and qualifications considered as the main instrument for VET policy frameworks (Tuck, 2007). It is argued that vocational qualification frameworks provide different long-term outcomes for national VET systems, including curriculum, involvement of social stakeholders, learning standards, assessment and monitoring, and cross-border recognition of qualifications (Grootings, 2007, Pilz, 2016). These national systems represent different welfare paradigms and approaches to the relations between labor market, economies, skills, and education (Dobins and Busemeyer, 2015; Pilz et al., 2017). In discussing these policy approaches adopted by different countries, the impact of socio-economic inequalities for implementation of VET policy is not a major consideration, especially with respect to territorial variations and disparities. Among the educational implications that determine qualifications, alternative debate is necessary to broaden the goals and targets of national VET policy frameworks.

In Lithuanian academic debates, VET policy has been analyzed as a part of the national education system, for example, reflecting on /considering the national policy reforms and policy response to labor market and economic development needs (Zelvys, 2004). The research underlines the need for vocational competences and national curriculum development (Laužackas et al., 2009, Tūtlys & Spūdytė, 2011; Vaitkute, 2016; Vaitkute et al., 2019; Tūtlys, Vaitkute, 2021), quality development of vocational training content and national policy response (Saniter & Tūtlys, 2016; Tūtlys et al., 2018) as well as development of national VET systems from the historical perspective (Saniter & Tūtlys, 2016). However, the question of the VET policy design as a response to territorial-driven social investment (SI) approach is insufficiently researched.

From the perspective of Social Investment (SI) policy, VET has been recognized as a field that contributes to resolving the puzzling problem of labor market integration and (re)production of socio-economic inequalities. It is argued that vocational education and apprenticeship-based policies focus on important training and educational components that contribute to a high-skilled labor market. The links with the labor market identify the strong functional interdependence between competencies and economic returns (Kazepov & Ranci, 2016). Qualifications in education and training directly affect work productivity and foster labor market integration for young people (Bosch, 2010; Morel et al., 2012). Additionally, Kazepov and Ranci (2016) point out that options for requalification and higher-skilled jobs could inevitably contribute to minimizing social exclusion as well (Kazepov & Ranci, 2016).

In our chapter, we focus on the VET policy that is analyzed from the Social Investment policy perspective. The Social investment policy approach underlines the importance of the connection between welfare state arrangements and the use of different resources in providing public services at different governmental scale (Kazepov, 2010; Martinelli et al., 2018). It is obvious that the VET system is deeply embedded within the national labor market and educational systems. Moreover, the spatial inequalities and regional trajectories in terms of multiscale territorial indicators, from employment and income to demography, education and public health, should likewise be considered in policy formation (Dijkstra, 2017; Iammarino et al., 2018). At this point, place-sensitive strategies would combine both territorial inequality indicators and growth-stimulating policy response to socio-economic development. It is important to focus on a few policy formation aspects that include SI policy perspective in the VET field, but also consider socio-economic factors (Hemerijck, 2017). Firstly, we should consider the VET policy return in terms of the institutional setting where the policy is regulated and implemented at national level (institutional framework). Secondly, policy returns that include public expenditure, participation, attainment, and policy realization (infrastructure and services) are important. Thirdly, VET contributes to wider socio-economic outcomes, for example, access to the labor market, employment, economic productivity, and income inequalities on a regional scale.

In the case of Lithuania, it is important to consider where VET policy is situated with regard to institutional design and its response to territorial needs that require a specific context-based response. The main question posed here is if there is any complementarity between national VET policy design and territorial needs. Can we draw the guidelines for more territorial-sensitive VET policy reflecting the territorial inequalities? This chapter presents the case of VET policy in Lithuania that exemplifies efforts to re-define the role of vocational training as more territorial-driven. The analysis reveals the aspects of the institutional setting: division of responsibilities between central authorities and municipal level, policy goals, planning, beneficiaries, expenditures, role of private actors, services provision. In the Lithuanian case, the VET system is highly consolidated at national level. The national standardization approach to vocational education informs the educational content, defines the need for professional skills and details the requirements for teachers. The municipalities do not have adequate functional discretion in implementing, managing, and supervising the VET system. This chapter employs the empirical data on VET policy instruments implemented in three different municipalities: urban, suburban and rural.

Designing standardization in vocational training: National framework and targets

VET policy goals, priorities, and beneficiaries. An insight into the national Lithuanian VET policy design and institutional setting reveals how the national vocational education and training has been embedded within the broader education and labor market policy context. The Welfare regimes approach differentiates between the VET systems in the various countries with reference to the dimensions of labor market, family policy arrangements, educational content and school-work transition (Vogel, 2002; Pastore, 2015). Referring to the Central European approach to work-based VET, the system and its curriculum should respond to the needs of the labor market. For decades, work related competences and functional analysis of occupations were understood as a basis for developing national VET systems (Tūtlys & Vaitkutė, 2021). The Anglo-Saxon approach was widely used in defining the national policy goals that emphasize skill formation and response to a dynamic labor market. However, the VET policy response to territorial needs as well as contextual factors were not utilized for policy interventions. If we look at the division of responsibility among different administrative levels, the VET system reflects the consolidated policy setting approach whereby central authorities enforce the policy design at lower tiers. Organization of the VET system is regulated by the following principal legal acts: Law on Vocational Education and Training (2018), Orders of the Minister of Education, Science and Sport: Description of Formal Vocational Education and Training Curriculum (2012), General Plan of the Vocational Education and Training Curriculum for the 2017–2018 and 2018–2019 (2017), Procedure for Consecutive Learning in Accordance with General Education Curricula (2012), Conceptual Framework of Non-Traditional Education (2010) as well as other important acts. VET is attributed to ISCED level 4 in Lithuania. As stipulated in the Constitution of the Republic of Lithuania (1992), compulsory education is regarded as completed at the end of lower secondary education (ISCED level 2). Subsequently, graduates can choose upper secondary general education, VET programs at ISCED level 3 or an EQF level 4 vocational qualification and an upper secondary leaving certificate which permits access to higher education. In Lithuania, VET schools provide a lower secondary curriculum and/or an upper secondary curriculum education along with vocational education and training for pupils typically aged from 17 to 19 years old. Vocational education and training is organized either in schools or using an apprenticeship system.

Another important characteristic of the national VET system is the implementation of the Lithuanian Qualifications Framework (NQF) introduced in 2006 and officially approved by government in 2010. The national NQF system was designed to implement the principles of coordination, collaboration with the employees, unions and stakeholders, study quality assurance, flexible learning pathways between different educational levels, skills assessment and workforce mobility (Tūtlys & Spūdytė, 2011). The collaborative administrative efforts enable the implementation of the NQF system; for example, the Ministry of Education, Science and Sport is responsible for the management of policy in this area together with the Ministry of Economy and Innovation which takes responsibility for recognition of regulated professional qualifications. The Lithuanian Ministry of Economy participates in shaping human resources development policy, takes part in developing and implementing VET policy, shapes national policy in recognition of regulated professions, and participates in the preparation of legislation pertaining to competences assessment. Together with the Ministry of Education, Science and Sports, the Ministry of Economy defines the structure of qualification and VET standards as well as and the procedure for their development and approval. The Ministry of Social Security and Labor remains responsible for social affairs, including training concerns related to the unemployed (Beleckienė, 2019). The governmental authorities together set and approve the procedures for a professional training standards structure and the preparation and modification of professional training standards. Further important institutional actors are multipartite sectoral professional committees – collegial and based on cooperation and advisory institutions, they coordinate qualification issues in a specific economic sector. In preparing education curricula, VET institutions cooperate with employers' representatives corresponding professional standards and other general skills requirements such as inter-personal communication, information literacy. With reference to VET policy monitoring and control, the national Qualifications and Vocational Education and Training Development Centre ensures development of the lifelong learning system which corresponds to the needs of the national economy within the global context. It develops sectoral qualification standards, organizes the development of modular programs, implements the LTQF, develops the VET credits system, assures quality, and represents the European Qualifications Framework.

Lithuanian national VET policy partly reflects the Anglo-Saxon tradition of specifying the formation of work-related skills and competences. On the other hand, the long-term tradition of centralized VET provisions also informs defines the national framework (Tūtlys & Vaitkutė, 2021). At the national level, VET is organized through laws and general procedures describing the principles and criteria for organizing vocational education, including education curricula content, general teaching plans, qualification standards, and staff qualification. With regard to institutional infrastructure and school network, 67 public vocational schools were accounted for in 2020–2021 (Lithuania Statistics, 2021). VET services may also be provided by freelance teachers or other VET providers (e.g., general education schools, institutions, organizations, or enterprises whose core business is other than the provision of VET) which have a statutory right to develop and/or deliver VET programs. Participation in vocational education and training (VET) is substantially below the EU average which in 2020 amounted to 4.5 % However, the general employment rate of vocational school graduates is among the highest in Europe and in 2020 amounted to over 62 % (Eurostat, 2021).

In the VET provision field, municipal autonomy is somewhat limited other than in the case of supervision of the institutional infrastructure, e.g., maintenance of the facilities. For example, the provisions for an institutional network of public and private vocational schools are approved at governmental level (Law of VET). These define the basic principles of how the municipality should manage and maintain the network of VET schools and set up, reorganize, or organize closure. According to these provisions, the national authorities negotiate with the municipality around re-organization of the VET schools' network at the particular local level.

From the perspective of national VET policy formation, teaching quality and the attractiveness of the teaching profession, the reforming of VET curricula to respond labor market needs and increasing participation in life-long learning are among the key points in policy agenda. A European Agenda for New Skills and Jobs adopted in July 2016, refers to the importance of improvement and relevance of skills as well as rendering skills more visible and competitive (European Skills Agenda, 2017). In 2021, a new Council Resolution on a strategic framework for European cooperation in education and training towards the European Education Area and beyond (2021–2030) (2021/C 66/01) also emphasized the importance of priority actions for inclusive training (EC resolution, 2021[1]). In

1 EC Council Resolution on a strategic framework for European cooperation in education and training towards the European Education Area and beyond (2021–2030) (2021/

December 2017, the Law on Vocational Education and Training (VET) (new edition) was adopted to reconcile with the European policy agenda and training requirements. Thereafter, the VET institutions network was being prepared for reform. The new law together with, and part of the re-organization of the VET institutional network, came into force from 1 January 2019. The reorganization of the network of VET institutions has been based on a comprehensive analysis of vocational education and training policy attainments. Together, all VET institutions operating in these regions were assessed – vocational education and training programs, their compliance with the needs of the economy, learners, pedagogical staff, accessibility, etc. The reform architects also evaluated the impact of regional demographic trends, economic and labor market needs in municipalities and inner migration. The network reorganization has been based on the review of vocational education and training programs and the identification of the optimal financial and organizational resources and training infrastructure needed to provide high-quality vocational education and training. Since 2021, several VET public schools in municipalities have been closed in line with the reform goals (see sub-chapters 6.1. and 6.2. for more detailed analysis).

Expenditures and policy funding mechanism. The funding mechanism of VET is not fully marketized. The basic principles of financing state educational institutions, including VET schools, are regulated by several legislative acts including the Law on Education, the Law on Vocational Education and Training, the Law on Higher Education and Research. According to the national educational financial subsidies model framework, state funds initiate vocational education and training vacancies. The state authorities annually decide on the number of vacancies and which vocational education and training institution to fund. This decision is made following an assessment of national human resources, vocational education and training institutions and qualifications, proposals from sector committees on organizing apprenticeships, etc. An institution holding founder status allocates household funds, while the continuing vocational education and training of companies, institutions, organizations, or farmers' holdings is organized by their own funds.

The state and municipal expenditures for VET system comprise 0.2 % compared to national GDP. From 2016 to 2020 the national expenditures allocated for vocational education decreased from 0.3 % to 0.2 %, despite the structural changes in state subsidized model (see Table 6.1).

C 66/01). Available online: https://eur-lex.europa.eu/legal-content/EN/ALL/?uri=CELEX:32021G0226(01).

Table 6.1. State and municipal budget expenditure on education, compared to national GDP in 2016–2020.

	State and municipal budget expenditure on education, compared to GDP | percent				
	2016	**2017**	**2018**	**2019**	**2020**
Total by educational service	4,5	4,4	4,4	4,4	5
Pre-school education	0,7	0,7	0,7	0,8	0,9
Pre-primary, primary, lower secondary, upper secondary education	2	2	1,9	1,9	2,2
Vocational education	**0,3**	**0,3**	**0,2**	**0,2**	**0,2**
Tertiary education	0,6	0,6	0,6	0,6	0,6
Non-formal education	0,4	0,4	0,4	0,4	0,4
Research and development activity	0,1	0,1	0,1	0,1	0,1
Additional educational service and other education-related issues	0,4	0,4	0,4	0,5	0,6

Source. Lithuania Statistics (2021).

On 1 September 2018, the funding model for pre-school, pre-primary and general education was modified according to significant regional demographic changes. It shifted from a "money follows the learner" principle (usually called the "pupil's basket") to a basic education costs basket, which is coherent with the implementation of curricula (usually called the "class basket"). This means that approximately 80 % of funding is allocated not to each pupil ("pupil's basket") but according to the size of a class. It is a purposive state subsidy that is distributed via the municipalities to the schools, or directly to the higher education institutions according to the actual number of pupils/students. Municipalities allocate the remaining less-than-20 % of the funds to the organization and management of the education process, education aid, the assessment of learning achievements, etc.

Another VET policy funding change refers to the amendments in The Law on Vocational Education and Training at the end of 2017 (Law on VET, 2017). The law establishes that the creation of conditions for validating non-formal and informal learning is one of the main aims of the vocational education and training system. It also states that a competence acquired outside formal education may be recognized as a qualification for an appropriate NQF level or part thereof in accordance with the procedure laid down by the Minister of Education and Science and the Minister of Economy. The law recognizes the right of a student to receive recognition of both non-formal and informal learning. According to the VET law, the assessment and recognition of competences and qualifications shall be funded from state budget (Beleckienė, 2019).

The role of private actors in defining VET goals. The coordination and management of VET are more centralized in Lithuania compared to the other EU countries. The national tradition of consolidation skills and competences formation policy has resulted in systematic challenges responding to regional needs. The Lithuanian VET needs more human resources able to administrate and cooperate in the field. Attempts to decentralize VET by including different stakeholders in the management of VET institutions have not been entirely successful. One of the reasons is unsatisfactory participation of enterprises or other social stakeholders unwilling to contribute to the development of VET. Between 2016 and 2018 there were 26 public institutions working in the field of VET. Twelve of them were managed by businesses, four – by both enterprises and municipality and ten – by the Ministry of Education, Science and Sports. In some cases, the benefits for private stakeholders could be described as highly questionable due to the lack of relevance to business needs (Profesinio mokymo būklės apžvalga, 2017).

Since the accession to the EU, the influence of labor market stakeholders has been strengthened by the involvement of the Central Professional Committee (CPC) (abolished in 2018 following a change to the Law on VET). The professional committee played a key role in the National Qualifications Framework implementation, notably in planning a framework for sector-based occupational standards. The professional committee was a tripartite committee, established under the Law on VET in 2007, signaling the need for active involvement of stakeholders outside of education and training. Sectoral professional committees: multilateral bodies at economic sector level, mainly responsible for the assessment and quality assurance of occupational standards and qualifications were also established. With an amendment to the law on VET in 2017, the role of sectoral professional committees has increased overtaking the functions of the central professional committee. It should also be mentioned that the stakeholders (employers and trade unions) initiate and support the development of new qualifications, occupational standards, education, and training programs. However, their participation is rather fragmented. Referring to Tūtlys and Spūdytė (2011), the design of a national qualification system and provision of high-quality training services requires specific institutional and organizational efforts and active participation of experts and stakeholders. For different reasons, the involvement of enterprises in policy design and skill formation remains relatively low (Tūtlys and Spūdytė, 2011).

To enhance stakeholder participation and encourage more active inclusion of business partners, during the period 2014–2017, 41 sectoral practical training centers were established in Lithuania. These centers comprise training workshops, practical workstations, and laboratories equipped with modern practical training facilities intended for one or several economic sectors of Lithuania. SPTCs were established in VET institutions. Services of the SPTCs are open not only to the students of various VET institutions, but to the students from general education schools, colleges and employees from sector enterprises, institutions, etc

Main shifts in transforming the national vocational education system: Towards a more regionalized approach

The past decade is characterized by dynamic developments in the field of VET policy design that emphasize changing relationships between work and education and public/private service provision. As was previously made apparent, the Ministry of Education, Science and Sports is the principal legislative body responsible for policy design, quality and coordination of VET and is the founder of VET institutions. The role of municipalities in designing and implementing VET is negligible. Thus, all initiatives for developing and changing VET policies were introduced primarily by the central government including the EU policy requirements for the financial period 2014–2020. Reforms implemented in the current period were predominantly driven by the drastic decline of the student age population, low enrollment in the VET institutions, and discrepancy between VET programs and labor market demands. The chief goals of the reforms were the optimization and increment of the efficiency of the VET institutional network in municipalities, higher quality and attractiveness of VET education, correspondence between local labor market demands and VET supply. The recent changes have not yet properly evaluated indirect effect on municipalities in terms of professional qualifications and labor market dynamics; however, the impact of VET qualification programs for the labor market were not monitored. Firstly, the changes in the amendment of the concept of VET to meet actual labor market needs and become more relevant to economic change. It resulted in the development of 10 qualification standards and 60 modular programs in accordance with the initiative by the Ministry of Education and Science. A further component of national VET reform is linked to competence-based curriculum changes that are widely discussed by Tūtlys and Spūdytė (2021). The importance of vocational teaching competence is acknowledged by national policy architects. Our chapter notes the main reform changes that reflect regional disparity and policy design solutions.

The first key reform of the VET policy shift connecting regional socio-economic discrepancies and institutional settings is **optimization of the network of educational VET institutions and consolidation of resource tendencies**. One of the challenges faced by the national VET system in the past decade is linked to demographic factors, namely the substantial decline of the student age population since 2008. For example, students numbered more than 563,000 in the 2004–2005 academic year and approximately 27,4990 in 2020–2021. The general participation trends in VET system remain negative (see Table 6.1). The total number of pupils has decreased dramatically by 42 % in the period between 2016 and 2021 (Statistics Lithuania, 2021). According to Eurostat, the proportion of pupils in Lithuania in 2015 who graduated from VET programs at lower secondary education (ISCED level 2) is only 2.1 %, at ISCED level 3.2, 26.8 %. The total proportion of pupils in the VET system is substantially below the 48 % EU average (Eurostat, 2018). Adult participation in professional learning also remains low – in 2018 it was 6.6 %, which is significantly below the EU average of 10.8 %. Consequently, the decreasing number of students involved in the system threatens the established network of VET institutions. VET students have some professional experience during their studies, (57 % of VET graduates took part in mandatory unpaid traineeships), but only 1.9 % had access to apprenticeship-type training in 2018–2019. The employment rate of recent upper secondary VET graduates dropped to 71.5 % in 2017, while the rate improved across the EU, reaching 76.6 % (Education and Training Monitor, 2018, Lithuania).

Thus, the sharp decline in the target student numbers decisively motivated the reform of the VET. In 2018, the Ministry of Education, Science and Sport adopted the Plan for the Development of Public VET institutions (2018 March 26)[2],

2 Plan for the Development of Public VET institutions, approved by Lietuvos Respublikos švietimo ir mokslo ministro 2018 m. kovo 26 d. įsakymu Nr. V-271 „Dėl Profesinio mokymo įstaigų tinklo vystymo tvarkos aprašo patvirtinimo". Available online: https://www.smm.lt/web/lt/smm-svietimas/profesinis-mokymas/tinklo-pertvarka.

General Development Plan for 2021 of the Network of State Vocational Education and Training Institutions in Which the Ministry of Education, Science and Sports Implements the Rights and Obligations of the Owner (Shareholder), 2021 April 22, No. V-597, Ministry of Science, Education and Sports. Available online: https://www.smm.lt/web/lt/smm-svietimas/profesinis-mokymas/tinklo-pertvarka.

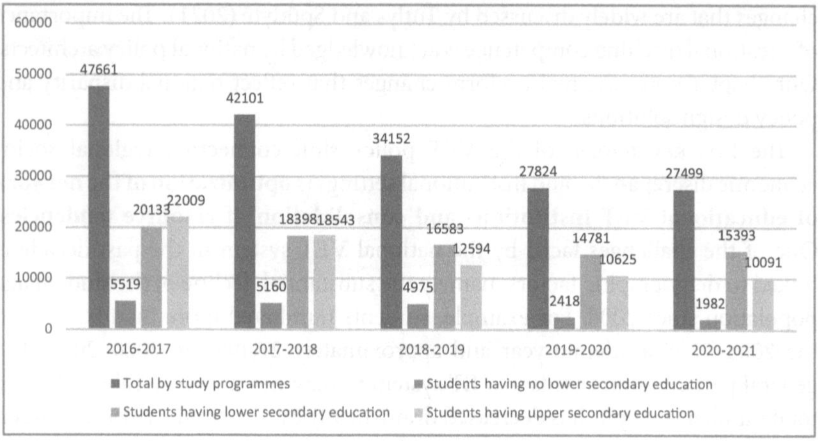

Figure 6.1. Number of students in vocational training institutions in 2016–2021.
Source: Lithuania Statistics (2021).

which amongst others, sets the optimization of the provision of VET study programs according "to the territorial principles" as a priority. The implementation of the restructuring of the VET network was a response to the significant demographic decline in regions of Lithuania. According to statistical data, the total number of VET schools has decreased from 74 facilities in 2016 to 67 schools in 2021. Almost all Lithuanian regions were affected by the closure of VET schools (Statistics Lithuania, 2021) (see Table 6.2).

As a result, 67 VET institutions, where the Ministry of Education and Science is main or partial founder, continued their activities in the period 2020–2021. It is expected that optimization of the network will reduce the overlapping of the study programs provided in the same territorial area by 50 %. The Plan emphasizes that: "*New re-structuring and optimization provisions are intended to combine the content of training programs delivered in vocational training institutions with the needs of business companies in the regions*" (Plan for the Development of Public VET institutions, 2018). Thus, there is no horizontal coordination regarding VET, local stakeholders are not involved in the VET domain. In January 2020, the Ministry of Education, Science and Sports suggested that the optimization of the VET institutional network should be fostered. Out of the 61 VET institutions currently operating, it is proposed that five be fully merged, and 25 enter into joint action agreements with general education schools in general education programs. Other options are offered to the rest

Table 6.2. Number of vocational training institutions in Lithuania in 2016–2021.

	Number of vocational training institutions | units				
	2016–2017	**2017–2018**	**2018–2019**	**2019–2020**	**2020–2021**
In total	74	76	73	71	67
Vilnius county	21	22	22	22	17
Alytus county	7	7	5	4	4
Kaunas county	13	13	13	13	14
Klaipėda county	10	10	9	9	8
Marijampolė county	1	1	1	1	2
Panevėžys county	6	6	6	6	6
Šiauliai county	6	7	7	6	6
Tauragė county	2	2	2	2	2
Telšiai county	3	3	3	3	4
Utena county	5	5	5	4	4

Source: Lithuania Statistics (2021).

of VET schools, for example, simply transferring their existing units on campus to a separate vocational training unit in secondary schools. There would also be adult education units provided in four VET schools. Among other initiatives, it is proposed that vocational training should be pursued as part of non-formal learning, with the possibility of obtaining a vocational school diploma at a later stage. In 2021, the General Development Plan for 2021 of the Network of State Vocational Education and Training Institutions was revised to re-consider the territorial dimension. The institutional re-organization plan was based on the idea of territorial equalization that should reflect the demographic decline and availability of VET services in rural regions. The priority from the policy perspective is the consolidation of educational services in rural areas where higher quality general education and vocational training could be realized (Plan, 2021).

In addition, the consolidation of the VET institutional network is aligned with the idea of developing specific economic specializations in the regions. VET institutions in the regions should offer a wider range of study programs that dynamically reflect the needs of local markets. In addition, in some areas, the general education schools will be merged with VET institutions to improve learning outcomes for pupils (General Development Plan, 2021). It is expected that this measure will increase the attractiveness of the VET services for youngsters and balance the proportion of students in VET and higher education, which currently is 30/70, while the goal would be 50/50 (Cedefop ReferNet VET in Lithuania report, 2018).

Second VET policy turn reflects the neo-liberal approach of better response to labor market demands. Several policy changes in defining the competences and national qualification standards were implemented; for example, since 2013, the modular VET programs approach was introduced as a flexible response to national economic growth needs. Modular training expedites the process r and enables program flexibility in reacting to the needs of the local business and labor markets, this type of training also offers diversity of learning forms. Moreover, the modular VET training programs better respond to market needs; for example, the number of hotel, restaurant and beauty sector programs will be reduced because the proportional market p demand for these services is only 6 % while currently there is an excess of qualified specialists in the field.

Development of the content of VET education in the last decade was also linked to the preparation and adoption of the national qualification standards. Qualification standards were adopted in 2010 and became the founding framework for reshaping the teaching content and competences of the VET education system (Andriušaitiene et al., 2008; Laužackas et al., 2009; Tutlys & Spudyte, 2011). The standards linked to VET were developed integrating two approaches: competence, and work-process analysis. The key advantage is identification and coverage of the professional qualifications required for the execution of work processes in the economic sectors, as well as mapping the links and interrelationships between the qualifications both inside and between the sectors (Tūtlys & Spoettl, 2017).

A further development in national VET policies was related to the validation of non-formal and informal learning. Lithuania has adjusted validation procedures so as to make it possible to assess non-formal or informal learning in VET. The skills and competences acquired outside of formal education are assessed against standards or programs used in formal education.[3] The validation

3 Asmens įgytų kompetencijų vertinimo tvarkos aprašas, Ministry of Education and Science, 2015, January 14, No. V-15. Available online: https://www.e-tar.lt/portal/lt/legalAct/43f8cf209cc411e48dcdae4eb2005eaf.

outcomes are recognized by the education system and may lead to a formal qualification linked to the national qualifications framework. Those wishing to formalize their non-formal and informal learning must apply to an appropriate VET. Additionally, life-long learning policy initiatives were linked to the development of VET policies. One of the policy aims was to foster the participation of adult learning in non-formal education activities. The changes to the Labor Code (new amendments introduced in 2017), entitle every employee to training leave for non-formal education activities. However, according to Tūtlys & Spoettl (2017), there is a huge discrepancy between policy planning goals and policy instruments. Despite an orientation to competence-based curriculum design, the important VET policy instruments and mechanisms that would foster the closer relationship between vocational learning and market needs have not been implemented, for example, apprenticeships, arrangements of work-based learning, informal and non-formal learning competences (Tūtlys & Spoettl, 2017, 57).

The model of apprenticeship was also considered as an important policy tool to respond to social stakeholders needs. National and European structural funding was allocated from 2013 to a pilot project to develop apprenticeship in Lithuania. It has been recognized that there is insufficient focus on the development of apprenticeship, especially in developing the links between competences-based VET curriculum and economic sector needs (Tūtlys & Spoettl, 2017). The Ministry of Education, Science and Sport aims to link the VET and the actual on-the-job training more closely and to enable the trainee to obtain formal qualification based on competencies acquired through apprenticeship. According to VET legislation, provisions for managing apprenticeship by employing an apprenticeship labor contract (between the employer and the VET student) and private companies, could implement a VET contract between an apprentice and a VET provider. The person can choose whether to study at a vocational school or go directly to the workplace and acquire a secondary education using distance learning. The Law on VET also states that sectoral professional committees should participate in planning the in-take of apprentices. However, apprenticeship still receives little attention from VET providers and companies. The usage of apprenticeship programs is very limited and not trusted by local business companies. For example, whereas the average number students using the apprenticeship program in the OECD countries comprises over 30 % per cent, in Lithuania it is only 2 % (citation).

If we turn to the demographic challenges facing the implementation of national VET policy, it is crucial to emphasize the problem of teaching staff and personnel aging, especially in rural regions. National VET strategic

Table 6.3. Pedagogic staff of vocational training institutions in 2016–2021.

		Pedagogic staff of vocational training institutions | persons				
		2016–2017	2017–2018	2018–2019	2019–2020	2020–2021
Males and females	Total by occupied position	3481	3263	3269	3035	3052
	Principal	69	64	65	51	51
	Deputy principal	234	228	229	208	215
	Teacher	1107	844	844	690	698
	Vocational instructor	1958	1822	1826	1811	1811
	Master	113	107	107	90	84

Source: Lithuania Statistics (2021).

planning documents have recognized that the VET system is rapidly being faced with the challenge of an aging teaching staff and a very limited influx of the young generation of teachers. During the period 2016–2021, the total amount of VET teachers has decreased by 25 % (see Table 6.3). The drop in numbers is directly related to the national plan of consolidation of VET schools in regions. Approximately 40 % of teachers are between the ages of 50 and 59, around 30 % are between 40 and 49 and only 3 %–5 % younger than 30 years old. The main reasons why the teaching profession is not attractive are the salaries (among the lowest in the EU countries), a limited possibility to upgrade professional qualifications and the unattractive perception of the profession in society (Cedefop ReferNet VET in Lithuania report, 2018).

Low salaries are one of the main constraints on attracting young skilled personnel to the educational sectors, including the VET. Consequently, in 2018 a new remuneration scheme was introduced with the aim of improving the working conditions of teachers, attracting younger teachers and increasing the prestige of the profession (VET Lithuania report, 2018). This is further linked to problems in the leadership of educational institutions. Although reform which limited the timeframe within which one person could lead the educational institution was introduced, low salaries, great responsibilities, administrative burdens, challenging competition when applying for the position and fixed-term contracts do not motivate people to apply for a managerial position.

Vocational education at local level: Services provision and territorial development

The previous sub-chapter focuses on the contextual aspects of the national VET policy design which reflect the general framework providing vocational education services. However, the national policy design does not consider the complementarities with the territorial development policy goals. Aspects such as the assignment of responsibilities and bodies within the VET policy area, the question of local autonomy and territorialization, funding mechanisms, the role of private actors, forms of public/private partnership and the role of municipalities are crucial to discussion of the social investment policy options. There are several challenges that define the VET policy framework at local level: for example, the assignment of responsibilities or implementation of territorial development policy goals as well as municipal response to creating high-income workplaces. Additionally, the policy design tools and mechanisms such as state subsidies, funding models, and supply constraints which impact on a flexible response to labor market needs in terms of governance and social partnerships, are major factors determining VET service provision.

Assignment of responsibilities within the VET policy area. Our analysis refers to the specificity of the Lithuanian VET system as a consolidated system supervised and controlled by the central authorities. The Ministry of Education, Science and Sports is the founder of public VET institutions which operate at municipal level. As defined by the Vocational Guidance Act (2012), the main educational institutions responsible for provision of VET services (e.g., career education, information, and counseling) are general education schools and VET institutions (vocational schools) which operate at municipal level. The municipal autonomy and functional discretion level are extremely limited in implementing VET policy. Municipalities are responsible only for the organization and coordination of professional guidance services at schools at municipal level. At national level, the Ministry of Education, Science and Sports is responsible for all stages of vocational policy system, including planning, monitoring, educational quality and qualification standards, staff, and overall supervision of VET institutional network in the regions. Almost no traces within local policies could be discerned in accordance with territorial development goals. The other central authorities, for example, the Ministry of Economy and Innovations play a minor consultation role in designing national VET policy. For example, the ministry prepares the predictions for future professional skills in the economic sectors, makes proposals for skills and qualifications needed for investors, and organizes apprenticeships and other on-the-job training courses. Despite the active municipal role in defining their needs and interests in economic growth policy, their impact on predicting and designing the market in vocational education and labor needs is less than adequate. The other social partners and business stakeholders participate in reforming the content of new qualification standards and VET programs, and in assessing whether VET programs should correspond to labor market needs. In 2018, the Ministry of Education and Science adopted the *Plan for the Development of Public VET institutions*, which among others specifies the priority to optimize the supply of the VET study programs according "*to the territorial principles*". The Plan underscores: "*New re-structuring and optimization provisions are intended to combine the content of training programs delivered in vocational training institutions with the needs of business companies in the regions*" (Plan for the Development of Public VET institutions, 2018). Nevertheless, the growth in participation and interest of private stakeholders in designing VET policy is an exception rather than a given. One of the exceptions was the development of a dual apprenticeship approach to acquiring qualifications that fostered higher engagement of business partners at national policy level during the period of 2014–2015 (Tūtlys & Spoettl, 2017, 62).

Territorial policy goals and VET territorialization. In general, the VET policy in Lithuania illustrates the example of a consolidated system where the lower tiers of governance are not considered an active part of policy formation and implementation. The policy design reflects different directions. Firstly, direction covers an institutional system that broadens the economic growth policy in terms of establishing complementarities between education, professional systems and the labor market. Secondly, national VET policy dispensations reflect the municipal autonomy level concerning the idea of the "municipalization" of the vocational education and training services provision. The approach raises the question of whether the VET schools should be decentralized for better integration of territorial assets and local economic needs rather than foster the top-down centralized approached (for example, Thelen, 2004; Pilz, 2016; Virolainen & Thunqvist, 2017).

As it was previously discussed, the first version of the Law on Vocational Education and Training (firstly approved in 1997) defines the VET system as designed for varying beneficiary groups: learners of different ages and educational backgrounds, learners who need to acquire their first vocational qualification and complete general lower or upper secondary education and upgrade current professional qualifications and skills. Another direction of national VET system is related to informal life-long learning and professional qualification programs. Formal continuing vocational training programs are carried out by 41 labor market training centers and other related education institutions. As stated in national legislation, non-formal vocational training is provided according to the needs of the business sectors in municipalities or regions. However, the VET legislation does not emphasize the importance of territorial policy goals that contribute to regional development in terms of developing professional qualifications. From the broader perspective, the exceptions are national strategic planning documents; for example, White Papers on Lithuania Regional Development for 2017–2030, National Education strategy 2013–2022, Employment Fostering Program 2014–2020 or sectoral short-term strategic operational plans (for example, Plan for the Development of Public VET institutions, 2018). The context of these documents defines the general priority to be focus on the labor market needs in terms of adjusting VET educational content and institutional VET network availability for beneficiaries. The regional role is to ensure the balance between supply and demand of VET qualifications as well as guarantee the effectiveness of provisions for students and business.

An additional strategic goal is related to professional qualifications and development of skills necessary for specific economic sectors; therefore, the individual regions should be responsible for discerning their specific economic specialization needs. A stated in the Development Plan of state VET institutions (2021), the strategic priority given to consolidation of VET schools should define the role of municipalities in determining their demographic and economic status first. Referring to the VET institutional consolidation plan, introduced by the Government in 2019, VET programs available in the largest cities could be limited to 2–3 specialties. Accordingly, VET institutions in the regions and municipalities should offer a wider range of vocational guidance choice. This approach reflects the need for better availability of VET provisions for beneficiaries in remote municipalities which could access specific training needed for local priorities. Consequently, it is expected that the consolidation tendencies could ensure better studying quality and attract more students (Plan for the Development of Public VET institutions, 2021). The service provision consolidation also escalates the question of whether the VET policy territorialization is achievable and municipal role in shaping their labor needs is limited.

Local autonomy and territorialization. The relatively low local autonomy level in implementing VET in Lithuania reflects the consolidated policy direction. As was previously noted, the Ministry of Education, Science and Sport supervisors all stages of vocational policy system, including planning, monitoring, quality and coordination of VET networks. Local authorities are involved in the VET only to a very limited degree and this is related to the national legislation provisions on vocational guidance services. In the other words, the municipal role involves the organization and coordination of vocational guidance services at schools. Indirectly, municipal impact is also observable in answering the needs of the local labor market and offering practical training for local employees in vocational schools or labor market training centers.

However, the standardization and equalization of the VET policies in the various territories could be seen in terms of financing mechanisms. The network of VET schools is allocated equally throughout the country regions. According to the national regulations, the direct state subsidies depend on the number of students admitted to vocational guidance, according to the so-called "student basket" financing principle. The state-controlled financial mechanism refers to the principle that the funds are allocated according to the total amount of students and teaching hours in an individual school. However, the consistently decreasing number of students in the VET system encourages optimization of the network and minimizing municipal resources. According to the survey on regional accessibility of formal vocational training institutions, the lowest geographical accessibility was found in the smaller rural regions of Taurage, Marijampolė and Telšiai. The best geographic accessibility of VET institutions is available in the more urban regions of Alytus, Klaipėda, Kaunas, Šiauliai and Vilnius (Report on VET, 2010).

Looking at the national VET financial costs, the state budget expenses for vocational training accounted for 116,4 million EUR which is only 5 % of total expenditure for public education in 2020 and comprises 2454,4 million EUR in total. Public expenditure for the VET system is estimated at only 0.3 %. of GDP which is among the lowest rates when compared to the other EU countries (VET Report, MOSTA, 2018). Statistical data also indicates that the funding resources for the VET institutions were rather increasing, for example, the total amount of public funds significantly increased by 32 % in the last decade (accordingly from 87,6 million EUR in 2016 to 116,4 million EUR in 2020) (Figure 6.2). The stable financial dispensation indicates that the state authorities consider the VET policy important even though there are some major discrepancies in territorial development policy.

Referring to statistical data, the general tendency demonstrates that the total expenditures per student was expanded during the period 2016–2020 (see Figure 6.3). The significant drop in numbers of students admitted to VET schools did not influence the governmental funding dispensation (see Figure 6.2). For example, during the period 2016–2020 the governmental funds per student in VET system doubled. Governmental subsidies comprise the largest proportion of vocational school budgets, including teachers' salaries, infrastructure and

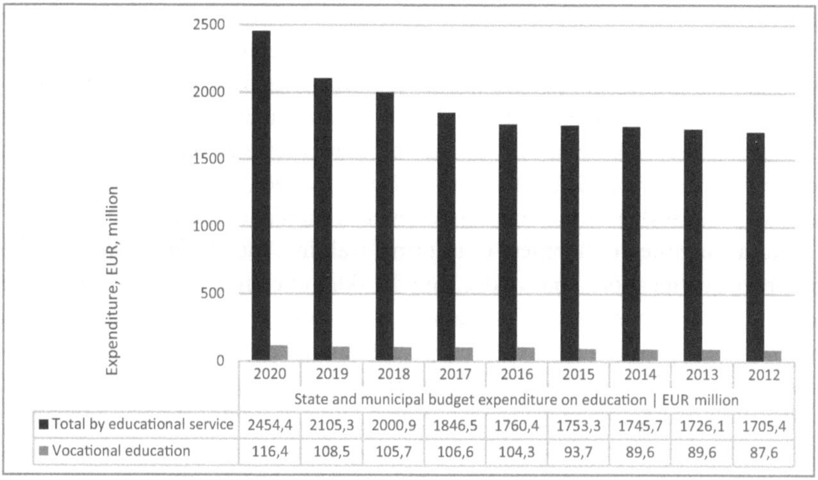

Figure 6.2. Expenditure change for VET institutions in Lithuania, EUR, million in 2012–2020. Source: Statistics Lithuania (2021).

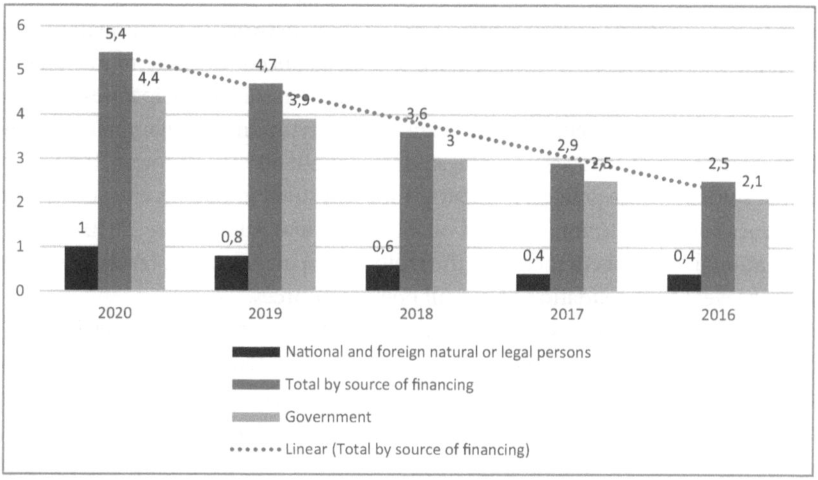

Figure 6.3. Total expenditure per student in vocational education, EUR thousand. Source: Statistics Lithuania (2021).

maintenance, and updating of training facilities. In total, the contribution from the national budget to formal vocational training comprises more than 83 % of total funding, while approximately 16 % emanates from private funding, the business sector and other funds (Report on Vocational Education and Training in Lithuania, 2018, CEDEFOP). VET schools may receive additional income from other business or public entities for services provided (such as training courses, rent of premises). This income is used for education and training purposes.

Regarding the development of informal training, the EU funds were used to improve qualifications, knowledge, and the skills of company employees to meet changes in the labor market. For example, the sectoral practical training centers in regions were financed from the European Regional Development Fund (ERDF) and European Social Fund (ESF) investments of more than EUR 100 million during the first EU financial period of 2007–2013. Recently, the training centers (41 institutions in total) have been challenged in the bid to ensure VET sustainability by the consistently decreasing number of admitted students. In contrast, the funding for informal life-long learning and training of employees is funded by private funds from the business sector or employees pay themselves.

Despite sufficient state subsidies allocated to consolidated VET schools network provisions, the vocational guidance services availability in terms of geographical dispersion is important. It should be noted that the network of vocational training institutions is geographically dispersed and unbalanced. In some municipalities there are no VET institutions, however, the large urban municipalities, such as Kaunas, Vilnius, Klaipėda, Šiauliai, Panevėžys, Alytus and Marijampolė have the highest number of VET schools and students (about 60 % of all county level vocational students). The greatest numbers of student study in Kaunas city and Vilnius city vocational institutions (Report on VET, National Audit Office, 2010). Hence, the national VET schemes created the regional disparities which result in an even higher level of consolidation of overall policy resources.

Role of private actors and partnerships. The question of partnerships and involvement of social stakeholders reflects the consistency of policy in relation to the affiliated parties, for example, the business sector. The question is how to recognize the future skill needs and define the need for professions. As was previously noted, the social partners and different stakeholders have participated in reforming the content of new qualification standards and VET programs, determining that VET programs should correspond to labor market needs. Business stakeholders were also invited to strategic negotiations about organizing practical training; for example, the Central Professional Committee and 41 sectoral professional committees (Lt. *Sektoriniai profesiniai komitetai*) were established to coordinate strategic issues related to development of the qualifications system for vocational training. Sectoral professional committees are advisory bodies whose role has been strengthened in the new VET law (in force from February 2018). They ensure cooperation between all VET stakeholders, update and approve qualification standards and assess vocational training programs. The tripartite bodies also submit proposals on qualifications that can be acquired through apprenticeships and new qualifications to be included in the national register of qualifications (the qualifications register). With regards to the role of private actors, the private companies are encouraged to support participation in VET system through tax initiatives that have been in place since 2005. The Law on Corporate Income Tax (approved in 2002) allows deductions for continuing training courses for employees that are linked to their present occupation. The new Labor Code (approved in 2016) sets out training leave conditions for employees participating in VET programs.

Referring to the question of better governance, the role of local actors, including the municipalities has so far been very limited in VET policy. The current reform alters the legal status of the VET institutions which enables more active inclusion of co-partners, whether municipalities, social partners or private legal entities. It is expected that changes in the government will increase the independence of the institutions but will additionally positively affect the quality of the services provided, the correspondence between services, and local labor market needs. In addition, the Boards were introduced as one of the actors in the government of the VET. However, we can observe, that the involvement of municipalities in VET governance is sporadic and limited (except the collaborations in cultural or sports events).

In summary, the underpinning principles for both vocational education at the local level and manner of service provision, assert that state authorities determine the main principles of policy specifics, including funding mechanisms, qualification standards and consolidation of the school system. However, the organization of VET systems have created top-down power-based relationships between municipalities, school boards and state institutions. The limited involvement of social and business stakeholders and local authorities has marketized provision in the context of demographic decline. The state paradigm of nationally controlled VET policy has turned in the direction where policy does not respond to contextualization. And thus, the territorially driven VET policy approach creates rather a complex challenge.

Vocational education in rural, urban, and suburban areas: Policy challenge of amortizing territorial differences

The previous sub-chapters address the arguments around national VET policy directives that uncover important aspects connected to territorial inequalities and social investment policy. National governance systems and strategic goals, financial tools, development of partnerships, inclusiveness of social stakeholders, and mechanisms for better policy territorialization define our analytical framework. Do we know enough about how the VET policy design and vocational services provision affects individual municipal decisions? When facing territorial inequalities in diverse municipalities, are there any innovative solutions to foster a territorial driven approach? We describe the basic aspects of the VET system at local level that are characteristic of three different municipalities: urban (Kaunas city municipality case), suburban (Kaunas district municipality case), and rural (Pakruojis district municipality case) localities (for a more detailed methodological description see Chapter 3). We do not claim here to establish a VET framework to incorporate social investment policy arguments, but rather to demonstrate the different roadmaps followed by municipalities with relatively limited autonomy for vocational service provision. The chapter will review the counter argument around the need for more territorially driven policy formation, for recognition of the territorial local community capital and for participation of stakeholders as well as a vertical governance approach. If we look at statistical data, in the period from 2016 to 2021, the overall number of VET schools has decreased from 74 units to 67 units. However, Kaunas region did not experience the same significant closure of VET schools compared to the Siauliai region. Accordingly, Kaunas city municipality has the highest number of VET facilities (9 in total) compared to rural Pakruojis district municipality. There are 9 VET schools under Kaunas city municipal jurisdiction (see Table 6.5), among them only 7 VET institutions provide basic and secondary education. According to the National Plan for the Development of Public VET institutions (last revision in 2021) the last vocational training school of Zeimelis was merged with Joniškis agricultural school in 2020 (see Table 6.4).

Challenges to VET governance. The relational dimension of territorial governance refers to the level of hierarchical arrangements between central authorities and municipalities in implementing different policies, including vocational training. There are many theoretical interpretations of territorial governance approaches and concepts (Healey, 1997; Rose, 2000; Jessop, 2021; Atkinson, Tallon, & Williams, 2019). We consider the territorial governance issues of vertical and horizontal coordination and the participation and involvement of social stakeholders' interests (Davoudi et al., 2008). Vertical coordination refers to the principle of re-scaling and subsidiary in self-governance systems. It also indicates the allocation of decision-making power at different governmental levels and distribution of competences for implementing decentralization policies in countries (Sellers & Lindstrom, 2007). The VET policy system provides

Table 6.4. Number of vocational training institutions in selected municipalities, in 2016–2021.

	Number of vocational training institutions | units				
	2016–2017	2017–2018	2018–2019	2019–2020	2020–2021
Country level, in total	74	76	73	71	67
Kaunas county	13	13	13	13	14
Kaunas city municipality	7	7	7	7	9
Kaunas district municipality	2	2	2	2	2
Šiauliai county	6	7	7	6	6
Pakruojis district municiality	1	1	1	0	0

Source: Lithuania Statistics (2021).

a case of top-down designed policy dispositions which cause unwarranted side-effects, such as loss of municipal control, state supervision, and discrepancies within territorial strategic planning. In three municipal cases, the role of municipal administration in implementing VET policy is marginal. The financial autonomy of the municipality which would allow implementation and control local VET is almost absent, except for in the case of career education, information and counseling in municipal secondary schools which is financed from the separate public funding for the secondary school system. On the local government agenda, VET services are marginal because the strategy and provision of these services are designed and supervised at national level. Previous field work has demonstrated that there are no local level strategic planning documents dedicated to the VET policy schemes. Consequently, local authorities do not participate in implementing, coordinating and monitoring the VET policy field.

As was previously noted, the Ministry of Education, Science and Sports adopted the *Plan for the Development of Public VET institutions in 2018*, which defines the priority to optimize the supply of the VET study programs according "*to the territorial principles*" (Plan, 2018). The document presents the top-down approach to standardize VET provision in defining the regional economic specializations. The Plan underlines the importance of responding to the needs of business companies in the regions by modifying the teaching content of the VET curriculum. However, the main concern in this reform is to identify requirements in large urban municipalities rather than in regional ones. The strategic document defines the directions for the optimization of VET institutions in large cities, including Kaunas city, based on the analysis and forecast of labor force demand. The role of urban municipalities underlines the necessity to meet economic competitiveness goals: "*The priority is VET in major cities (Vilnius, Kaunas, Klaipėda) that should implement solutions leading to more specified schools' specialization and more rational infrastructure use. The economic specializations of the cities are consolidated with the activities of practical training centers*" (Plan, 2018). According to the structure of the economy, the VET institutions in Kaunas aim to implement the VET study programs related to business administration, IT technologies, engineering and construction, the labor force for furniture, paper industries and services. Documents conclude that generally, the existing structure of the study programs correspond to the demands of the local economy.

Additionally, the national VET policy agenda identifies the overlaps between urban and suburban zones in delivering vocational training. According to the Plan provisions (2018), the main economic fields in Kaunas district municipality are transport and logistics, construction, furniture, textile, plastic industries, and agriculture. The Plan states that the existing VET institutions in Kaunas city municipality are sufficient to cover labor force demand in suburban Kaunas district municipalities. The Plan sets the directive to develop specialized VET schools because of overlapping teaching and qualification programs provided by different VET providers. The competition creates the discrepancies in student admission rates, for example, Vilkija agricultural school in Kaunas district municipality offers study programs that other than the car mechanic specialization, are not linked to the agricultural industry.

The case of the rural Pakruojis district municipality demonstrates the results of state consolidation plans for VET institutions across the country. By 2020, the municipality hosted only one VET institution – Žeimelis agricultural school located in the rural eldership on the border with Latvia. The rural locality reflects the general tendency of low participation in VET at upper-secondary education level. According to recent data, the school had 217 pupils in 2018. The number of students dropped significantly by 37 % from 2016 to 2018 (Lithuania statistics, 2019). The first reason is related to the preference of young persons and their parents for higher education over VET. Another important reason is the VET system funding specificity for secondary and VET schools which is dependent on the number of students. The state subsidies mechanism leads to competition between these two educational levels in attracting and retaining pupils. Faced with significant demographic decline, Ministry of Education, Science and Sports adopted the National Plan for the Development of the VET Network (2019). The document motivates the restructuring of the school based on the results of the analysis of the costs, efficiency, and demographic trends in the area. Consequently, in 2020 Žeimelis agricultural school become a branch of Joniškelis vocational school located in a neighboring municipality.

Involvement of public/private partnerships. Because of the national VET policies and their implementation mechanisms, there is very little space for innovative public/private partnerships and collaborations related to VET. The case studies analysis has demonstrated that there is a limited relationship between VET institutions and the local labor market due to the centralized top-down governance approach. Sporadic social partnerships and initiatives could be claimed as a particular form of horizontal governance. For example, the interviews with the local authorities in Kaunas city municipality have demonstrated that there is an indirect impact of VET systems in the city on answering the needs of the local labor market and offering practical training for local employees in vocational schools or labor market training centers. As one respondent from urban municipality argued, there is a rather limited connection between VET institutions and the local labor market needs because of the centralized governance of the VET institutions in Lithuania. VET institutions do not participate in the preparation of strategic documents of Kaunas city and their involvement in the territorial governance or introduction of place-based needs in the policy agenda is limited (Public Authority Actor, Kaunas city municipality). In the suburban case, Vilkija agricultural school operates in the rural eldership that is 30 km from the metropolitan zone of Kaunas city. The school plays an important role for the local community in Vilkija eldership in participating in cultural or educational activities. The provision in the Strategic Plan of Vilkija agriculture school for 2018–2020 defines the measures to develop the partnership with local business in terms of signing cooperation agreements and practice places for students. However, institutional partnerships with the business sector or other social stakeholders are not developed sufficiently to sustain the territorial driven policy approach.

National level VET policies resulted in VET offering educational programs which do not correspond to the local economy demands. In the rural case, the VET school in Pakruojis district municipality previously had programs linked with agriculture, but in the past decades shifted to the more general service sector programs (training of the salespersons, welder, cook, etc.). Zeimelis VET school has so far limited opportunities to participate in the lifelong learning programs because much of the short-term professional training was provided by the Labor exchange office, where the training was of ashorter duration compared to the VET schools. According to the abovementioned *Plan for the Development of Public VET institutions (2018),* the VET institution in the rural municipality merged with the gymnasium in 2020. The local community mobilized and protested this re-organization, however they failed to protest against the state initiative for consolidation (Public Authority Actor, Pakruojis district municipality).

The summary of the similarities and differences among the three case studies (urban, suburban and rural municipalities) demonstrates the specificity of the VET policy arrangements in each area (see Table 6.5). The comparison also uncovers the tensions inherent in implementing territorial driven policy design that has been designed as a top-down roadmap. The urban regions have more competitive advantages in terms of higher quality vocational guidance service provision and number of students compared to rural areas.

The chapter reviewed the spatial diversity arguments around designing and implementing VET policy at municipal level. It is important to understand that the top-down vocational policy approach is hardly compatible with the municipal context, especially when policy tools and mechanisms are not able to equalize the territorial diversities. Demographic decline, the consolidation of VET schools, teacher qualification, financial state subsidies approach and the low impact of local business stakeholders in formation of skills and qualifications define the similarities in all municipal cases; urban, suburban, and rural. However, the main difference comprises the involvement of social stakeholders that have more impact in rural areas compared to urban ones.

Conclusions

The chapter on VET policy demonstrates that an expected impact of a social investment (SI) policy approach can be reached when institutional and contextual parameters are synchronized. Lithuanian VET policy is a case of a strongly consolidated system with relatively low impact of local authorities. Vertical coordination and centralization are used as guiding principles to shape the vocational policy dispositions. However, policy territorialization is challenging due to the nature of state institutional agendas and external socio-demographic factors, for example, state subsidies mechanisms depend on the number of students admitted into VET schools. The chapter asked, what are the policy tools and (inter-)institutional mechanisms of vocational training that facilitate or hinder SI strategies; for example, vertical coordination and centralization versus horizontal coordination based on local partnerships and involvement of business

Table 6.5. Similarities and differences in VET policy arrangements.

Comparison of VET cases	Localities	Characteristics
Similarities	Kaunas city municipality (urban case) Kaunas district municipality (suburban case) Pakruojis district municipality (rural case)	10. Negative impact of decreasing number of students on institutional network and top-down costs optimization and consolidation tendencies. 11. Dependence on state subsidies mechanism defined by "student-basket" unit costs. 12. Low attractiveness of VET programs for students. 13. Low support for youth entrepreneurship and self-employment and fostering re-qualification programs for adults. 14. No clear traces of local labor market needs and focus on low-income services sector professions. 15. Low participation of social and business stakeholders in school boards and modification of training and qualification programs adopted to local needs. 16. Low level of outsourcing and innovative teaching practices.
Differences	Kaunas city municipality (urban case)	1. Higher competition between VET schools in the urban and suburban area and discrepancies in supply and demand in VET programs. 2. Focus on low-qualification professional qualifications rather than responding to local business needs in industries and services. 3. Low level of inter-institutional cooperation and engagement in local policy agenda on labor market needs, professional skills, and re-shaping professional qualifications.
	Kaunas district municipality (suburban case)	10. Low competition and supply and demand in VET programs and non-formal education for students and adults. 11. Low engagement in local policy agenda on recognizing local economy needs and competitive advantages. 12. Focus on low-qualification professional qualifications rather than responding to local business needs in industries and services.

(*continued on next page*)

Table 6.5. Continued

Comparison of VET cases	Localities	Characteristics
	Pakruojis district municipality (rural case)	8. Low competition and supply and demand in VET programs and non-formal education for students and adults. 9. High level of engagement in recognizing local needs and advantages and encouraging local community participation in VET policy formation. 10. High negative impact of demographic decline and spatial remoteness of the VET school. 11. Spatial coverage issues for students from neighboring municipalities.

stakeholders. The urban, suburban and rural municipal cases were selected as a means of illustrating the phenomenon of interconnectedness between top-down policy design and municipal efforts for place-sensitive approach.

Considering VET policy design in Lithuania, it is obvious that the system challenges different problems in terms of the attractiveness of VET studies, modification of formal and non-formal teaching programs to local labor market needs, inclusiveness of adult learning, marketization, and resources consolidation policy pressure. The low number of admitted students and negligence on the part of employees in advising on the needs for professional qualifications signalize the weaknesses of the national approach. The negative stereotype that suggests VET institutions are chosen by the least advanced students is typical among youngsters and their families. The national level challenges and problems of the VET system also create pressure at municipal level to sustain the inclusiveness of the overall system for the territorial governance. The analysis of the Lithuanian VET policy field also suggested proposals to increase the capacity of the system and define the social investment related priorities:

(1) **Response to the decreasing number of students and re-consolidation of VET institutional networks**. Our chapter demonstrates that the participation in VET system is relatively low in terms of admitted student numbers and study attractiveness in Lithuania. The government initiatives to improve the balance between the VET system and labor market demand by developing formal and informal VET programs, supporting youth entrepreneurship and self-employment, fostering re-qualification programs are not operating effectively. To face the challenge of an attractive VET system,

since 2016, a network of sectoral practical training centers has been established. However, collaborative initiatives with the business sector are rare and ineffective. The state agencies (e.g., the Vocational Education and Training Council, the Central Professional Committee, the Centre for Quality Assurance in Higher Education, and others) are expected to foster this process by continuing efforts to collaborate with local companies and other social stakeholders.

(2) **The financial subsidies mechanism for VET system.** The state subsidies mechanism for VET institutions is based on the "student basket" principle which fosters intensive competitiveness among the vocational schools to attract higher numbers of students by offering attractive study programs. The supply and demand of VET teaching programs is largely dependent on liberal market principles, offering attractive programs rather than applying to local economic sector needs. In Lithuania, the impact of municipalities on funding mechanism in policy implementation is inadequate. Accordingly, the financial challenge is also related to the demographic structure of vocational teachers where older teachers comprise the largest proportion of the overall VET institution staff. To address the problem, it would be important to enable young personnel to work as vocational education teachers.

(3) **Regional dispersion in service provisions.** The top-down designed VET schools consolidation reform (since 2018) underlines the discrepancies between large and small regions. According to the reform provisions, VET programs available in the largest cities of the country would be subjected to specialization (limiting to 2–3 specialties). In this regard, VET institutions in the regions should offer a wider range of teaching programs which reference territorial needs and economic and employment structure. The VET reform is better tailored to fulfill the needs of large regions and cities rather than focusing on peripheral ones. It reflects the main tendencies of the state regional policy to foster the economic growth in urban regions. Furthermore, there are provisional plans to consolidate VET institutions in rural Lithuanian municipalities and localities to ensure better learning conditions and higher numbers of students. Any form of consolidation has an impact on regional development. Hence, the national agencies and policymakers cannot yet define the outcomes of policy contextualization.

(4) **Participation of social stakeholders and recognition of territorial needs.** The New Skills Agenda for Europe (adopted on 10 June 2016) invites the social partners, industries and other stakeholders to raise the quality and relevance of professional skills training to enable better career choices for

employees (Agenda, 2016). In the case of Lithuanian VET policy, the network of social and private stakeholders in enhancing and restructuring the VET system does not support joint collaborations. For example, the trade unions and business associations express very limited interest in tailoring VET policies mostly because of the negative perception of VET qualifications and skills. The participation of local municipalities is very ill-defined having no direct impact on policy implementation. The "White Papers on Lithuania Regional Development for 2017–2030" (approved on 2017 December 12) focuses on the regional economic specialization initiatives to modify vocational education programs. The new VET program design addresses the needs of foreign and local investments and specialized business infrastructural needs. As an example, to balance the business needs and VET policy tools, the apprenticeship programs could be used as a policy tool. The goal of the central authorities is to enable the VET student to obtain a professional qualification based on the competencies acquired through apprenticeship. However, the number of students in VET apprenticeships comprised approximately1.9 % in 2018–2019 (National Audit Office Report, 2020). 40 % of VET schools did not implement apprenticeship programs because of the lack of teaching competence, organizational skills, municipal support, and inadequate connections with local business. The state's ambition to increase the number of students in apprenticeships by 20 % was not realized. With reference to the National Audit Office Report (2020), a quarter of surveyed employers (larger companies) work with VET schools on professional training or in-service training. Larger companies and those working with VET schools are more likely to employ skilled workers than those less qualified (National Audit Office Report, 2020).

(5) **Better inclusiveness of beneficiaries with different socio-economic backgrounds**. Providing learning opportunities for people from disadvantaged socio-economic backgrounds or those with special needs is still a challenge. The more open enrollment policy which reflects the general state educational guidelines fostering better inclusiveness of children with disadvantaged backgrounds has been introduced by few VET institutions. For example, in the 2018–2019 school year, 26 vocational education institutions (out of 67) had admitted students with special education needs, and there is a lack of educational support staff in schools. Another challenge is scholarships and material support to reduce social exclusion of students. The cost of living is difficult for some students from socially vulnerable families. Due to low family income, many young people after completing their primary education, move into low-skilled and low-paid jobs

> for which employers do not require qualifications. The number of children not attending school and the young people who have not qualified in a profession is increasing. The tendency is especially critical for small towns and rural areas (National Audit Office Report, 2020).

Finally, referring to theoretical assumptions; a social investment policy approach is important to reconcile social cohesion and economic growth goals but seems too insubstantial to recognize the contextual pre-conditions. VET policy design requires the contextualization of tools and mechanisms. However, the Lithuanian national VET policy roadmap separates itself from municipal problems. Our conclusions around options for social investment (SI) policy approach is define the list of main priorities in the local policy agenda for developing VET field. Firstly, the aspect of targeting users; increasing accessibility and quality of vocational service provision and participation of stakeholders in defining local needs in relation to the priorities of a social investment approach are important. For example, special attention should be paid to VET measures that support lifelong learning, assessment and recognition of formal and informal learning, and adult requalification mechanisms and their interrelation with the labor market needs in individual regions. The statistics indicates the growing demand for a younger labor force. However, the increasing emigration rates enable us to discuss the more active involvement of older generations and re-shape of their professional qualifications.

The second argument relies on the socio-demographic profile of students. The issues around decreasing numbers of students in VET institutions and changing labor market needs also need to be considered. The situation is critical in the rural (mostly, border) regions that have the highest drop in population size and emigration rates. The demographic context is also directly related to the central authority initiative for VET network consolidation reform since 2018. The government plans to establish several multi-profile regional vocational VET centers and schools that address recent labor market needs and meet local employer expectations. The initiative to re-organize the VET institutional network is also crucial for foreign companies located in these zones. However, the government still lacks a clear vision of the use of VET schools, mostly because of dramatically decreasing number of young students in peripheral regions.

The final argument for connecting VET and social investment policy is cooperative initiatives and higher local autonomy of municipalities. The policy directives need to re-consider the attractiveness of the VET system to students by fostering effective cooperation between employers, local NGOS, trade unions, state agencies, municipalities and VET institutions. The notion of how to involve all municipal stakeholders and social partners in VET qualifications development is important. Social partners, VET providers, and other stakeholders should be able to initiate VET programs in developing new professional qualifications and prepare highly skilled employees for the local economies. Finally, we have to look at municipal autonomy and decisive powers that can be shared in the formation of vocational training policy profiles. The underpinning principles and traditional divide between state authorities, vocational services providers and municipalities could be replaced by modifying the power from vertical to more horizontal governance.

References

Anderson, D. (2009). Productivism and ecologism: Changing dis/courses in TVET. In *Work, learning and sustainable development* (pp. 35–57). Dordrecht: Springer.

Andriušaitiene, D., Gurskiene, O., Jovaiša, T., Laužackas, R., Pukelis, K., Spudyte, I., & Tutlys, V. (2008). Lietuvos kvalifikacijų sistemos metodologija, Lietuvos darbo rinkos mokymo tarnyba prie Socialines apsaugos ir darbo ministerijos, Vilnius.

Asmens įgytų kompetencijų vertinimo tvarkos aprašas, Ministry of Education and Science. (2015). January 14, No. V-15. Available online: https://www.e-tar.lt/portal/lt/legalAct/43f8cf209cc411e48dcdae4eb2005eaf

Atkinson, R., Tallon, A., & Williams, D. (2019). Governing urban regeneration in the UK: A case of 'variegated neoliberalism'in action?. *European Planning Studies*, *27*(6), 1083–1106.

Beleckienė, G. (2018). European inventory of validation on non-formal and informal learning, 2018 update, Lithuania report. Available online: https://cumulus.cedefop.europa.eu/files/vetelib/2019/european_inventory_validation_2018_Lithuania.pdf.

Beleckienė, G. (2019). Profesinis mokymas Lietuvoje. Online: https://strata.gov.lt/images/tyrimai/2020-metai/svietimo-politika/20200316-profesinis-mokymas-lietuvoje-2019.pdf.

Beleckienė, G., Zimina, N., Corcoran, T., McKerracher, M., & Faudel, H. (2002). *Vocational education and training and employment services in Lithuania. Monographs: Candidate countries*. For full text: http://www.etf.eu.int/WebSite.nsf/Pages/8E6F84C50A104E71C1256D660052BE7D/$FILE/LITH_VET_NAT_03_EN.pdf.

Bosch, G. (2010). *The revitalization of the dual system of vocational training in Germany.* London: Routledge.

Cedefop ReferNet, Vocational education and training in Europe: Lithuania report. (2018). Available online: https://cumulus.cedefop.europa.eu/files/vetelib/2019/Vocational_Education_Training_Europe_Lithuania_2018_Cedefop_ReferNet.pdf.

Chakroun, B. (2010). National qualification frameworks: From policy borrowing to policy learning. *European Journal of Education*, *45*(2), 199–216.

Conceptual Framework of Non-Traditional Education. (2010). The Minister of Education, Science and Sport.

Davoudi, S., Evans, E., Governa, F., & Santangelo, M. (2008). Territorial governance in the making: Approaches, methodologies, practices. *Boletín de la Asociación de Geógrafos Españoles*, *46*, 33–52.

Description of Formal Vocational Education and Training Curriculum. (2012). The Minister of Education, Science and Sport.

Dijkstra, L. (2017). My region, my Europe, our future. Seventh Report on Economic, Social and Territorial Cohesion. Luxembourg: Publications Office of the European Union.

Dobbins, M., & Busemeyer, M. R. (2015). Socio-economic institutions, organized interests and partisan politics: The development of vocational education in Denmark and Sweden. *Socio-Economic Review*, *13*(2), 259–284.

EC Council Resolution on a strategic framework for European cooperation in education and training towards the European Education Area and beyond (2021–2030) (2021/C 66/01). Available online: https://eur-lex.europa.eu/legal-content/EN/ALL/?uri=CELEX:32021G0226(01).

Education and Training Monitor Lithuania (2018). European Commission. https://education.ec.europa.eu/sites/default/files/document-library-docs/et-monitor-report-2018-lithuania_en.pdf.

Employment Fostering Program. (20142020). Ministry of Social Security and Labor. Available online: https://socmin.lrv.lt/lt/veiklos-sritys/darbo-rinka-uzimtumas/uzimtumo-ir-darbo-rinkos-politika/uzimtumo-didinimo-2014-2020-metu-programa.

European Skills Agenda. (2017). Available online: https://ec.europa.eu/social/main.jsp?catId=1223.

Eurostat. (2018). Official database: https://ec.europa.eu/eurostat/data/database.

Eurostat. (2021). Official database: https://ec.europa.eu/eurostat/data/database

EURYDICE. Key features of the Lithuanian Education system. Available online: https://eacea.ec.europa.eu/national-policies/eurydice/content/lithuania_en.

EURYDICE. Secondary and post-secondary non-teriary education, Lithuania. (2019). Available online: https://eacea.ec.europa.eu/national-policies/eurydice/content/secondary-and-post-secondary-non-tertiary-education-30_en#LS.

General Development Plan for 2021 of the Network of State Vocational Education and Training Institutions in Which the Ministry of Education, Science and Sports Implements the Rights and Obligations of the Owner (Shareholder), 2021 April 22, No. V-597, Ministry of Science, Education and Sports. Available online: https://www.smm.lt/web/lt/smm-svietimas/profesi nis-mokymas/tinklo-pertvarka.

General Plan of the Vocational Education and Training Curriculum for the 2017–2018 and 2018–2019. (2017). The Minister of Education, Science and Sport.

Grootings, P. (2007). Discussing national qualification frameworks. Facilitating policy learning in practice. In: ETF Yearbook 2007. Quality in Vocational Education and Training (Turin, European Training Foundation).

Healey, P. (1997). *Collaborative planning*. London: MacMillan Press.

Hemerijck, A. (2017). *Social investment uses*. Oxford: Oxford University Press.

Education and Training Monitor Lithuania (2018). European Commission. https://education.ec.europa.eu/sites/default/files/document-library-docs/et-monitor-report-2018-lithuania_en.pdf.

Eurostat (2018). Official database: https://ec.europa.eu/eurostat/data/database.

Eurostat (2021). Official database: https://ec.europa.eu/eurostat/data/database.

Iammarino, S., Rodriguez-Pose, A., & Storper, M. (2018). Regional inequality in Europe. Evidence, theory and policy implications. *Journal of Economic Geography*, *53*, 898–924.

Kazepov, Y. (Eds.). (2010). *Rescaling social policies: Towards multilevel governance in Europe* (Vol. 38). European Center Vienna: Ashgate Publishing, Ltd.

Kazepov, Y., & Ranci, C. (2016). Is every country fit for social investment? Italy as an adverse case. *Journal of European Social Policy*, *27*(1), 90–104.

Laužackas, R., Tutlys, V., & Spudyte, I. (2009). Evolution of competence concept in Lithuania: From the VET reform to the development of National Qualifications System. *Journal of European Industrial Training*, *33*(8/9), 800–816.

Law on Amendment of the Law on Vocational Education and Training of the Republic of Lithuania. (2007). Valstybės žinios. 2007-04-19. No. 43-1627. Vilnius.

Law on Vocational Education and Training. (2018). Lithuanian Parliament (2017). Lietuvos Respublikos profesinio mokymo įstatymo Nr. VIII-450 pakeitimo įstatymas [Law on vocational education], 2017, No. XIII-888. *Teisės aktų registras* [Register of legal acts], 27.12.2017, No 21305.

Lietuvos Respublikos švietimo ir mokslo ministerija. (2017). *Profesinio mokymo būklės apžvalga 2017*. [Overview of Lithuanian Vocational Education and Training status 2017]. http://www.kpmpc.lt/kpmpc/wp-content/uploads/2015/08/Profesinioapzvalga-Lithuania.pdf.

Lithuanian Government. (2010). Resolution approving the description of the Lithuanian qualifications framework. Resolution No 535 of 4 May 2010. *Valstybės žinios* [Official Gazette], 2010, No 56-2761.

Lithuania Statistics (2021). Official database. https://osp.stat.gov.lt/pradinis.

Lithuanian Parliament. (2013). Lietuvos Respublikos Seimo 2013 m. gruodžio 23 d. nutarimas Nr. XII-745 "Dėl valstybinės švietimo 2013–2022 metų strategijos patvirtinimo" [National education strategy 2013–22]. *Valstybės žinios* [Official Gazette], 2013, No 140-7095. https://www.etar.lt/portal/lt/legalAct/b1fb6cc089d911e397b5c02d3197f382.

Martinelli, F., Anttonen, A., & Matzke, M. (Eds.). (2018). *Social services disrupted. Changes, challenges and policy implications for Europe in times of austerity*. Cheltenham, UK, Northampton, MA, USA: Edward Elgar Publishing (New horizons in social policy).

McGrath, S. (2012). Vocational education and training for development: A policy in need of a theory?. *International Journal of Educational Development*, *32*(5), 623–631.

Morel, N., Palier, B., & Palme, J. (Eds.). (2012). *Towards a social investment welfare state?* Bristol: Policy Press.

National Education Strategy. (2013–2022). Ministry of Education, Science and Sports. Available online: https://www.sac.smm.lt/wp-content/uploads/2016/02/Valstybine-svietimo-strategija-2013-2020_svietstrat.pdf.

Operational Plan for Development VET schools' network, 2018–2020, No.V-305, Ministry of Education, Science and Sports. Available online: https://e-seimas.lrs.lt/portal/legalAct/lt/TAD/094a5111345511e884a38848fe3ec9e2?jfwid=zaydj60p3%20.

Outline of the National Qualifications Framework of Lithuania. (2007). National labour market training authority. Vilnius.

Pastore, F. (2015). *The youth experience ga explaining national differences in the school-to-work transition*. Heidelberg among others: Springer.

Pilz, M. (2016). Typologies in comparative vocational education: Existing models and a new approach. *Vocations*, *9*(3), 295–314.

Pilz, M., Junmin, L., Canning, R., & Minty, S. (2017). Modularisation approaches in initial vocational education: Evidence for policy convergence in Europe?. *Journal of Vocational Education & Training*, *70*(1) 1–26.

Plan for the Development of Public VET institutions, approved in 2018 March 29, Ministry of Education and Science, later amendments, 2020 January. Available online: https://www.smm.lt/web/lt/smm-svietimas/profesinis-mokymas/tinklo-pertvarka.

Procedure for Consecutive Learning in Accordance with General Education Curricula. (2012). The Minister of Education, Science and Sport.

Profesinio mokymo būklės apžvalga. (2017). Ministry of Education, Science and Sports. Available online: https://www.sac.smm.lt/wp-content/uploads/2017/09/Profesinio-mokymo-bukles-apzvalga-2017.pdf.

Report on VET, National Audit Office. (2010). Available online: file:///C:/Users/28925/Downloads/IT-Profesinis-mokymas.pdf.

Saniter, A., & Tūtlys, V. (2016). Comparison of historical development pathways of initial vocational education and training in Lithuania and Germany: How does history matter for policy learning?. *History of vocational education and training in Europe: Cases, concepts and challenges/editors Esther Berner, Philipp Gonon*. Bern: Peter Lang.

Sellers, J. M., & Lidström, A. (2007). Decentralization, local government, and the welfare state. *Governance*, *20*(4), 609–632.

The New Skills Agenda for Europe (adopted on 10 June 2016), European Commission. Available online: https://ec.europa.eu/social/main.jsp?catId=1223&langId=en.

Thelen, K. (2004). *How institutions evolve: The political economy of skills in Germany, Britain, the United States, and Japan*. Cambridge: Cambridge University Press.

Tuck, R. (2007). *An introductory guide to national qualifications frameworks: Conceptual and practical issues for policy makers*. Geneva: ILO.

Tutlys, V., Gedviliene, G., & Vaiciukyniene, S. (2018). Legal regulations for advertising vocational education and training services: Case study of Lithuania. *European Scientific Journal, ESJ*, *14*(22), 202–222.

Tūtlys, V., & Spoettl, G. (2017). From the analysis of work-processes to designing competence-based occupational standards and vocational curricula. *European Journal of Training and Development 41*(1).

Tūtlys, V., & Spūdytė, I. (2011). Implementing a national qualifications framework in Lithuania. *Journal of Education and Work, 24*(3/4), 429–448. https://doi.org/10.1080/13639080.2011.584701.

Tūtlys, V., & Vaitkutė, L. (2021). Knowledge formation practices in the context of the VET curriculum reform in Lithuania. *Journal of Vocational Education & Training, 74*(1), 1–20.

Vaitkute, L. (2016). Key competences in vocational education and training: Lithuania. Report. https://www.cedefop.europa.eu/en/country-reports/key-competences-vocational-education-and-training-lithuania

Vaitkute, L., Perini, M., & Tacconi, G. (2019). Implications of competence/learning outcomes-based VET curriculum reforms for the vocational teachers and trainers in Italy and Lithuania. *Barbara E. Stalder and Christof Nägele (Editors)*, 405.

Valk, A. (2009). Recognition and qualifications frameworks. *Assessment in Education: Principles, Policy and Practice, 16*(1), 83–95.

Virolainen, M., & Thunqvist, D. P. (2017). Varieties of universalism: Post-1990s developments in the initial school-based model of VET in Finland and Sweden and implications for transitions to the world of work and higher education. *Journal of Vocational Education & Training, 69*(1), 47–63.

Vocational Education and Training in Europe: Lithuania. (2018). Available online: https://www.cedefop.europa.eu/en/publications-and-resources/country-reports/vocational-education-and-training-europe-lithuania-2018.

Vogel, J. (2002). European welfare regimes and the transition to adulthood: A comparative and longitudinal perspective. *Social Indicators Research, 59*(3), 275–299.

White Papers on Lithuania Regional Development for 2017–2030. Ministry of Internal Affairs. Available online: https://www.nrp.vrm.lt/data/public/uploads/2018/01/baltoji_knyga_galutinis-2018-01-15.pdf.

Young, M. (2005). *National qualifications frameworks: Their feasibility for effective implementation in developing countries.* Geneva: ILO.

Zelvys, R. (2004). Development of education policy in Lithuania during the years of transformations. *International Journal of Educational Development, 24*(5), 559–571.

Jurga Bučaitė-Vilkė

Chapter 7 In summary: Is a social investment approach compatible with territories? Lessons to be learned

This summary reflects on the theoretical arguments of previous chapters that outline the importance of a place-based social investment policy approach sensible to territorial development patterns. Territorial sensitivity and the enactment of municipal potential should become a crucial resource for re-inventing national welfare policies at different scales, both regional and local. The main objective when selecting the chapters was to choose texts which would respond to questions around the possibility that social investment policies could be tailored differently to address territorial capacities and individual territorial needs. The book cites three examples of social investment policy fields that follow the life span of families from early childhood, family and work reconciliation, participation in labor market, and development of professional skills. Research findings from Lithuanian policy fields in ECEC, ALMP and VET exemplify how institutions have developed the potential for addressing territorial inequalities in a variety of urban, suburban and rural municipalities. In addition, the chapters reveal the failures and risks when highly consolidated state policies based on subsidies and in-cash contributions for regions are implemented Theoretical implications for developing the relationship between socio-spatial configurations and territorial cohesion is also important. The chapters analyze and discuss the territorial potential in the provision of public infrastructure and delivery of services, the reduction in patterns of socio-economic segregation and means of minimizing the negative impact of urban concentration processes in the country.

The challenges of a territorially driven social investment policy are emphasized through the lens of multi-scale governance and policy design. Social investment policy domains comprise a multi-scale complex of public services, implementation of public infrastructure, policy objectives and beneficiaries, decision-making, leadership, and response to local life. One of the central challenges involves the complexity of multi-scale governance concerned with balance between horizontal and vertical coordination, organizational fragmentation, a shift to municipal responsibilities and efficient delivery of public services in urban as well as rural regions. Referring to regional socio-economic inequality analysis presented in Chapter 3, the social investment policy architecture should take into account the urban-rural development patterns. Over the last decade, the Lithuanian regional profile has been characterized by strong metropolitan agglomeration and the emergence of lower indications of socio-economic development in lagging-behind territories. The compilation of political and academic discussion around the re-arrangement of territorial scales of government is a lengthy process. Debates on decentralization, devolution and delegation of competencies to local authorities dominate the European context. However, in the Lithuanian case, analysis demonstrates the strong shift to a centralization policy based on vertical coordination and financial state subsidies rather than expansion of municipally autonomous public services.

In summary, we propose several mechanisms that could be put into practice to identify the best options for territorialized social investment policy domains. We hope that the lessons Lithuania is learning could be useful for other countries, especially in the CEE region with strong state consolidation traditions. Experimentations with governance modes could become an alternative strategy to tackle territorial disparities. What makes the territorialized social investment policy work? How to realize the place-based policies that are adaptive to changing socio-economic and demographic contexts? What coordinating actions of institutions and actors could be important for integrating different policies? What works for different countries?

Firstly, in this book we offer a re-consideration of the concept of **territory and territorial governance**. In summarizing the theoretical debates around territorial governance, the dimensions of the participation and consensus-building among public and private actors, the devolution of powers and resources to lower levels of decision-making and territorial cohesion implementation could be identified (Lidström, 2007; Faludi, 2012; Stead, 2013, 2014). Further, the aspect of different forms of collaborative efforts for decision-making in different policy domains is important. For example, the ESPON report on "Towards Better Territorial Governance in Europe" (2014) refers to the dimensions of coordinating actions of inter-related stakeholders, integration of policy sectors, mobilization of stakeholders and importance of territorial context and territorial specificities (ESPON, 2014). Referring to Davoudi et al. (2008), the elements of participation, coordination and conception of the territory define the territorial governance (Davoudi et al., 2009). It is important to consider the relational aspect of governance, clustering vertical and horizontal coordination modes that in addition enable the implementation of social investment policies. The relational dimension of territorial governance refers to the level of hierarchical arrangements between central authorities and municipalities in implementing different policies. Contributing to this discussion, Chapter 5 provides a comprehensive overview of territorial governance dimensions across Lithuanian cases in terms of different analyzed policies (VET, ECEC, ALMP). The municipal authorities are the main actors taking responsibility for the integration of analyzed place-based policies in planning, development and implementation of collaborative projects or initiatives to tackle territorial challenges. Nevertheless, due to a centralized top-down approach, active labor market and vocational training are less considered in the agendas of local authorities. The policy implementation mechanism and provision of these services are designed and supervised at the national level where municipal role is limited. Despite ongoing debates on de-centralization, the book chapters demonstrate that the role of central authorities is significant in delegating the functions and defining the level of financial autonomy of municipalities. For example, ECEC policy is subsidized by the Ministry of Education, Science and Sports but fully implemented and coordinated at municipal level.

Vertical and horizontal coordination networks are additionally important as stakeholder's interest's negotiation and decision-making mechanism. The involvement of different municipal stakeholders and community actors is necessary for the design and implementation of the territorial governance process. Many authors argue that the horizontal dimension of territorial governance is concerned with decision-making in the public sphere (Stead, 2013). Our book demonstrates that the horizontal inter-institutional and neighboring networks combine the territorial strategies providing a formal basis for negotiations, public consultancy, and deliberations, especially important to design context adaptive policies. Local inter-organizational networking and interconnectedness are less important for VET and ALMP programs compared to the ECEC policy field that is more flexible than local arrangements. The governance actors address the ongoing tensions between the variety of interests of different stakeholders, especially business. Although the local community organizations are active in small-scale interventions, their voice in developing the place-based social investment decisions is unarticulated. The second problem is that the different interest groups and stakeholders with dissimilar practices and understanding of territorial needs are too diffuse.

Secondly, the book presents the argument around **community capacity and inter-institutional networking between different actors and institutions**. Theoretical arguments on the importance of relational resources, mobilization capacities, community capital and institutional partnerships are exclusively confined to the literature on urban studies and planning (Healey, 2004; Blokland & Savage, 2008). As seen previously in this book, authors reveal different levels of participation and stakeholder involvement in implementing childcare services, promoting active labor market engagement, or adapting vocational training systems to recent professional needs. The analysis of selected Lithuanian municipalities demonstrates that local communities do not acquire sufficient capacities to intervene in the implementation of social investment policy measures. Their impact could be described as small-scale local welfare services interventions. Further, the inadequate leadership and expertise of local community activists are the chief impediments to successful implementation of public services. On the other hand, the communities, local councils, neighboring initiatives and local NGOs are proactive in small-scale and short-term projects related to cultural projects, public infrastructure and interventions in public infrastructure (for example, maintaining recreational zones). Local communities are characterized as the most active units in improving the local quality of life. The lack of common understanding of public interests and ineffective negotiations between the municipality and businesses limits the initiatives of entrepreneurs from more active role in territorial development. As an example of more efficient collaborative initiatives relates to implementation of ECEC services case where joint efforts of local authorities, local entrepreneurs and community initiatives are implemented to ensure childcare services. The services are high on the municipality agenda, and there is a mutual understanding of the relevance of the high-quality childcare services. The municipality, ECEC institutions, and communities have strong links in securing the ECEC provision as a result of which the services are coherent and adapted to local needs, for example, demographic change in early-age groups of children or changing number of young families who prefer suburban lifestyles. Additionally, we found that the municipalities encourage both formal and informal local activity groups because this is necessary for collective efforts and efficacy. On the other hand, the relationships between local communities and municipalities are often colored by distrust and lack of institutional recognition.

Finally, we should be aware that the theoretical debates of territorial governance elaborate the complex and multi-dimensional understanding of the dimensions of participation and consensus-building among public and private actors, the devolution of powers and resources to lower levels of decision-making, and territorial cohesion implementation. The dimensions of coordinating actions of inter-related stakeholders, integration of policy sectors, mobilization of stakeholders and the importance of territorial context and territorial specificities are the main domains of territorial governance understanding. This book has tried to capture the issue of territorial sensitivity. It makes an important contribution to further considerations of multi-level governance, public engagement, the role of authorities and local welfare.

References

Blokland, T., & Savage, M. (2008). Social capital and networked urbanism. In T. Blokland & M. Savage (Eds.), *Networked urbanism – social capital in the city* (pp. 1–20). Aldershot: Ashgate.

Davoudi, S., Evans, E., Governa, F., & Santangelo, M. (2008). Territorial governance in the making. *Approaches, Methodologies, Practices, Boletin de la A.G.E., 46*(2008), 33–52.

ESPON – European Spatial Planning Observation Network. (2014). Towards better territorial governance in Europe. A guide for practitioners, policy and decision makers based on contributions from the ESPON TANGO Project. Available online: https://www.espon.eu/topics-policy/publications/guidance/towards-better-territorial-governance-europe.

Faludi, A. (2012). Multi-level (Territorial) governance: Three criticisms. *Planning Theory & Practice, 13*(2), 197–211. https://doi.org/10.1080/14649357.2012.677578.

Healey, P. (2004). The treatment of space and place in the new strategic planning in Europe. *International Journal of Urban and Regional Research, 28*(1), 45–67.

Stead, D. (2013). Dimensions of territorial governance. *Planning Theory & Practice, 14*(1), 142–147.

Stead, D. (2014). The rise of territorial governance in European policy. *European Planning Studies, 22*(7), 1368–1383.

List of Figures

List of Tables

About the authors

Artelaris, Panagiotis, Dr., Assistant Professor of Spatial Economic Analysis, Department of Geography, Harokopio University, Athens, Greece. His research interests are in the areas of Spatial Economics, Economic Growth and Decline, Spatial Inequalities and Spatial Econometrics. He has been involved in several European research projects and has published several papers in international academic journals including, among others, Environment and Planning C, Regional Science Policy & Practice, Regional & Federal Studies, Geoforum, International Regional Science Review, Growth & Change and Journal of Economic Studies. Contact: Harokopio University, 70 El.Venizelou Ave., Athens 17671, Greece, e-mail: partelar@hua.gr.

Baranauskienė, Viktorija, Researcher, Dr., Institute of Sociology, Lithuanian Centre for Social Sciences. Her research interests include Geography of the population, regional and urban studies, regional development and regional policy, regional differences, regional inequalities, sparsely populated territories of Lithuania, socio-spatial exclusion, change of network of public service infrastructure, peripheralization and metropolization studies. She has published several articles and book chapters on socio-spatial exclusion, problems of unequal regional development, typology of the level of urbanization, regional linguistic aspects (sociolinguistics). Contacts: Lithuanian Centre for Social Sciences, A. Gostauto st. 9, LT-01108 Vilnius, e-mail: baranauskiene.viktorija@gmail.com.

Boczy, Tatjana, Ph.D. candidate and lecturer at the University of Vienna, Department of Sociology. Her research interests include comparative urban and regional research, social change and institutional transformations, political and environmental sociology, as well as mixed-methods research. In her Ph.D.-thesis, she investigates the urban as well as regional intricacies of welfare under recent social, economic and environmental challenges such as climate change policies in England and Austria. Her contributions to urban futures will be in applications of mixed-method research as well as empirical and theoretical detail of territorial social and climate justice from a sociological perspective. Contacts: University of Vienna, Department of Sociology, Rooseveltplatz 2, 1090 Wien, e-mail: tatjana.boczy@univie.ac.at.

Bučaitė-Vilkė, Jurga, Assoc. prof., Dr., Faculty of Social Sciences, Vytautas Magnus University. Since 2020 she has been head of the Department of Sociology.

Her research interests include local governance systems, participatory and representative democracy, community development and territorial policies. She has published several articles and book chapters on local democracy, civic participation and municipal governance. Contacts: Vytautas Magnus University, Jonavos g. 66, LT-44191 Kaunas, e- mail: jurga.bucaite-vilke@vdu.lt.

Cefalo, Ruggero, Post doc University Assistant at the University of Vienna, Department of Sociology. His research interests include multilevel governance, territorial policies, comparative welfare policies, school-to-work transitions. He has published several papers and book chapters on spatial disparities and youth labor market. Among his recent publications: *Territorial disparities in youth labor market chances in Europe* (Regional Science, Regional Studies, 2021, with R. Scandurra). Contacts: University of Vienna, Department of Sociology, Rooseveltplatz 2, 1090 Wien, e-mail: ruggero.cefalo@univie.ac.at.

Marta, Cordini, Junior Research Fellow at Department of Architecture and Urban Studies (DAStU), Polytechnic of Milan. She is part of the Laboratory of Social Policies and she teaches Urban Sociology. Her main research interests include housing, urban sociology, educational and territorial inequalities and sociology of migration. Among her recent publications "*Families between care, education and work. The effects of the pandemic on educational inequalities in Italy. The case Of Milan*" (European Journal of Education, with Gianluca De Angelis, 2021). She has been recently involved in a Horizon 2020 project on territorial inequalities and she is still working on Ersamus+ Project on School segregation. Contacts: Polytechnic of Milan, Via Bonardi 3, 20133 Milan, e-mail: marta.cordini@polimi.it.

Maslauskaitė, Aušra is Professor of Sociology at Vytautas Magnus University and a senior researcher at Lithuanian Center for Social Research. Her research interests lie in the area of family sociology and family demography, including topics such as family formation and dissolution, causes and consequences of divorce, post-divorce parenting, gender and intergenerational relationships in families, family policies. She has focused on implications of structural changes on family dynamics, interconnections between system of socio-economic inequalities and family processes. Her research has been published in Demographic Research, Men and Masculinities, Journal of Divorce and Remarriage, The History of the Family.

Mavrommatis, George, Dr., Assistant Professor of Political Geography, Department of Geography, Harokopio University, Athens, Greece. His research interests are in the areas of migration, integration, transnationalism, mobilities, urban studies, political movements, territorial issues etc. He has been involved in several European research projects and has published several papers in international academic journals including, among others, Journal of Ethnic and Migration Studies, Mobilities, Ethnic and Racial Studies, Population, Space & Place, Journal of Rural Studies, Ethnicities. Contact: Harokopio University, 70 El.Venizelou Ave., Athens 17671, Greece, e-mail: gmavrommatis@hua.gr.

Tereškinas, Artūras is a Professor of Sociology and Head of the Social Research Centre at Vytautas Magnus University in Kaunas, Lithuania. His research interests include cultural sociology, sociology of gender, men's studies, social exclusion, and prison studies. He is the author of ten research monographs and edited collections and more than fifty articles. Contacts: Vytautas Magnus University, Jonavos g. 66, LT-44191 Kaunas, e-mail: arturas.tereskinas@vdu.lt.

Baltische Studien zur Erziehungs- und Sozialwissenschaft

Baltic Studies in Educational and Social Sciences

Herausgegeben von Gerd-Bodo von Carlsburg, Natalija Mažeikienė und Airi Liimets

Edited by Gerd-Bodo von Carlsburg, Natalija Mažeikienė and Airi Liimets

Band 1 Gerd-Bodo Reinert / Irena Musteikienė (Hrsg.): Litauische Gespräche zur Pädagogik. Humanismus – Demokratie – Erziehung. 1999.

Band 2 Gerd-Bodo Reinert / Irena Musteikienė (Hrsg.): Litauische Gespräche zur Pädagogik II. Staat und Schule. 2000.

Band 3 Jaan Mikk: Textbook: Research and Writing. 2000.

Band 4 Gerd-Bodo Reinert / Irena Musteikienė (Hrsg.): Erziehungswandel und moderne pädagogische Verfahren. 2001.

Band 5 Airi Liimets (Hrsg.): Integration als Problem in der Erziehungswissenschaft. 2001.

Band 6 Gerd-Bodo Reinert / Irena Musteikienė (Hrsg.): Wissenschaft – Studium – Schule auf neuen Wegen. 2002.

Band 7 Palmira Jucevičienė / Gediminas Merkys / Gerd-Bodo Reinert: Towards the Learning Society. Educational Issues. 2002.

Band 8 Gerd-Bodo Reinert / Irena Musteikienė (Hrsg.): Bildung im Zeitalter der Informationsgesellschaft. 2003.

Band 9 Dalia Ohlinger: Argumentation in der Erst- und Fremdsprache. Pragmalinguistische und grammatikalische Aspekte anhand von Argumentationen deutscher und litauischer Studierender. 2003.

Band 10 Inga Šukevičiūtė: Interkulturelle Interferenzen im Bereich Wirtschaftskommu-nikation. Zur Analyse von Geschäftsbriefen im Vergleich Deutschland, Litauen und Russland. 2004.

Band 11 Gerd-Bodo Reinert von Carlsburg / Irena Musteikienė (Hrsg./eds.): Innovation durch Bildung. Innovation by Education. 2004.

Band 12 Gerd-Bodo von Carlsburg / Palmira Jucevičienė / Gediminas Merkys (eds.): Learning and Development for Innovation, Networking and Cohesion. 2005.

Band 13 Gerd-Bodo von Carlsburg / Irena Musteikienė (Hrsg./eds.): Bildungsreform als Lebensreform. Educational Systems Development as Development of Human Being. 2005.

Band 14 Gerd-Bodo von Carlsburg (Hrsg./ed.): Entwicklung erziehungswissenschaftlicher Paradigmen: Theorie und Praxis. Development of Educational Paradigms: Theory and Practice. 2007.

Band 15 Gerd-Bodo von Carlsburg (Hrsg./ed.): Bildungs- und Kulturmanagement. The Management of Education and Culture. 2008.

Band 16 Jaan Mikk / Marika Veisson / Piret Luik (eds.): Reforms and Innovations in Estonian Education. 2008.

Band 17 Gerd-Bodo von Carlsburg (Hrsg./ed.): Qualität von Bildung und Kultur. Theorie und Praxis. The Quality of Education and Culture. Theoretical and Practical Dimensions. 2009.

Band 18 Airi Liimets (Hrsg.): Denkkulturen. Selbstwerdung des Menschen. Erziehungskulturen. Festschrift für Professor Dr. Dr. h.c. Dr. h.c. Heino Liimets. 2010.

Band 19 Ellu Saar (ed.): Towards a Normal Stratification Order. Actual and Perceived Social Stratification in Post-Socialist Estonia. 2011.

Band 20 Marika Veisson / Eeva Hujala / Peter K. Smith/ Manjula Waniganayake / Eve Kikas (eds.): Global Perspectives in Early Childhood Education. Diversity, Challenges and Possibilities. 2011.

Band 21 Airi Liimets / Marit Mäesalu (eds.): Music Inside and Outside the School. 2011.

Band 22 Gerd-Bodo von Carlsburg (Hrsg./ed.): Enkulturation durch sozialen Kompetenzerwerb. Enculturation by Acquiring of Social Competences. 2011.

Band 23 Reet Liimets: Ich als raumzeitliches Konstrukt. Die Fiktionen vom Leben der estnischen und deutschen Jugendlichen. 2012.

Band 24 Raivo Vetik (ed.): Nation-Building in the Context of Post-Communist Transformation and Globalization. The Case of Estonia. 2012.

Band 25 Airi-Alina Allaste (ed.): ‚Back in the West'. Changing Lifestyles in Transforming Societies. 2013.

Band 26 Gerd-Bodo von Carlsburg (Hrsg./ed.): Bildungswissenschaft auf der Suche nach globaler Identität. Educational Sciences in Search of Global Identity. 2013.

Band 27 Airi Liimets / Marika Veisson (eds): Teachers and Youth in Educational Reality. 2014.

Band 28 Gerd-Bodo von Carlsburg / Thomas Vogel (Hrsg./eds.): Bildungswissenschaften und akademisches Selbstverständnis in einer globalisierten Welt. Education and Academic Self-Concept in the Globalized World. 2014.

Band 29 Marika Veisson / Airi Liimets / Pertti Kansanen / Edgar Krull (eds.): Tradition and Innovation in Education. 2015.

Band 30 Robertas Jucevičius / Jurgita Bruneckienė / Gerd-Bodo von Carlsburg (eds.): International Practices of Smart Development. 2015.

Band 31 Gerd-Bodo von Carlsburg (Hrsg./ed.): Strategien der Lehrerbildung. Zur Steigerung von Lehrkompetenzen und Unterrichtsqualität. Strategies for Teacher Training. Concepts for Improving Skills and Quality of Teaching. 2016.

Band 32 Gerd-Bodo von Carlsburg (Hrsg./ed.): Denk- und Lernkulturen im wissenschaftlichen Diskurs. Cultures of Thinking and Learning in the Scientific Discourse. 2017.

Band 33 Palmira Pečiuliauskienė / Aleksa Valdemaras: Motivation of New Generation Students for Learning Physics and Mathematics. 2018.

Band 34 Gerd-Bodo von Carlsburg (Hrsg./ed.): Transkulturelle Perspektiven in der Bildung. Transcultural Perspectives in Education. 2019.

Band 35 Giedre Kvieskienė / Vytautas Kvieska / Gerd-Bodo von Carlsburg: Social Clustering: Paradigm of Trust. 2021.

Band 36 Natalija Mažeikienė (ed.): Learning the Nuclear: Educational Tourism in (Post)Industrial Sites. 2021.

Band 37 Gerd-Bodo von Carlsburg / Annette Miriam Stross (Hrsg./eds.): (Un)pädagogische Visionen für das 21. Jahrhundert. Geistes und sozialwissenschaftliche Entwürfe nach dem Ende der ‹großen› Menschheitsgeschichte. 2022.

Band 38 Jurga Bučaitė-Vilkė (ed.): Social investment and territorial inequalities: mapping policies and services in the Baltic states. 2022.

www.peterlang.com